OIL CHANGE

Perspectives on Corporate Transformation

THE LEARNING HISTORY LIBRARY

Series Editors

George Roth
Art Kleiner

Car Launch: The Human Side of Managing Change

Oil Change: Perspectives on Corporate Transformation

OIL CHANGE

Perspectives on Corporate Transformation

Art Kleiner

George Roth

with

Ann Thomas
Toni Gregory
Edward Hamell

New York   Oxford
OXFORD UNIVERSITY PRESS
2000

Oxford University Press

Oxford   New York
Athens   Auckland   Bangkok   Bogotá   Buenos Aires
Calcutta   Cape Town   Chennai   Dar es Salaam   Delhi   Florence   Hong Kong
Istanbul   Karachi   Kuala Lumpur   Madrid   Melbourne   Mexico City   Mumbai   Nairobi
Paris   São Paulo   Singapore   Taipei   Tokyo   Toronto   Warsaw

and associated companies in
Berlin   Ibadan

Published by Oxford University Press, Inc.
198 Madison Avenue, New York, New York 10016
http://www.oup-usa.org

Library of Congress Cataloging-in-Publication Data

Kleiner, Art
    Oil change: perspectives on corporate transformation / Art Kleiner, George Roth
        p. cm - - (The learning history library)
    ISBN 0-19-513487-7 (cloth)
    1. Petroleum industry and trade -- United States -- Management -- Case studies. 2.
    Organizational change -- United States -- Case studies. I. Roth, George, 1957 - II. Title. III.
    Series.
    HD9565.K574 2000
    333.8'23'0973 -- dc21   99 - 55140

                                                            CIP

9 8 7 6 5 4 3 2 1

Printed in the United States of America
on acid-free paper

CONTENTS

PREFACE

◆ The OilCo transformation

Only a handful of corporations have ever set out to deliberately transform themselves as a whole—to change from top to bottom their ways of conducting business, their attitudes, and their organizational structure. It is particularly audacious to take on such a transformation just after a time of layoffs and cutbacks, when most managers instinctively want to hunker down and wait for better times to return.

Yet the senior leaders of OilCo, an American oil company, embarked on just that sort of comprehensive change initiative in 1993, soon after the worst round of layoffs in their history. During the next three years, the "OilCo transformation," as they called it, profoundly altered every aspect of the company. OilCo's business practices, corporate governance structure, team management approaches, leadership style, and values came into question. Many policies and structures were abruptly altered. A host of assumptions and attitudes, long ingrained in OilCo's culture, no longer seemed to fit as well as they once did, and these too were brought up for reexamination and renewal. The act of change itself, once the exclusive purview of the senior-most executives, was propelled and cascaded to many far-flung parts of this large corporation.

Between 1993 and 1997, OilCo actually did most of the things that large companies are exhorted to do by management "gurus," by leadership books, and by the Harvard Business Review. But OilCo didn't just follow a set of management fads blindly. Its leaders, and people throughout the company, thought in depth about the changes they adopted and crafted them into a relatively coherent program. Few companies have gone so far, and rare indeed is the opportunity to look behind the corporate curtain to see what happened from within.

The document you are about to read was created to provide an inside glimpse of OilCo's transformation—so readers can decide for themselves the significance and impact of this experience. Originally written in late 1996 and 1997, it follows the course of OilCo's change from the groundwork laid in the late 1980s, through to the beginning of the 1997 denouement. The managers whose story is told here agreed to allow the document to be published so that people in other companies (and in their own evolving system) can learn from their unique experience.

Oil Change is the second in a series of a new kind of case history—the "learning history," told by the people who directly took part in a critical organizational story. Learning histories are a new approach for transferring learning from innovative team efforts within and between organizations. The learning history work is part of a larger research effort on fostering collective learning—conducted at the Massachusetts Institute of Technology (MIT) Sloan School of Management and at the Society for Organizational Learning (SoL), an international multidisciplinary consortium based in Cambridge, Massachusetts. Learning history documents (and the group processes that have been developed for using these documents) have evolved, during the past few years, into a form of assessment that aims, in itself, to help people throughout an organization (and outside, in business schools) build the kind of collective judgment they need to assess and evaluate innovation on its own terms.

This learning history tells the story of OilCo's transformation firsthand in the words of people in the company. Using a "learning history" technique developed at MIT's Center for Organizational Learning, the authors of this document interviewed about 150 people between August 1 and September 15, 1996. Interviewees included people at all levels, from hourly workers to members of the Executive Council, working in all four primary OilCo businesses—Exploration & Production, Refining & Retail, Chemical, and OilCo Consulting—as well as the professional firms—Human Resources, Legal, Tax and Investment Services. All quotations were approved by the people who made them, and the report has been validated to make it as accurate as possible.

The resulting document includes the decisions that some people have made, the results they noticed, and the ways in which their attitudes changed. It recounts both negative and positive aspects of transformation, and the varied points of view that different people held about the same events. It describes some of the things that OilCo has learned as a company and many things that its people have learned as individuals.

In this document, the names of the company and all internal individuals have been omitted. This was a condition of OilCo's willingness to see the document published, and it was also part of our agreement with interviewees. People took part in these interviews with the understanding that they would never be quoted by name; this allowed them to speak candidly. We also feel it is desirable to maintain anonymity because we want to focus attention on what people learned and what roles they played within the company—not on personalities or public perceptions. Similarly, mentioning the company by name might call up preexisting associations that would probably not have much to do with the underlying story here. We think there is more to learn from the story on its own terms. (One side effect of this decision, of course, is the necessary alteration of some key details—enough to disguise the company without distorting the critical aspects of the story or the interviews.)

As you make your way into *Oil Change,* you will see that it does not resemble a conventional case study. For one thing, it is not intended to be read just by individuals. It is a tool for collective learning and for ongoing study and practice. The unusual two-column format allows for more in-depth group discussion by putting the "ground truth" of the story, as told by participants, side by side with key questions and perspectives that explicitly show why quotes were chosen and that impart some of the significance that otherwise might not be evident.

Learning histories like *Oil Change* are deliberately designed to reward the intensive involvement of its readers. Reading the OilCo story, you will "hear" company executives, employees, and consultants reflect upon their role in the transformation and their response to the events around them. Each will speak from his or her own perspective, telling his or her own part of the story. With access to these multiple voices and multiple perspectives, you don't have to accept any particular "moral" to the story; rather, you can come up with (and develop) your own understanding of the reasons things happened this way and how you could effect similar changes in your own organization.

If the OilCo story is meaningful to you, you may find it valuable to establish a "book group" of your own—a group of people who meet several times, each time visiting a different part of the story in the context of your own issues and priorities. (We have found that it takes two or three hours, at minimum, for a group of six to eight people to consider any one of the themes in this document.) It will not necessarily be easy to meet this way. Collective learning is unexpectedly difficult. It requires ongoing study and practice, which requires a certain amount of time set aside for learning and a certain amount of support. But it also yields unexpected rewards, by helping a group develop "actionable knowledge": knowledge embedded in the form of new skills, capabilities, and innovations.

"Here's a segment," a discussion group leader might say, "in which some OilCo executives struggle to create a vision statement and then get challenged by a mid-level manager who says it's not 'noble' enough. What does this suggest about our own efforts to galvanize our people?" As they talk about their own insights, and the differences in the assumptions and attitudes underlying them, the group members cocreate their own collective understanding of their own situation, based on the narrative of the learning history.

Although we have tried to represent most points of view faithfully, you may feel that some comments are inaccurate, or that we have missed critical attitudes or perspectives. Some of this kind of inaccuracy is to be expected. This document is, after all, full of people speaking subjectively. However, it is completely accurate in one sense: All quotations have been checked with, and approved by, the individuals who stated them. Though the speakers are anonymous, they have carefully considered their comments. The quotes faithfully represent the way that people perceived events.

Of course, only a fraction of the relevant stories can be told from interviews with 150 people. An estimated 3,000 people or more have directly participated in efforts related to OilCo's transformation. Literally hundreds of initiatives took place as a result; people created high-performance teams, adapted the financial literacy approach in new ways, and made new kinds of commitments to alliances and joint ventures. We chose the particular cases in this volume because they were reasonably representative of stories going on throughout the company or because they raised questions about the transformation that could not be ignored. (For example, the "OilCo Services" clash with "OilCo Refining & Retail" was included precisely because it showed how new governance structures led to new sorts of dilemmas.)

The document is also incomplete in another way; it ends in late 1996. The events described here continued, more or less expanding, throughout 1997. Then, in 1998, the oil industry, as a whole, underwent a period of turbulence. And the organization, without repudiating the transformation to date, began another phase of activity that is not documented here. (See the epilogue, page 227, for more detail.)

Despite these limitations, we continue to see this document as a powerful record of the effects of a broad change initiative. Everyone at any company undergoing profound change faces the concerns, challenges, and opportunities that people describe herein.

◆ THE CHANGES AT OILCO

The OilCo transformation was based on a variety of organizational change theories. First, it adopted a "revolutionary leadership" approach developed at General Electric under Jack Welch, and later at the University of Michigan at Ann Arbor, in which senior leaders initiate a full-scale move toward candor and speed, and away from bureaucracy. Allied with this was an in-depth effort in financial literacy: an effort to make managers keenly aware of the profit-and-loss ramifications of every act they took, even if (like most of them) they hadn't been required to pay attention to the company's economic indicators in the past.

Second, the CEO and executive board launched a full-scale shift in OilCo's governance structure. They sought, following the model of "subsidiarity" as articulated by British management writer Charles Handy, to devolve power and accountability to lower levels of the hierarchy. This meant setting up a string of new minicompanies throughout OilCo.

Finally, a learning-oriented initiative aimed at reframing attitudes and behavior, particularly among senior executives, took hold in various ways throughout the OilCo system. Based on a series of in-depth counseling and "team learning" practices, and grounded in the theories and practices of the MIT Center for Organizational Learning, this initiative couched the value of transformation in terms of mental and emotional shifts. Managers struggled to remove their "corporate masks" and to embrace a style of mutual acceptance and support instead of the top-down judgment and political gamesmanship typical of OilCo in the past.

None of these initiatives was completely realized. Nonetheless, after three years of work under them, a host of "noticeable results" were evident at OilCo. These visible changes ranged from the growth of new businesses, to the public voicing of discord and frustration, to gains in financial performance, to financial losses, to new feelings of vitality and engagement, to dramatic new relationships with outside companies. Some individuals reported enormous levels of improvement: in their capabilities, in the authenticity they brought to the job, in the levels of responsibility they handled, and even in their personal lives. Some parts of the company, bolstered by the new autonomy they were given, took unprecedented risks with varying results. As a whole, OilCo's financial performance improved noticeably—even during an industry-wide slump. (A list of OilCo's "results" can be found on page 6.)

Any two readers of this document might disagree about the meaning of these results or perceive them as stemming from different aspects of OilCo's transformation. But every reader would agree that a significant change has taken place at this company—a change that few other companies have matched in scale or scope and a change that is still not fully understood.

Within OilCo, people disagree about the final impact of the transformation. Many observers from within OilCo argue that the transformation was the right thing to do; the alternative would have been continued stagnation and even full-fledged decline. Others believe that OilCo would have been better served by a more charismatic, authoritarian warrior-leader who would have bullied the company toward prosperity (as happened at some other mainstream American companies). And still others believe that the transformation didn't go far enough; that it would not have been effective unless it had ultimately led to a full devolution into a group of associated, but separate, companies.

Was the OilCo transformation successful? There are no easy ways to answer that question. Indeed, as you tackle the OilCo story you will confront a series of universal questions, questions raised by every organizational change initiative. And there are no easy answers to any of them:

- When a large company needs to change, should it happen all at once, in an abrupt "big bang" revolution driven from the top? Or should it take place in a gradual, evolutionary fashion? Can either approach make a large, stolid organization flexible enough to face the changing vicissitudes of its environment?

- Does increasing the autonomy of personnel (and building new business capabilities among less-experienced managers) lead to better performance? Or does performance require more top-down direction than the CEO of OilCo was willing to provide?

- How can an organization facing bad times best prepare itself for good times (and vice versa)? Between 1985 and 1999, OilCo went through at least two complete cycles of boom and bust. Many people perceive themselves as learning only when they are in a crisis, but OilCo tried to stretch itself during one of the "boom" parts of the cycle. How did the learning that occurred during good times affect the company's ability to deal with hard times?

• How far into peoples' hearts and minds can a change initiative reach? Senior leaders worked hard to involve people throughout OilCo on a level of genuine commitment, instead of merely asking them to comply with new rules and practices. Some OilCo people enthusiastically embraced this approach; others found it disturbing. Given the need for full-bore commitment, how should an organization handle this dilemma?

This last question is particularly worthy of consideration. Since World War II, a growing number of management theorists have posited that people who merely "go along with the rules" will not develop into a high-performance work force. To genuinely change a company, at some deep level, they must be prepared to give themselves to the enterprise. That, in turn, means that they must have enough autonomy to take meaningfully large risks.

OilCo's story was clearly such an initiative. The OilCo leaders sought to create an environment that would help people through psychological changes that would then lead to deeper and more profound behavioral changes than were possible otherwise. Instead of following "what the bosses want," OilCo people were expected to develop their own understanding. Not surprisingly, many found it a very difficult task—including the bosses themselves. Readers of the OilCo story will notice a continual "dance" between hard and soft elements: between commands that were followed and calls for psychological commitment. Sometimes the people in this story spend a great deal of time and reflection trying to figure out which parts of the effort belong to them, versus which belong to OilCo, and how they should view their own efforts.

◆ COMMENTARIES ON OILCO'S TRANSFORMATION

We chose the three commentators in this volume precisely because each one, in his work, has dealt with the ramifications of the relationship between the changes within people, a culture, or the environment.

In his commentary on the OilCo learning history, Edgar Schein, professor of management at MIT and author of many books on process consultation and organizational culture, examines the transformation as a planned change process. The theory of planned change suggests that, for change to be enduring, it must develop at multiple levels. Changes in organizational behavior, interpersonal relationships, and psychological development must take place simultaneously, all complemented with organizational structural changes in the governance system. Schein notes that change at multiple levels is enormously challenging. Taking a fifty-year view of organizational development history, he suggests that the tensions in the OilCo story—such as the tensions between the new implicit humanism of the change process and the technical and financial habits of the company—were fundamental and unavoidable.

Schein notes that when a corporate change initiative, fueled by personal commitment and motivated through learning, unleashes forces for change, it moves these changes along faster than those connected above and outside the organization can keep up. The gap between the innovators and others creates anxiety and triggers resistance.

How can leaders of transformation deal with this type of problem? As Schein insightfully points out, they must bring others along in their own learning before the growing body of anxiety and resistance squashes the new initiative. The leaders, paradoxically, must slow down their efforts so as to stay connected with others.

(In his commentary, Schein also looks at the issues of research and intervention that are implicit in the learning history form. Perhaps like other readers of the document, he finds the form frustrating at times because answers are not provided. They must be found by the reader. But this is also, to Schein, a critical reason why the learning history form has value. We are grateful for this part of his commentary and include it, in part, because it may help readers make sense of and use this new form of case reporting.)

Sense making is the cornerstone of Karl Weick's commentary—which is fitting for the theorist who has done more than anyone else to conceptualize organizational action as, at heart, a mutual way of making sense of the world. Weick looks at transformation not as a revolutionary change but as a continuous change—even when it is perceived as revolutionary by its protagonists. By looking at the microinfrastructure of people's sense-making process, Weick suggests that the OilCo "transformation" simply represented an acceleration of the ordinary process of continuous change, already embedded in OilCo's ethic.

Weick's proposition, in taking a sense-making perspective, is that the greatest single factor in determining the effectiveness of change is the quality of interaction among people who must deal with the ambiguities of change. The quality of change is determined by the characteristics of the microinfrastructure, rather than, as change agents and leaders would have us believe, by the nature of the change and its facilitation and leadership. Weick points out the paradox of transformation from a sense-making perspective—as a call to action it doesn't provide for the reflective time and space for people to do anything but enact what they've learned previously. In reality, people don't start with blank sheets, they act to address the crisis and return to the way they were, perhaps thankful that it's over (for now). The continual change that underlies what we see as transformation and revolutionary change may actually be decelerated because the problems of sense making interfere with needs for adoption.

The third commentary, by management theorist/author Charles Handy (a former executive in the oil industry), starts by comparing the transformation at OilCo with the throes of a totalitarian state as it evolves into a democracy. Handy looks at transformation as a political act, built upon changes in the governance system that start out as a platform for greater efficiency and organizational effectiveness, but evolve into much more. In this context, Handy carefully teases out concepts of authority, control, empowerment, and decision making and the impact of the governance structure on them. Building on his research on forms of governance, particularly federalism, he notes opportunities and challenges in the ways in which OilCo's organizational changes have positioned it for the future.

Why include several commentaries, instead of just one correct "explanation"? Because we recognize the complex and contextual nature of change in large corporate settings. There are no single responses or recommendations that will direct managers how to be successful in improving their own organizations. Each of the three commentaries in this book suggests different courses of action: Schein's around intervention in the system, Weick's around the develop of a more complex and fruitful "micro-infrastructure," and Handy's around designing appropriate governance models. Anyone seeking to emulate OilCo's example, or the best of it, would do well to consider the prescriptions that are explicit (and implied) in each of these commentaries.

◆ LEARNING FROM THE OILCO LEARNING HISTORY

Consider the prescriptions—but make your own diagnosis and treatment. Having multiple commentaries is meant to further encourage you, as a reader, to use the learning history in your own teams, to develop your own insights, and to apply them in your own settings. You may find yourselves disagreeing with the commentaries and with your fellow readers' assessments or conclusions. The spirited dialogue and debate that might follow are worthwhile; the idea of learning through open conversation lies at the heart of learning history methodology.

In fact, we specifically suggest you avoid basing your thinking and sense-making process on the commentary of any one of the "experts" (in this volume or elsewhere). Don't argue that one of the points raised in this volume is "right" or "wrong." When you find yourself making insightful statements, link them to their source—on what you read in the learning history. In what ways did you interpret it? How might others have seen it differently? Extend OilCo's experiences to your own: How can your own everyday activities be considered in light of this company's transformation experience? What actions would you and your team naturally take?

Organizational learning is a process of collective sense making. You don't just produce results; you produce a "theory of how you got there." Thus, this document has no "answers." It is designed as a conversation starter: a way for you to articulate—either on your own or in a learning group or team—your own answers about how to move forward.

By offering this learning history for reading and discussing as a team, we hope to help you and your organization develop new ways of seeing, thinking, and learning together. We encourage you to use the learning history to create a "transition time," a time for cultivating your judgment about past experiences, when your vision and your memory meet and you can collectively generate the possibilities for a new future.

As you make your way through *Oil Change*, pay attention to your own reactions. How credible do you find the stories? How would your team have handled the events at OilCo? How could your team have handled those events differently? What influences made it easy or difficult to learn at OilCo, and what would make it easy or difficult in your organization? What capabilities and factors sustain a team's learning as it interacts with the larger organizational system? How do we know when an investment in learning provides discernible business results?

The OilCo leaders may not have found all the answers to these questions; but they asked them and took them seriously. Other companies will do the same in forthcoming years. Building capabilities that combine inner development with more tangible "spiritual" skill is the single most critical task of the organization of the twenty-first century, where knowledge is the key asset and what people think is the key resource. If you are trying to make your organization competitive, in an era of knowledge-based commerce, then OilCo's example is highly relevant to you; its task is your task, and its challenges, large and small, are poised in wait for you, no matter how simple the path seems at the outset.

Welcome to the OilCo story. We think you will enjoy it.

George Roth and Art Kleiner, editors

ACKNOWLEDGMENTS

This is the second volume in the Oxford University Press Learning History Library. In the first volume, *Car Launch*, we thanked the many people whose ideas and influences helped define the learning history form. In this volume, we wish to focus our thanks on the people who contributed to this book. Once again, managing editor Nina Kruschwitz is responsible for the design and production of the book—overseeing editorial work, creating graphics and diagrams, and organizing the layout and production process on the authors' end. She played an enormous role in helping the critical messages of the OilCo story shine through the complexities of detail and dialogue.

Ken MacLeod, academic editor at Oxford University Press, developed the prototype for this volume and worked with us to define and develop Oil Change. Others at Oxford University Press who deserve credit include: Peter Ban, editorial design manager Elyse Dubin, and Oxford University Press marketers Scott Burns and Sally James. Literary agent Joseph Spieler managed the contractual underpinning for the book; Helen Basilesco of the Ford/MIT Collaboration, where George Roth is executive director, provided valuable support, as did Maggie Piper of the Fieldbook Project.

Ordinarily, we would effusively and gratefully acknowledge our colleagues at OilCo by name—the people who commissioned the learning history, who coauthored and coedited the document, who designed the workshops in which OilCo people talked about it, who championed it at all levels of the organization, who "midwifed" the process that allowed it to be publically available, and whose comments provided the substance from which we drew our intellectual understanding. We would also thank the OilCo executives who recognized the value of this document and who gave approval and support for its general release. We would especially acknowledge the OilCo employees, managers, and executives who permitted themselves to be interviewed and painstakingly made sure their quotes were accurate. For three years (and more), they dedicated their workdays (and often much more) to one of the most comprehensive experiments in organizational learning that any corporation has ever attempted. Unfortunately, anonymity—and the agreement that allows us to make this story public—prevent us from mentioning any of these people by name. Nonetheless, we wish to offer them our heartfelt thanks and appreciation.

The staff and members of the former MIT Center for Organizational Learning, now the Society for Organizational Learning, provided an intellectual home, supportive community, and financial support that both helped OilCo's transformation effort and made this learning history possible. The OilCo learning history, in particular, has been nurtured by the support and critical insight of a number of renowned organizational researchers, who have not hesitated to help us understand the opportunities and pitfalls that they saw in this form. We wish to thank Peter Senge, Edgar Schein, Charles Handy, Charlotte Roberts, and Karl Weick for their comments and (in three of their cases) for their contributions to this volume.

We also wish to single out with gratitude the coauthors who put their time into this learning history on the Reflection Learning Associates (consulting organization that worked with OilCo people to produce the original internal document) side: Ann Thomas, Toni Gregory, and Edward Hamell.

Finally, with the greatest thanks, we wish to acknowledge our wives and daughters, whose love and support enable us to give part of ourselves to work like this. Thank you to: Linda Rafferty, Maggie Roth, Erika Roth, Faith Florer, and Frances Kleiner.

George Roth and Art Kleiner, editors

CAST OF CHARACTERS

This learning history was written as part of an effort to engage thousands of managers and employees in OilCo in a company-wide change initiative. We sought to evoke the experience and insight of one hundred and fifty people, from all levels and branches of the company, who had been directly involved in some part of the change initiative (or "transformation"). The interviewees included a wide variety of OilCo people and some outside consultants; most were interviewed individually, but about thirty were interviewed in groups as part of project teams where they had been active. To provide a degree of confidentiality to the people we spoke to, and to direct readers' attention away from personalities toward more universal themes, we have identified people only by their titles or roles. This helps focus the document on the universal roles, responsibilities, and relationships that people have in an organization undergoing transformation, so that people can more easily see their own situation reflected in part of this one.

When people held more than one relevant title, they were identified by the most salient dimension of their connection with the OilCo transformation. For example, some members of the Executive Council were also members of the Corporate Executive Team and managers of a particular department. We asked them how they wished to be identified for any particular quote.

◆ ORGANIZATIONS

ACTION LEARNING CONSULTANTS: The first set of consultants called in to deliver a design for the transformation and leadership initiatives, this group was influenced by the successful transformation at Jack Welch's General Electric. They recommended or helped develop the Initiative Teams, the early work of the Executive Council, the word "transformation," the work on financial literacy, and much of the initial momentum-building activity.

BUXTON FALLS: A refinery in the U.S. Midwest that underwent dramatic changes using a self-organizing teams approach.

DUCK COVE: One of the most high-profile and productive refineries in the OilCo system, located near OilCo headquarters in Los Angeles.

EXPLORATION AND PRODUCTION (E&P): One of the four main OilCo businesses, engaged in finding oil and getting it out of the ground. Also known as the "upstream" business, this is the traditionally glamorous side of the oil industry, the most technologically-oriented and capital intensive.

HOLISTIC LEADERSHIP ASSOCIATES: A second set of consultants called in to facilitate and design the post-1995 wave of transformation-related activities. This group was influenced by ideas of organizational learning, such as those described by MIT lecturer Peter Senge in his book *The Fifth Discipline*. The work of this consulting group included in-depth coaching and counseling of OilCo leaders, the creation of large-scale workshops for galvanizing shared vision, and the development of informal networks and support teams.

HUMAN RESOURCES: A professional staff service at OilCo, handling personnel and conventional training functions. During transformation, it was reorganized and asked to justify its services in P&L terms.

OILCO CONSULTING: One of the four main OilCo business divisions, engaged in information technology and business support services. This represents a new effort to turn a former staff function (and thus a cost center) into a viable business that would sell its computer-consulting services to other oil companies besides OilCo.

OILCO CHEMICAL: One of the four main OilCo business divisions, engaged in the manufacturing and sale of petrochemical-based products, generally to other manufacturers (such as plastics manufacturers). Most oil companies have a vibrant petrochemicals business, but the petrochemicals industry has faced increasing commoditization and lowered revenues during the past few years. OilCo Chemical is no exception.

REFINING AND RETAIL: One of the four main OilCo business divisions, engaged in refining and making oil-based products from crude, distributing, marketing, and managing service stations. The most diverse part of the organization, this "downstream" segment represents the part of

OilCo's business traditionally seen by consumers. It is evolving into much more of a generic retail and service industry, and it is also consolidating rapidly, as oil companies acquire or merge with each others' refining and retail operations.

SOUTHERN COMPANY: A newly independent operation of OilCo operating on the Gulf of Mexico, with exploration and production as well as some refining within its business.

THE OILCO COMPANY: An American oil company, employing thousands of people worldwide.

◆ TEAMS

CORPORATE EXECUTIVE TEAM (CET): A 100-member group representing senior levels of management in transformational activity, formed as part of the preparation for the second Learning Conference (early 1995). One of the perennial controversies of the OilCo transformation concerned the CET, whose members were sometimes regarded as "not walking the talk"—i.e., not fully living up to the new values espoused by transformation. This group met as a whole in the annual Winter-time "OilCo Learning Conferences," which kicked off the following year's transformation activities.

CORPORATE TRANSFORMATION GROUP (CTG): The internal consultants charged with training OilCo employees in financial literacy: they spearheaded the "Improving Our Economic Value" project and helped managers and employees innovate ways to increase growth and revenues.

DIVERSITY IMPERATIVES TEAM: A third-year imperatives team focused on finding ways to value and leverage a heterogeneous workforce. The diversity team's experience was particularly evocative of the changes taking place in OilCo as a whole; their story is described in Chapter 11.

EXECUTIVE COUNCIL: A working committee of the ten senior-most executives of OilCo, responsible for much of the planning and execution of transformation. This group, assembled by the CEO in 1993, included the CEO himself, the heads of the four major divisions (E&P, Oil Products, Chemical and Consulting) and the heads of various internal staff functions and businesses (HR, Legal, Technology, Planning and Finance, and Taxes).

FUTURE IMPERATIVES TEAM: In the second and third year of transformation, the Executive Council established eight action teams that focused on particularly important topics for OilCo's future development. These cross-functional teams, and the experience of the people on them, were important to the company.

GROWTH IMPERATIVES TEAM: A second-year imperatives team focused on identifying growth options and fostering a culture of innovation at OilCo.

HR IMPERATIVES TEAM: A second-year imperatives team focused on recommending changes to the human resources system in line with the needs of a transforming company.

IT IMPERATIVES TEAM: A second-year imperatives team focused on developing an information-technology improvement strategy that would work well in a transforming company.

PLANNING IMPERATIVES TEAM: A second-year imperatives team focused on developing an operating plan for OilCo and new ways to help monitor performance.

RECOGNITION AND REWARDS IMPERATIVES TEAM: A third-year imperatives team focused on devising a framework for official recognition and rewards that would foster alignment, motivation, commitment, and increasing capability among OilCo employees.

◆ KEY MEETINGS

CORPORATE TRAINING CENTER: A full-scale learning environment located about 25 miles from OilCo headquarters, set up to facilitate team learning during transformation.

GEORGIA PINES: Key meeting of the OilCo Consulting leaders, late in 1996.

KEY WEST: The first meeting of the Executive Council, late in 1993.

LEARNING CONVENTION: Annual meeting of the Executive Council and Corporate Executive Team, held each February to set the agenda for transformation during the following year.

OILCO HOTEL: A meeting place near headquarters, partly owned by OilCo.

WINTERGREEN: A critical meeting of the Executive Council late in 1995.

◆ PEOPLE

ADMINISTRATIVE ASSISTANT, CORPORATE: One of several clerical staff members interviewed for this learning history.

ADVISER, EXECUTIVE COUNCIL: A former information technologies manager with a background in organizational learning, who was commissioned by the CEO to advise and abet the Executive Council's transformation work. This individual was the primary OilCo sponsor of the learning history you are reading.

APPLIED LEARNING CONSULTANT: One of two consultants who were interviewed out of the several who worked at OilCo through Applied Learning Consultants, facilitating meetings and suggesting strategies related to the early stages of transformation.

CEO, OILCO: Appointed in 1993, this senior-most executive of OilCo was the most visible figure, internally and externally, at OilCo, and the "prime mover" of the company's transformation initiative.

CLERK, OILCO CHEMICAL: One of several administrative staff members interviewed for this learning history.

CONSULTANT, HOLISTIC LEADERSHIP ASSOCIATES: Three external consultants were interviewed from this group, the second of the two main groups of external advisers to the transformation initiative.

CUSTOMER, OILCO CHEMICAL: Several staff members were interviewed from this part of OilCo Chemical, in which a well-regarded effort to develop self-managing teams was underway

DATA ANALYST, OILCO: Staff employee who helped propose an innovation that was implemented at the corporate level.

DATA ANALYST, SOUTHERN COMPANY: A member of Southern Company's technical staff, who was interviewed for this learning history.

EMPLOYEE "A," OILCO CONSULTING: A fairly junior employee in the OilCo Consulting hierarchy, who spoke up publicly in a system-wide meeting.

EMPLOYEE, OILCO CHEMICAL: One of a number of non-managerial employees of this part of OilCo, interviewed for this learning history.

EMPLOYEE, OILCO CONSULTING: Member of the OilCo Consulting Staff.

EXECUTIVE, E & P: One of several senior managers in the E&P division who were interviewed and who were also members of the Corporate Executive Team.

EXECUTIVE, OILCO CHEMICAL: One of several senior managers in the Chemical division who were interviewed and who were also members of the Corporate Executive Team.

EXTERNAL CONSULTANT: An outside consultant, one of several independents brought in to help OilCo during the transformation stages.

FORMER FOREMAN, BUXTON FALLS: One of several operators at this refinery who, before the advent of self-managing teams, had been foremen.

FORMER HIGH-LEVEL EXECUTIVE, E & P: This senior executive moved to another part of OilCo; when quoted under this name, the quote refers to his E&P career.

FORMER MANAGER, BUXTON FALLS: One of several higher-level managers in this refinery who were interviewed for this learning history. All played roles in developing the self-managing team effort there, and all subsequently left for other parts of OilCo.

FORMER MEMBER, CORPORATE STAFF: This individual, working for corporate staff during the early stages of transformation, moved on to another part of OilCo.

FORMER ORGANIZATIONAL EFFECTIVENESS (OE) MANAGER, BUXTON FALLS: Training specialist who had helped develop the self-managing teams concept at Buxton Falls and subsequently moved on to other jobs in OilCo.

FORMER SENIOR ADMINISTRATION EXECUTIVE: A long-standing OilCo executive who acted as an informal mentor to CEO before transformation was underway, and who left OilCo before 1993 to work for the shareholder group that owned most of the company.

HEAD APPLIED LEARNING CONSULTANT: Internationally known organizational change consultant who organized and directed the Applied Learning consultation group.

INDIVIDUAL CONTRIBUTOR, HUMAN RESOURCES: Staff member in the HR organization, who chose to be named "individual contributor" for this learning history.

INTERNAL CONSULTANT: This organizational effectiveness staff person was assigned to coach and abet the efforts of a senior executive in one of the OilCo businesses.

MANAGER, E & P: One of a number of mid-level E&P managers interviewed for this document.

MANAGER, HEALTH, SAFETY, AND ENVIRONMENT: The only manager from this staff function who was interviewed for this learning history.

MANAGER, HUMAN RESOURCES: One of about ten managers at various levels of the HR staff who were interviewed for this learning history, and who observed the changes at OilCo from the vantage point of their traditional role as "change agents,"although they were not always given leadership roles in this new transformation.

MANAGER, OILCO: One of many possible interviewees, identified here only as a manager from one of OilCo's four core businesses, describing an event germane to the system as a whole.

MANAGER, OILCO CHEMICAL: One of a half-dozen managers interviewed from OilCo's Chemical business.

MANAGER, OILCO CONSULTING: One of a dozen or more managers interviewed from the new OilCo Consulting business, formerly known as OilCo Services.

MANAGER, OILCO E & P: One of several managers interviewed from OilCo's E&P business.

MANAGER, OILCO REFINING AND RETAIL: One of several managers interviewed from the Refining & Retail (downstream) business; some were refinery managers, others managed various aspects of the retail business.

MANAGER, SOUTHERN COMPANY: One of a dozen managers of the semi-autonomous Gulf Coast subsidiary of OilCo who were interviewed for this learning history.

MEMBER OF EXECUTIVE TEAM, SOUTHERN COMPANY: One of a few members of Southern Company's top-level team interviewed for this learning history; Southern's executive team was analogous to the OilCo Executive Council and took on many of the same roles.

MEMBER, _____: See the team identified in the title. For example, for "Member, Diversity Imperative Team," see, "Diversity Imperatives Team."

MEMBER, CORPORATE EXECUTIVE TEAM: One of many senior managers at OilCo, members of the Corporate Executive Team, interviewed for this learning history. The CET represented more than 200 senior managers handpicked by the Executive Council to play significant roles in fostering transformation.

MEMBER, CORPORATE STAFF: One of a dozen or more professionals interviewed from the staff functions at OilCo, which include: HR (which included media relations); Legal; Planning/Investments/Finance; Health, Safety, and Environment; and Taxes.

MEMBER, CORPORATE TRANSFORMATION GROUP: One of several internal consultants who were interviewed for this learning history from this visible group, set up in the first year of transformation to help the organization learn financial literacy, along with other skills later.

MEMBER, EXECUTIVE COUNCIL: One of the ten senior executives of OilCo, all of whom worked closely with CEO as the transformation unfolded.

OFFICE ASSISTANT, SOUTHERN COMPANY: This administrative assistant worked closely with the President of Southern Company.

OPERATIONS FOREMAN, SOUTHERN COMPANY: An operations-level employee at this semi-autonomous Gulf Coast subsidiary.

OPERATOR, BUXTON FALLS: Workers in the Buxton Falls refinery who underwent a conversion to self-managing teams—some enthusiastically, some with no enthusiasm at all.

OPERATOR, OILCO REFINING AND RETAIL: Worker at the Buxton Falls Refinery who chose to be named in this document as a worker at OilCo R&R.

PRESIDENT, OILCO CHEMICAL: The highest-level executive at Chemical, and a member of the OilCo Executive Council, this official had come to OilCo from another company.

PRESIDENT, OILCO REFINING & RETAIL: The highest-level executive at OilCo Refining & Retail, and a prominent member of the OilCo Executive Council.

PRESIDENT, E & P: The highest-level executive at E&P, and a member of the OilCo Executive Council, this official was, in effect, the director of a large company-within-a-company.

PRESIDENT, OILCO CONSULTING: The executive leader of the OilCo Consulting business, who was also a member of the OilCo Executive Council.

PRESIDENT, SOUTHERN COMPANY: Senior-most executive of the semi-autonomous Southern Company, an oil company owned by OilCo.

SENIOR EXECUTIVE: One of a number of top-level executives interviewed from the various OilCo businesses.

SENIOR LEADER, HUMAN RESOURCES: One of the highest-level executives in the Human Resources organization at OilCo.

SENIOR MANAGER: A member of the Executive Council with a reputation as a primary advocate and role model for transformation.

SENIOR MANAGER, BUXTON FALLS: Manager with current line accountability for the Buxton Falls refinery.

SENIOR MANAGER, E & P: One of several senior managers interviewed from the E&P division, each with line accountability for a department or project.

SENIOR MANAGER, OILCO: A veteran manager somewhere in OilCo with profit-and-loss responsibility for a department or project.

SENIOR MANAGER, OILCO CHEMICAL: One of the higher-level managers in this part of OilCo.

SENIOR MANAGER, OILCO CONSULTING: One of the members of the OilCo Consulting leadership group, its equivalent to the Executive Council.

STAFF MEMBER, CORPORATE TRANING CENTER: One of several employees coordinating classes and workshops at this center, established in 1996, for developing competencies among leaders and employees of the transforming OilCo.

STAFF MEMBER, OILCO HEADQUARTERS: One of several employees at the OilCo corporate center.

STRATEGIC PLANNER: OilCo professional whose work included developing the OilCo strategies and plans.

SUPERVISOR, OILCO CONSULTING: One of several middle-level managers interviewed from the OilCo computer and accounting services division, which had become a separate company (OilCo Consulting).

TECHNICAL MANAGER, SOUTHERN COMPANY: One of a few managers of Southern Company interviewed for this learning history.

TECHNICAL STAFF, DUCK COVE: Staff member at one of the most prominent refineries in the OilCo system.

THE SAME BOSS AS IN THE PREVIOUS STORY (AS IDENTIFIED ON PAGE 112): Senior executive at OilCo, coached by Internal Consultant.

UNION SHOP STEWARD, BUXTON FALLS: Labor representative for Buxton Falls throughout the period when self-managing teams were established.

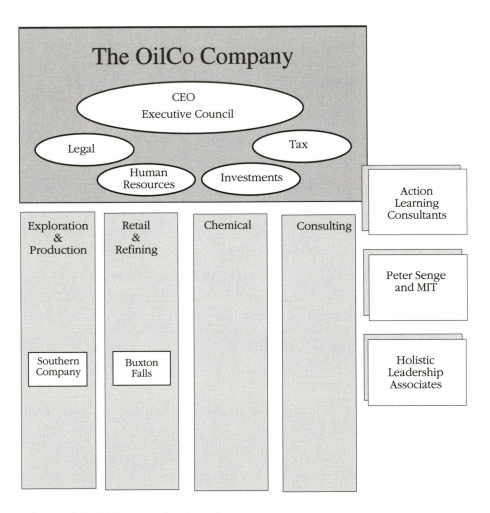

Figure 1-0 *OilCo organization chart*

INTRODUCTION

CHAPTER 1

INTRODUCTION

◆ CONTENTS OF THE LEARNING HISTORY

The learning history materials are divided into eleven chapters that follow the Introduction:

2) Genesis: The Early Years: The forces and events that led up to the transformational "kick-off": the 1994 Learning Convention.

3) The Quest for Financial Literacy: The story of OilCo's company-wide financial literacy initiative, its influence, the responses it engendered, and the cultural shifts prompted by the need to develop a new concept of business performance.

4) Southern Company: How a major component of OilCo spun off into its own company—providing an early major example of the implications of the new governance structure and financial literacy initiative.

5) Governance: New structures for focusing power and accountability: OilCo's new governance system, the "Federalist" ideas that support it, and the effects that it has had upon day-to-day work life.

6) Noble Purpose: The OilCo Consulting governance story: How the new autonomy of OilCo Consulting has raised questions about relationships with other OilCo entities—and the purpose of the enterprise.

7) The Glass House of Leadership: The paradoxes of leadership as people struggle to undo hierarchical dependency and build performance.

8) Buxton Falls' High-Performance Teams: Experiences with new team structures have focused attention on leadership and cultural change.

9) Three Siblings and the Pace of Change: The pace of transformation may depend upon the interrelationships among existing attitudes at OilCo.

10) Downsizing During Transformation: The OilCo Chemical story: Cutbacks and restructuring take on new dynamics after transformation begins.

11) The Diversity Corporate Initiative Team: The experience of this strategic team offers insights for anyone trying to explore new values in OilCo's culture.

12) "Who Am I?": The transformation's emphasis on "learning" raises fundamental questions of human identity.

Chapters 2, 3, 5, 7, 9, and 12 represent "themes" that emerged in the research of this document. Chapters 4, 6, 8, 10, and 12 are self-contained stories that embody key themes. All of the chapters represent facets of the same underlying "system" of transformation at OilCo. All of these themes and stories have influenced each other. But telling them separately allows you to focus attention on areas of particular interest.

In all of these sections, a clear message exists. It can be expressed in four words: "You are not alone." No matter what level you occupy, and no matter where you work, many others within the company face similar dilemmas and opportunities.

◆ HOW TO READ A LEARNING HISTORY

A learning history is a new format for presenting the story of a project. The document is designed to spark conversation. Thus, it will seem unfamiliar at first. However, it generally does not take long to get used to the two-column format.

Each theme is presented in the form of a "jointly told tale," separating the researchers' comments from participants' narrative. There are four different types of material in these "jointly told tales," as illustrated in Figure 1-1.

In reading the two-column format of the "jointly told" tale sections, you will find yourself having to make a choice. Which column do you read first? Do you skip back and forth, and when do you do so? There are no "rules" for reading a learning history; different people read segments in different orders.

As you make your way through the story, however, try to pay attention to your own reactions. How credible do you find the story? What decisions might you make in similar situations? How can the experiences described here help inform the decisions that you (and your associates) have to make in the future? We recommend that you highlight and add your own notes, particularly in the minor (commentary) column, as the basis for further conversation. It is through discussion and dialogue with colleagues about the contents of this document, that we believe your own, your fellow course members', and your team's learning will best be served.

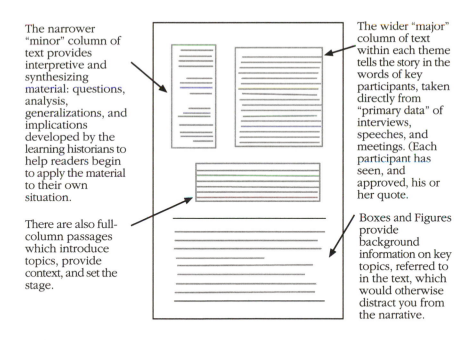

The narrower "minor" column of text provides interpretive and synthesizing material: questions, analysis, generalizations, and implications developed by the learning historians to help readers begin to apply the material to their own situation.

There are also full-column passages which introduce topics, provide context, and set the stage.

The wider "major" column of text within each theme tells the story in the words of key participants, taken directly from "primary data" of interviews, speeches, and meetings. (Each participant has seen, and approved, his or her quote.

Boxes and Figures provide background information on key topics, referred to in the text, which would otherwise distract you from the narrative.

Figure 1-1 *Learning history formats*

◆ NOTICEABLE RESULTS

These noticeable results were used as conversation starters during our interviews. They represent a preliminary list of evident indicators of change, seen from the perspective of late 1996. Interviewees were invited to select from this list the events they felt were most significant and that they had seen first-hand.

Subsequently, some of these "results" changed, especially as the price of oil decreased; we include here the results that were evident at the time the learning history was produced. Observers at that time would not have agreed, even then, on what each of these results meant. All observers would have agreed that the results listed here had taken place, that they were observable, and that they were significant. The extensive and diffuse nature of OilCo's transformation resulted in many different indicators of improvement. The following list is organized in categories OilCo leaders regarded as important.

FINANCIAL RESULTS

- OilCo had experienced growth in revenues with growth in return on investment (ROI) since transformation began.

- A 10 percent ROI goal was set for the future.

- The crisis of the late 1980s/early 1990s had turned to "recovery."

- The second quarter 1996 financial performance: "Best in our history but millions of dollars behind target."

- OilCo stock had done very well in 1995-1996.

- Analysts' evaluations of OilCo had become more enthusiastic.

CORPORATE LEADERSHIP AND CORPORATE MISSION

- "We will be a premier company": showed a shift in attitude had taken place.

- A prominent civic leader had been appointed a board member. (Interestingly, no interviewees chose to talk about this "result".)

- Early 1995: a vision/values report was published.

New governance structures and mechanisms

- A universal pay scale review had taken place.

- Variable pay was pegged to organizational performance. (This led to some dissatisfaction.)

- OilCo had undertaken a comprehensive alliance development/out-sourcing review. (Alliances were begun with other large oil companies.)

- Organizational restructuring within businesses was going on.

- The new governance structure had established new business units beginning January 1995.

- Reduced levels of work force were evident in the organization.

- The number of signatures required for a financial expenditure of $100,000 had gone from approximately twelve to one.

- OilCo had adopted self-approved, on-line expense statements.

- More alliances and strategic partnerships existed.

- Outsourcing had dramatically increased. (This created job security concerns.)

- An E&P joint venture with [a large energy company] had begun.

- A FlexTime work schedule had been proposed and implemented.

- New integration structures were oriented to being competitive in business. (These included both marketing and exploration projects.) These new corporate structures aligned across old "stovepipes."

- A joint E&P group was formed to break down barriers or practices or perceptions.

- OilCo people were working on brand identity in a new cross-functional group.

- A new growth initiative gave impetus to new projects and risk-taking.

- Real projects got freedom to take risks. One Chemical plant, for instance, entered a new business and "saved the plant." Strategic teams commissioned and accomplished cross-functional goals. (Some of these teams produced controversial results.)

- Momentum from the Corporate Transformation Group, in particular, fostered an understanding of the financial ramifications of work performed throughout the company.

- A job-posting system significantly altered people's perceptions of their horizon, of "what is possible."

- OilCo's new Corporate Training Center was established.

- An Enterprise Leadership Group was created of 100 senior managers, aimed at fostering transformation.

OPERATIONS/TECHNOLOGY

- "Top drawer" technological prowess was enhanced since 1993.

- Outside entities recognized OilCo's technological capabilities.

- Deep-water offshore platform production had begun in the Gulf of Alaska.

- New "team-based" operations had taken hold.

SOUTHERN COMPANY

- Southtern Company had been spun off.

- Southern Company embraced financial literacy.

CORPORATE CULTURE

- New openness or personality shift had occurred in a key leader, observed from below by people working in the business unit reporting to that person.

- Learning conventions were taking place at a business unit within OilCo.

- "We are more open now."

- People were much more accountable.

- People were accepting much more responsibility relative to costs. Technical people were more attentive to the business side (ROI).

- Behavior in meetings had changed: Team meeting structures were different.

- There was a commitment to results.

- People talked to each other across functions.

- Anxiety was still high, re: downsizing. Job security concerns were fueled by new alignment and outsourcing structures.

- In 1995, people said: "I don't feel trusted." This year, they said: "I worry about my future." This was seen as a more honest expression of peoples' anxiety.

- Explicit awareness existed in senior circles of doubts, ambivalence, and skepticism among middle managers.

- Serious problems persisted in areas such as discrimination (the class-action suit).

- Misalignment was identified; there was less "hiding in the weeds."

- Criticism of previous OilCo leadership decisions was articulated within the company.

- Competitiveness between the four OilCo companies continued.

- "We are not serious about growth." New venture ideas emerged but were not implemented.

◆ CHRONOLOGY

Many diverse elements took place as part of OilCo's transformation. The Chronology in Figure 1-3 represents an attempt to put them in context with each other on a timeline.

1991
Crisis: "abysmal financial results"
Cost reduction and asset restucturing begins
Pretransformational efforts at Administration, E&P, Buxton Falls, etc.

1993
[CEO] becomes CEO (summer)
Early organizational learning announcement
Applied learning begins regular consultation with OilCo
Executive Council formed (Aug.)
Key West Executive Council meeting (August)

1994
Learning and Development Initiative announced (January)
Learning Convention (February
Mission, vision ("premier company"), values (belief in people, trustworthiness, excellence, innovation, urgency)
Financial literacy ("Improving Our Economic Value") project begins
Operational projects (June)
Corporate Initiative Teams begin work (August): Growth, Sustained Low Cost/High Value, Human Resources, Investing, OilCo Brand/Corporate Reputation, Information Technology
Vision Survey: "We want to see corporate transformation" New governance concepts announced (November/ December)

1995
Corporate Initiative Teams' recommendations to Executive Council (January)
New governance model operational (January)

Figure 1-3 *Chronology*

Learning Convention (February)

Corporate Transformation Group begins training

Southern Company spun off into separate entity

Two new Corporate Initiatives (August): Recognition and
  Rewards, Diversity

"Generative interviews" process launched

Holistic Leadership Associates begins in-depth work with
  OilCo

Wintergreen Executive Council meeting (October)

Community Service Initiatives

Financial performance reaches ten-year high, but not new
  10 percent ROI goals

Enterprise Leadership Group launched

1996 OilCo Consulting begins new governance strategy
  (January)

Learning Convention (February)

Independent refining companies created in OilCo Refining
  & Retail

Deep water Gulf of Alaska venture featured in Wall Street
  Journal

New Corporate Training Center begins operation

CD-ROM produced, "rolling out" corporate transformation
  (August)

OilCo learning history commissioned

1997 Learning Convention, including the first public presentation of this learning history (February)

OIL CHANGE

CHAPTER 2

GENESIS:
THE EARLY YEARS

How did the OilCo corporate transformation begin? One factor was the appointment of a CEO who set the company on a deliberate course of learning and transformation. At the same time, the organization was poised to change.

◆ THE CULTURE OF THE 1980s

The roots of corporate transformationhave much to do with OilCo's long-standing history and culture. Later, when crisis would strike, a number of people within OilCo began to recognize that they could not blame out-side circumstances alone. Somehow, the company's own attitudes had contributed to its misfortunes.

SUPERVISOR, OILCO CONSULTING: In the early 1980s, things were booming. Nobody thought about laying off people. You didn't worry too much about where you spent your money. We were buying Univac machines just as fast as we could. There was a naiveté on my part and on the part of many others, and we were paid well to be naive. I think we expected those times to last for ever.

MANAGER, OILCO CHEMICAL: It was not really like a real business. It was more like a giant government agency. It wasn't like having real customers. People tended to be pretty far removed from direct business results.

Judging from our interviews, this culture of formalistic non-candor existed not just at the Executive Council level, but throughout the company. If you spoke candidly about events in someone else's domain, you might spark a hostile reaction.

MEMBER, EXECUTIVE COUNCIL: In the past, you didn't think about authenticity. You would hear a decision that would hurt, but would think "Maybe he knows what he's doing, so let's just play the game."

MEMBER, EXECUTIVE COUNCIL: Our conflicts would seethe below the surface. When it got tense we would ratchet up to become even more formal and more polite.

We had an informal understanding at the senior level: "You don't plow my field, and I won't plow yours." If a vice president made a presentation to the CEO, the other senior executives wouldn't mess up his field. They might think, "This is the dumbest thing I ever heard," but they would never say it. They might ask a polite question in support, or make a brief inquiry. But there were never any penetrating, tough questions, other than from the former CEO. There was no constructive challenging.

What does this anecdote say about OilCo's old culture? About competitiveness? Risk aversion? Political gamesmanship?

How might this type of practice affect behavior, such as openness and the ability to create trust?

SENIOR MANAGER, E&P: The vice president of E&P used to call each of the senior managers every Monday morning and ask how the business was going. In my case, that meant that I had to know, every Monday morning, what the state of the wells had been on Friday. And I guess it meant that the CEO was calling him up every Monday, and he had to be prepared.

This meant that everybody in the week before, toward the end, started gearing up. There was a thick little black book prepared every week. It contained notes for the division manager to use for the call from the general manager, who would use it for the call from the vice president, who would use it for the call from the executive vice president, who would use it for the call from the president. I remember having to get two or three sentences about my well into the book, even though it probably fell on the cutting room floor. You had to get it in, because if you didn't, it looked as if you weren't doing anything.

That book was a visible symbol of totally wasted energy. We stopped using it years ago, and yet business is doing quite well.

Box 2-1

OILCO'S LONG-STANDING HISTORY AND CULTURE

OilCo's culture and business style have grown and evolved over a period of more than six decades. The company's history began in the 1900s when the founders began shipping gasoline from overseas to America. By the turn of the century, these traders had begun drilling for oil and marketing their products in the United States. Refineries were opened during the next two decades; the resulting "OilCo" company expanded operations dramatically during the oil boom of the 1920s, and ultimately became a well-known producer of fuel and chemicals.

Within the industry, OilCo's great strength was technological innovation. OilCo engineers and scientists developed a variety of technologies for agricultural production, for specialized fuels, and for new materials production. Some of this innovation was critical to the Allies during World War II. During the postwar period, OilCo established technological leadership in offshore deep well drilling; in refinery technologies; in plastics and other chemical research; in gasoline formulation; in fuel transportation systems; in new technologies for exploration and production; in geologic research; and in the corporate use of information technology. OilCo was also known for its brand name at retail stations in some states.

By the mid-1970s, OilCo's characteristic traits—technological leadership in the oil industry and high financial security—had held steady for the entire length of most OilCo employees' careers. Then came the "oil crises" of the 1970s, which had the effect of pushing oil prices and revenues higher. High-capital-investment projects produced strong returns, and with its privileged resource position, OilCo prospered. This gave the company an incentive for continuing to acquire assets and extend its resource base.

Then, between 1979 and 1986, the industry began to change. Markets became more energy-efficient, the balance of power among the oil-producing nations shifted, and the oil price collapsed in 1986. OilCo's culture of "winners," accustomed to having its strategies pay off, had a hard time recognizing these new realities. By the early 1990s, the setbacks in the oil and chemical businesses were impossible to ignore, or to rationalize. Expert technological leadership would, in itself, no longer be enough.

◆ 1986-1993: The slide and the crisis

In 1986, the fall of the oil price set in motion a series of events that caught people at OilCo unaware. The difficult environment, combined with some decisions made at senior levels, led to a gradually worsening financial situation. It reached crisis proportions in the early 1990s.

People still struggle with the memory of the cutbacks and layoffs that they were forced to endure and implement. For a while, it seemed that the crisis would never end.

This story describes how some leaders at OilCo misjudged the company's long-term financial health.

What indicators could have been used at the time to judge financial health?

During early 1990's, people at OilCo sometimes assumed the crisis was temporary.

MEMBER, EXECUTIVE COUNCIL: Prices started falling in 1985. They fell off the cliff in early 1986.

We had invested heavily on the idea that oil and gas prices would continue to increase. So the return on our investment was lousy and we were out of step with many of our competitors. The whole E&P industry was lousy, because other companies had done the same thing—but not to the same extent that we had. We had bet on our technology, but the prices would just not support that technology to the point where we could make a reasonable return on our investment.

So as prices fell, we tried to cut our costs without changing the way we worked. We sold some of our businesses. We laid off about half of our staff. That took place from 1986 to about 1993. And we did it in several increments.

SENIOR EXECUTIVE: I was in corporate planning then, and the story told there was: "There was a funny aligning of the stars. All the businesses happened to go in the tank the same year. But lightning only strikes once, so we're okay." But if you really looked, you could see that it hadn't happened to other companies. We really had lost competitive ground.

I found it personally frustrating because we hired an awful lot of good people. I didn't see much of a plan to get better; only excuses.

MEMBER, EXECUTIVE COUNCIL: We had thought we were the greatest thing since sliced bread, and then, in 1991, our net income went down to a significant amount. But we still were given our huge budgets. We still would say, "Boy, if I don't spend my budget this year, I won't get the same amount next year." And no one held us accountable. So it looked as if nothing was going to change.

MANAGER, OILCO REFINING & RETAIL: In 1991, we had our first broad-based staff reductions. I realized then that the old cradle-to-grave implied commitment—the expectation that "if I get hired on with OilCo and do satisfactory work, I could be here thirty years and retire with all the benefits"—would have to change.

As the next few comments suggest, many interviewees described feeling blind-sided or even devastated by the staff reductions. Several interviewees noted that it was tougher on the rank and file staff, who were directly affected, didn't know why it was being done, and had the strongest feelings of anger, mistrust, and betrayal.

We had targets that year for reducing staff, but the targets were not based on an analysis of the work to be done. It was "cut and cope." We had to drive cost out of the system. We had some latitude to try to be smart about it, but at the end of the day we were expected to deliver reductions of a certain percentage. The question "What if we really need all those people?" was not acceptable.

To select the people who would be offered severance choices, we used lists of people in similar skill groups, ranked from best performance to worst. The worst didn't mean awful; it just meant relative performance. In some cases, we had to go fairly high up on the list, up into the really solid contributors, to offer severance. And since everyone knew the list was based on performance, a terrible stigma was associated with the voluntary offer.

From a statistical perspective, the ranking approach to severance seems compassionate. But does it have unintended consequences? What could be done to make severance less devastating?

Meanwhile, there were other people who ranked high in performance, but who wanted to leave, because it fit their personal circumstances. They wanted to step up and sign up for the lucrative severance opportunity, but the answer was "no." So they felt like they were being denied an advantage.

I had sleepless nights over this; partly because I didn't agree with the philosophy of this rigid performance focus.

I believe the way we went about this contributed to some of the disenfranchisement or distance that some of the employees still feel about the transformation process. People are still fearful that the next time things get tight, the grim reaper will come around again.

MANAGER, OILCO: I was at the exploration labs, and our work was cut way back. I heard, "You are very expensive. We don't like paying for you." Personally I went through a low time. I felt as if six years of my life had been thrown away. At an intellectual level, I could understand that our costs were high and our refineries were in bad shape. But at a gut level, it was a traumatic era.

MANAGER, OILCO: It was a pretty hateful climate. When the senior leaders came to address middle managers at OilCo Chemical at an off-site, they had to appoint a young MBA to edit the questions from the floor so that the more embarrassing questions wouldn't get to the podium.

There were questions like, "You hold us accountable for results, but here are the results that you have done." Or, "Why haven't you been fired?" That speaks to some kind of relationship, right?

There was basically a total breakdown of respect. It cascaded all the way down to the factory floor level. People looked for scapegoats instead of reasons.

MEMBER, CORPORATE STAFF: There was a lot of tension and anxiety. People were unsure what was next. Who would go? What would go? Were we valuable as employees? As people? We watched a lot of brain trust going out the door, and there was an uncertainty about whether OilCo—or the oil industry—would be able to recover.

I was working in media relations. I had to be the public voice for the downsizing. Since I had an external role in the community, people would ask me in restaurants: "How's OilCo? Are you still with OilCo?" That was

Some interviewees are outspoken in blaming the company's management for the 1989-1991 episode. They accuse senior leaders of failing to acknowledge their own part in OilCo's troubles.

Other interviewees refuse to be quoted, even anonymously, as critical of past leaders. This is in part, they say, because they do not want past leaders to see themselves being maligned.

What do these two attitudes imply for what might still exist at OilCo?

For comments about the aftermath of "breaking the employment contract," see page 131.

a downer. You always want your company to be in the best light. People in the outside world realized that the community—beyond our immediate OilCo family—was also going to be impacted. There were suppliers who counted on us, and governments which counted on contribution to the tax base. They were asking good questions but we didn't necessarily have the answers.

There was also an underlying feeling among some that we may have gotten too complacent. Maybe a shakeup was really what we needed to get us thinking in new directions.

◆ 1991: Precursors to corporate transformation

Before the current CEO was appointed, several change programs existed, all experimenting with management innovation. Some of the initiators were senior people in the company; others were comparatively obscure. All of them kept a low profile on their "change" efforts. In the early 1990s, the rest of the organization did not seem ready to pay attention.

But when the corporate transformation developed into a company-wide action in 1993-1994, some OilCo people wondered what the big deal was. They were already engaged in their own transformation, and had been for years. At the same time, they felt recognized. Transformation had made their own efforts part of something larger.

CEO, OilCo: The idea that I am the architect of the transformation is not on target. A pre-existing host of people were predisposed to this process of transformation. I wouldn't call it a network, but they had been reading the same things, and experiencing different ways of doing business in other corporations they interacted with. They were ready and willing to effect any kind of transformation of this kind, and a lot of them were involved in that early work.

Might the CEO's most significant role in corporate transformation be that of a lightning rod for the already visible energies in OilCo?

President, E&P: In 1991, before the "OilCo Corporate Transformation," we started trying to change the culture in E&P. We had tried everything we knew; all the quick hitting things. Prices continued to deteriorate and the busi-

What implications do the multiple initiatives already taking place have for the ability of an organization to undergo and sustain a corporate transformation?

Some people described a dilemma they faced in promoting "soft" approaches—based on changing human behavior, instead of simply implementing "hard," easily measurable business or technological fixes. The old OilCo culture was not openly supportive of "soft" change approaches.

In the face of skepticism, what is persuasive about such "soft" efforts as leadership training, team building, and organizational learning?

In what ways is skepticism justified?

This manager felt that this quote, though accurate, seemed "sugarcoated." He does not want to imply that the entire OilCo Chemical transformation story is positive.

ness didn't show signs of revival. We were at wits' end.

There must be a better way, we decided, and we could not wait for somebody to come forward with it. We had to develop it ourselves.

We brought in a group of "effective leadership" consultants and started talking about "soft" as well as "hard" things that we could do to improve. We made training available to everybody in E&P, to change the way we did business and learn to work together as teams. This took place over four or five years.

At first we had a difficult time convincing people this wasn't another "flavor of the month." There was a low level of trust in E&P, between the staff and the management. There was great concern about job security. Everybody was in a survival mentality and looking out for themselves personally. Who could blame them? Since 1986, almost one-half of the work force had been severed, either through asset sales or staff reduction programs.

I think there was also a sincere attitude: "You guys are getting paid to lead this organization; now lead it. Lead us out of this situation."

EXECUTIVE, E&P: We used a team process approach to provide the framework for ongoing improvement. We provided coaching resources for training and behavior support to each one of our teams. Within the first three years, our organization within OilCo saved hundreds of millions of dollars of operating costs and capital. We moved from being a high-cost producer in all areas to one of the lowest in the three-year time frame.

MANAGER, OILCO CHEMICAL: In the late 1980s, OilCo Chemical was in the forefront of the quality initiative that started at OilCo. And circa 1988, OilCo Chemical crystallized a set of guiding principles by which we judged ourselves, called the Mission and Guiding Principles. It had concepts like: commitment to our people, growing with our customers, profit leadership, and a real strong people and customer focus.

When [CEO] became CEO, and began to focus on how he wanted to run the corporation, Mission–Vision–Values came along. I drew a picture for my troops: one box portrayed the OilCo-wide Mission–Vision–Values, and an overlapping box contained our Mission and Guiding Principles. I said, "Isn't seventy percent of it the same?"

"Yeah."

"And isn't this different stuff better?"

"Yeah."

"So, what's the big deal?"

"Nothing."

Actually, I think most of us at OilCo Chemical are proud that the company sort of adopted the path that we were on.

At least two OilCo refineries had similar stories of middle-ranks initiatives that anticipated the corporate effort when it finally appeared.

What does this suggest about effectively melding top-down and bottom-up efforts so they reinforce each other?

FORMER SENIOR ADMINISTRATION EXECUTIVE: In 1987, after the drop in crude oil prices, Administration was under particularly great pressure to reduce costs. When today's CEO, then VP of Administration, went to his direct reports, he got pretty much the same response: "We've done everything we can. To cut costs more dramatically, we'll have to run the business differently."

[CEO] was quite supportive. He had a very open view about learning how to find world class best practices. He brought in a leading consulting firm to executives and some other consultants, including a reengineering guru to bring new views to the table. Once we began opening up, listening to new ideas, and even setting a vision, we began to see new opportunities and directions.

Our new approaches needed a leader like [CEO], who could say, "Here is the direction we're going in. We don't know all the answers. But we're looking for all the people in the organization to help figure it out."

Each executive was experimenting with different approaches to save costs. In some cases, cost-savings became a spur to innovation.

Is there enough encouragement for people to look outside OilCo for world-class best practices?

With many different efforts under way, would there be a need to achieve synergy?

EXECUTIVE, E&P: Corporate initially was not on board with a comprehensive improvement process. Therefore, President, E&P was taking some "risk." Corporate was just interested in the bottom line. The organization did not relate to anything other than financial data. At that time, we didn't know how successful we were going to be and the process was fragile. So for these reasons it wasn't widely shared with the rest of the organization.

Then the new CEO came in. With the change, there was more support from the top. But that brought other activities that were being generated outside of our organization, so there was almost an overload situation. We were faced with: "How do we integrate the E&P initiatives with the OilCo transformation?"

Some of these quotes are notable because they show a commitment to the future of the company that had to be kept hidden. Managers saw themselves as having to fight "guerrilla wars" and skunk work projects to promote needed changes, in an almost clandestine fashion, until they could feel secure of more support from the top. If it was valuable for OilCo then to have people challenging the status quo, what does it suggest about challenges when the new status quo is "Corporate Transformation?" How might these new challenges be handled?

Many initiatives were also brewing at OilCo. (See, for example, the Buxton Falls story on page 119.) Within the corporate central offices, an informal "skunk works" team was assembled in early 1993, as a transitional team for the new CEO. This team began working on concepts such as cultural change and the governance model, to give form and shape to these concepts and to present alternatives when the CEO was appointed.

◆ THE APPOINTMENT OF THE NEW CEO

A new CEO was appointed by the OilCo board of directors in mid-1993. We do not include the reasoning behind the selection of the CEO, because we did not interview people who had made the decision.

To some people, the CEO was seen as the obvious choice; others saw him as an unlikely "dark horse" candidate. At the time, he was Vice President of Administration. Originally trained in physics, he had spent much of his career at OilCo in Exploration & Production. He had also held positions in Public Affairs, with the US government as an exchange manager, and (like many senior OilCo managers) in international management.

In this segment, people talk about their expectations before a CEO was named; he talks about his own thought process after receiving the assignment.

CEO: I don't think I was chosen because anyone hoped I would initiate a corporate transformation. I don't know if a lot of the transformation would have been viewed as wise.

MANAGER, OILCO REFINING & RETAIL: The CEO spoke at a management course that I went to in 1992. He was awful; he seemed to be a cold, stern man, who managed by the numbers. He basically pleaded with us to do a better job so that the leaders of OilCo could continue to lead the company.

Several people noted, like this manager, that they originally expected the CEO to continue traditional leadership... or worse.

My private reaction was: "I'm doing my part, buddy. You are the ones whose decisions have screwed the place up." The rest of us had essentially been minions, carrying out what we had been told to do. So it made me very angry.

Several people spoke of the corporate "mask" that senior managers must wear to get to positions of power.

Then I heard that he was going to be CEO, and I started getting resumes out. I expected his regime to be very dehumanized, command and control-oriented. There would be a blood bath of cost-cutting. I saw no sense of hope, no vision for the future.

MANAGER, OILCO CONSULTING: [CEO] is like Gorbachev. Somehow, he had survived in the old power structure for years. I would like to see [CEO] talk about the years when he believed one thing deeply, and the people he reported to believed something different—and how he came to grips with that.

When leaders seek change, does the implicit benefit of that "mask" become a liability?

MEMBER, EXECUTIVE COUNCIL: I've asked [CEO] on a number of occasions, "Why did you do this? How were you smart enough to see this when nobody else did?"

He will say that he didn't have a series of planned moves. He had two or three in mind, and then he would take it from there, depending on how things worked out.

The plan for transformation was not disclosed ahead of time. Indeed, there was no delineated plan; but a goal and process in mind

The idea that OilCo can be "outstanding place to work" is linked, inevitably, to the implicit employment contract.

A skeptical point of view would say: Outstanding for whom? A new and less expensive work force?

At the same time, the CEO's comment is powerful precisely because it recognizes that the trauma, and the aspiration that OilCo could be outstanding, exist in context with each other.

This passage shows the evolution of a process of thought.

Is this type of reflection important? For leadership? For people throughout the company?

CEO: The period after you find out you're probably going to take over a job like this, but before you take it over, is a time of real reflection. So for eight months, I conducted a personal examination. What was I going to do? Did I want to preside and take all the nice things that come with higher office? Or did I want to make a significant difference? I think almost everyone would choose the latter.

So I tried to analyze the company's position. I had been involved in its management at a high level for many years. I could assess my own mistakes, what we had done wrong and right, and our fortunes as a company. We had conducted traumatic layoffs and other actions that were out of character for OilCo. Those actions had been necessary, but not sufficient, to make the company into what I thought it should be: a truly outstanding place to work and a widely respected company.

I could see that we had to find a way to grow the company substantially. We had to get significantly better performance out of every element and probably do a lot of restructuring and changing. What could I do to help?

One of the fundamental things I wanted to do was to significantly alter the distribution of power. We had a centrally controlled management style—very much based on a hierarchical and military model. Senior management basically made the decisions. People looked there for direction: "What do we do now, coach?"

I have had a fundamental belief, all of my life, that this is a flawed style of management. It had led us to significantly under-use the talents of the organization. When you think about someone's performance, you can either think in terms of the mistakes they will inevitably make —we all make mistakes constantly—or you could think about what they could do if they really tried. If you give them that room, people can perform much better than we usually give them credit for.

So I felt we had to create an environment based more on freedom and open flow of communication. People would have more control of their jobs and their own development; they would make decisions with which people above them might not agree, and we would get more out of the human element of the company. That is pretty easy to say, but very difficult to accomplish. In some ways, it's not fair to do, if you have a group of people who have not been conditioned or trained to take care of their own affairs.

What resources and attitudes would encourage a leader, at any level of the company, to engage in this type of reflection?

Thus, there would have to be a very significant new process of learning—in particular, to develop two kinds of skills.

First, we were an undisciplined business organization. I included myself very much in this. Historically, we had been run by technical people. We never invested any time or effort in developing business skills in people. It was almost seen as a mark of intellectual contempt that people would be considered commercially as opposed to technically competent.

These two sets of needed new skills fore-shadowed the two forms of "transformational" consultation brought into the company: The "quest" for financial literacy (see page 41) and the work on leadership and organizational learning (see page 99).

Second, we had not developed in our people the skills or behaviors that would allow them to operate easily or well in this new environment of freedom and open communication. We would need a lot of development in people skills and changing behaviors.

How would we go about all this? I will confess that I didn't have a clue. But I explicitly knew that it would require a focus on learning. I've always thought of learning as the fundamental process of change—the way in which people gain new insights and capabilities, and begin to behave differently.

During late 1992 and early 1993, I looked at a host of people who were advertised to be experts at transformational learning and changing companies. From my discussions and reading, I developed not a blueprint, but a sort of topographical map and general mental picture of where and how we should go. I decided to use Applied Learning Consultants as the initial instrument—the shock troops who could begin the wrenching change.

Why, if learning is intrinsic, do companies look to external consultants to help with transformational learning efforts.

ADVISER, EXECUTIVE COUNCIL: [CEO] began to talk openly about his intentions. He would do away with the General Executive Office, which consisted of the CEO and the

The General Executive Office ceased to exist, without being formally dissolved, because the CEO never called a meeting of it.

executive vice presidents of the three major organizations. In its place [CEO] wanted to create an Executive Council.

◆ THE FORMATION OF THE EXECUTIVE COUNCIL

The transformation effort formally began with the Executive Council's first off-site session, in August 1993, at the Key West resort. It wasn't yet called the Executive Council; it was a meeting of everyone at the level of corporate vice president or above.

Previous high-level meetings had generally consisted of formal presentations. This meeting was intended (by the CEO and Applied Learning) to get people to talk more informally about fundamentals: What was wrong with the company? What direction should they take? There were no preconceived "solutions" to OilCo's problems. Finding solutions would require managing through experimentation, continual reflection, and collaborative teamwork—new norms that seemed counterintuitive.

APPLIED LEARNING CONSULTANT: They didn't call themselves the Executive Council at that point; they were trying to determine their name. Were they a governing body? How much authority would they have, versus the authority of the business units? The feeling was "We can't call ourselves a team, we're not really a team."

MEMBER, EXECUTIVE COUNCIL: We were a little uncomfortable. We had never worked like this as a group of people sharing ideas across the tables.

MEMBER, EXECUTIVE COUNCIL: This was the first time that the vice presidents ever got together, except for Christmas parties. The old CEO and General Executive Office had made all the decisions. So there had been no reason to bring everybody together.

Knowing that new behaviors never come easily, where does one find the willingness to begin to make fundamental change?

Now we were together. We fumbled around. After the first day, I called [CEO] and said, "I'm out of here. This is a waste of time. All we're doing is singing your praises." But he told me to wait it out. At the end of three days, I still wasn't pleased, but I did notice that we had made some change.

APPLIED LEARNING CONSULTANT: At that first off-site, I saw the OilCo leaders as being cautious, courteous, conflict-averse, bureaucratic game-players. I liked them as individuals; they were nice people. Very gentlemanly. They spent a lot of time on process and procedure instead of results. They would ask, "What is the correct way to communicate our decision to the people?" As opposed to, "What is the right decision?"

Old norms had people seeking for the "right" behaviors.

I had the feeling that they didn't see their destiny in their hands. It was somewhere in the ground.

CEO: I had very severe doubts. From what I had read, I knew that the probability of success for transformation exercises is pretty low. Most of them result in an awful lot of work and a high degree of cynicism; they create Dilberts. Moving this way was the right thing to do, but it would probably be a dry hole.

Most of the Executive Council members made similar assessments of their early meetings—noting the stiffness and inability to focus on key issues. They wanted to communicate effectively, but (as in the rest of the company) it would take time and learning new skills to evolve that new form of behavior.

I did not know if the participants were willing to go on this kind of trip. I had known them all for many, many years. Some I considered good friends. I knew I could not force this on them. No one can; I don't care if you're Jack Welch or god almighty.

The meeting itself was probably one of the most dysfunctional gatherings I have seen. Not that peoples' attitudes were bad. But we were illiterate, incapable of even engaging with each other.

In one key exercise, the Head Applied Learning Consultant suggested they write a mock Fortune article about OilCo, as if it were published several years ahead in the future.

MEMBER, EXECUTIVE COUNCIL: We all wrote that results will be good. "And it's all through the leadership of [CEO]."

CEO: Everybody said the same things with a slightly different twist. We'd all get involved; we'd have extremely high profits and happy employees. I got a little sick of it. It didn't seem real. And I had written the same story myself. So I decided, at the last minute, to put a different spin on it.

MEMBER, EXECUTIVE COUNCIL: [CEO] went last. "I listened to the rest of you," he said, "and I'm not going to read you what I wrote." Instead, he went on to tell a story that: "The board of directors announced today that OilCo is being liquidated. The headquarters in Los Angeles are being closed down, employees are being let go, and all the assets are to be sold to other companies."

That made everybody sit up and notice. "Wait a minute, he's serious." Something similar had already happened at another large oil corporation, and a lot of other companies were going under. The light bulbs went off: "He's going to change this company."

MEMBER, EXECUTIVE COUNCIL: The room went quiet. We all looked at each other. Wow. Looking back on it now, it almost seems contrived. But at the time, it was powerful.

That was the first clue that I remember, that we would go down the path on this transformation.

Here is an outsider's perception.

APPLIED LEARNING CONSULTANT: At the end, they split up in different teams to work on pieces of the mission, vision, and values. The backdrop was: "Okay, there's a lot of competition. There aren't many oil reserves left that are easy for us to access. Our rate of return is not great. Do we need to transform? What does this mean we need to do?"

What actually takes place, on the inside, beneath the surface of this "lack of energy"? Might it be: Fatigue? Procrastination? Fear?

I was amazed at the lack of energy. I had done a little bit of background research and knew that things weren't fantastic for OilCo. These senior executives were being paid a lot of money and, except for a couple of people, I didn't get the sense of urgency that I might have expected.

CEO: I look back on that meeting as a great success. It was like the first time a child stands up on its feet; you

don't need to take a lot of steps to have a strong beginning. We worked out some things and looked toward further actions.

Thereafter, in our meetings, we would sit in small
groups actually doing things—instead of at long conference tables or audience-style, with one person speaking
on a platform.

◆ DEVELOPING A "MISSION, VISION, AND VALUES"—AND THE FIRST
STIRRINGS OF ROLL-OUT

At the Key West meeting, the CEO announced that this group would
develop a "mission, vision, and values" for the company.

CEO: For the previous few years, the idea of "vision driven
management" had been getting pretty hot. A lot of people
in OilCo had picked up on it. Different sectors of the company were creating their own visions. But when I gave
talks in my old job, the question always came up: "We
don't know if our E&P or Chemical vision is consistent
with the corporate vision. Where is the corporate vision?"

There was no corporate vision articulated. People
were crying out generally: "Where are you taking us?
What are we trying to become? All we've seen is blood
and carnage for the last three years. Is there anything else
out there?"

*A push-pull phenomenon begins to
take shape. The impetus for
transformation comes, as with a
see-saw, alternating from above
and below.*

MEMBER, EXECUTIVE COUNCIL: [CEO] got up at the Key West
meeting and said, "We've got to do a vision, mission and
values." Many of us had been exposed to this sort of
thinking. You spend three or four days off-site, working
on a vision statement. It means a lot to you, because you
fought over every word. You bring it back to people who
stare at you with blank faces and say, "What have you
been smoking down there?" It goes into a desk drawer,
and nobody does anything as a result.

But the CEO led us in the right direction.

*Often, the process of putting the
vision together has more impact
than the actual words of a vision.*

Box 2-2:

MISSION, VISION, AND VALUES AT OILCO

From the beginning, the Head Applied Learning Consultant argued that no progress could be made in OilCo's transformation without a well-designed statement of the company's mission, vision, and values. At General Electric under Jack Welch, these three sets of guiding principles had given people a framework for action that allowed them to make autonomous decisions in an aligned fashion. The mission expressed why a company was in business; the vision articulated an image of where the company was ideally headed (where it "wanted to go"); and the values described key principles for individual and team behavior that would help realize the company's mission and vision.

Here are excerpts from the statement of the mission, vision, and values, as articulated by the OilCo Executive Council:

Mission:

OilCo is in business to excel in the oil, gas, petrochemical and related businesses... In doing so, our mission is to maximize shareholder value by being the best at meeting the expectations of customers, employees, suppliers and the public.

Vision:

Our vision is to be the premier U.S. company, with sustained world-class performance in all aspects of the business. We will be a dynamic company, characterized by our integrity, customer focus, profitable growth, the value placed on people and superior application of technology.... People will be proud to work for OilCo because we consistently attain superior business results, offer fulfilling work and provide the opportunity for individuals to achieve their full potential. The communities in which we operate will welcome us because of our sensitivity and involvement.

Values:

1. Belief in People: Our corporate performance is the sum of our individual performances.... The understanding that each person must find ways to add value has opened up more opportunities for creativity and leadership, more opportunities for learning, more opportunities to be all that we can be.
2. Trustworthiness, which is closely related to integrity and ethical behavior, has deep roots in the OilCo tradition.... But as part of our transformation we also want to explore a few, less obvious aspects of this value. One of those is doing what we say we will do. A look at our business plans for the past five

years shows that we have not always turned in the performance we said we would…. Leaders must "walk the talk." And so must each and every one of us if we are to earn the trust and respect of others.

3. Excellence: We need to go beyond creating excellent products to creatinng the products our customers want… All excellence starts with the individual. That's why personal commitment is so important. But a complex, competitive future will also demand excellence from teams, from work groups, from our individual businesses, and from OilCo as a whole.

4. Innovation: In the old OilCo culture, with its proven and accepted ways of doing things, innovation often took a back seat. But in the company we are creating, innovation occupiees a place of honor…. Would-be innovators must also be risk-takers… Although we should never become complacent about failure, we must understand that a certain amount of it iss the price of admission to a faster-paced, rapidly changing, and highly competitive future.

5. A sense of urgency: If change is the new status quo, speed has become the only acceptable response…. A sense of urgency suggests that a fast solution that's 80 percent effective may work better than a 100 per cent solution perfected after the window of opportunity has closed.

The single element that most captured the attention of OilCo people was the idea of becoming a "premier" company. Throughout the interviews, OilCo people used this term again and again. They seemed to have internalized it as a yardstick for the transformational content of any thought or action. If it was truly worthwhile, then one could easily imagine it as characteristic of the premier company of the U.S.

MEMBER, EXECUTIVE COUNCIL: We divided up into teams of three and four people. One team would write a mission and vision statement; another would work on relationships. The third would work on values for the corporation. We divided up to begin to write down the kinds of things that we would like to see happen at OilCo.

Later, after the organization had an opportunity to respond to the mission, vision, and values, the Executive Council would rethink them. See page 99.

MEMBER, EXECUTIVE COUNCIL: In our subteam, we went off into a room with a facilitator. We met a dozen times or so to try to define the elements of a mission ("who you are"), vision ("where you want to go"), and values ("how you want to live"). We developed that into a draft. We told ourselves that it was 80 percent complete.

We took it back to the Council for debate and discussion. For instance, we had a vision of being the premier company. Did that mean the premier oil company, or the premier company in America? Could we achieve the latter?

APPLIED LEARNING CONSULTANT: At the Executive Council sessions, they didn't always agree on the mission, vision and values specifics, but there was a lot of energy in the group. It was clear that it was important for the Executive Council to have these conversations, even if they weren't going to govern, so they could do the right things for their business units.

They came back and decided that they weren't going to solve all their unanswered questions right away. Instead, they would ask the next level of leadership in the company, a group of about 100 people, for feedback as they refined the document.

◆ EARLY TRANSFORMATIONAL LEADERSHIP

A few signals filtered out to the company about transformation at this time. A mysterious announcement, for example, appeared in January 1994.

When they read the announcement (see Box 2-3) some people were concerned that it was a signal of further layoffs. Others recognized it as a statement of the visible need to develop peoples' capabilities for improvement at OilCo. In the following months, most of the visible effort to promote the transformation seemed to stem directly from the CEO's own activity. He seemed serious in intent, but interviewees recall having no clear idea of where he was going, or what would happen next, as if he were still testing the waters. Bit by bit, people began to get an idea that something new was going on.

ADVISER, EXECUTIVE COUNCIL: After an early assignment on a special project for transformation, I was assigned to a

---

Box 2-3

EXCERPTS FROM THE FIRST ANNOUNCEMENT OF CHANGE

January, 1994

The Executive Council of OilCo is launching an initiative to strengthen and enhance learning and development. To achieve our business objectives in today's difficult environment, we will need a continually improving performance from everyone....

Investment in people is critical to OilCo's performance and this initiative is intended to impact everyone. We need to improve our processes for learning and developing our full potential. We expect open communications, listening and dialogue across the Company....

The initiative will complement other learning and development activities already under way in OilCo organizations. The initial thrust in 1994 will be to provide learning experiences that develop a shared vision and understanding of OilCo's direction and business objectives.

---

different job, which had nothing to do with transformation. But [CEO] kept calling on me to do things.

One day, I told him: "You know, this is a full-time job supporting you in this transformation, and I've just been given another full-time job." In reflecting back, I'm quite surprised that I said this, but I'm glad I did. He asked me, "Well, what would you like to do?" And the words that came out of my mouth were: "I have fire in my soul for this transformation."

The fire came from a couple of things. In part it came from a conversation I had had with [CEO] himself, before he became CEO. I had had thirty minutes in which to describe how we might go from quality to business process re-engineering to organizational learning. And I became aware that this man was listening to me with full attention. It was so unusual and exceptional to feel that from someone at his level. I will never forget what that felt like. It felt very good.

The CEO sought people with passion and vision to help him improve the company. Is this typical for change efforts?

In several accounts, people described how they were impressed by the CEO's honesty, receptive attitude, and frankness.

MEMBER, CORPORATE STAFF: The CEO came to our plant and talked about what a humbling experience it was for him to be named president. He acknowledged that he didn't have the skills by himself to turn this ship around. He would need a lot of help. He showed a vulnerability and authenticity that made me want to join with him and be part of the solution. People knew that he was part of the past, because he had been in senior positions for so long. We'd never heard a CEO talk like this before.

MANAGER, OILCO CONSULTING: [CEO] came to some off-site session, where he answered questions people had written on cards. One question was: "Do you have any idea how difficult it is to get up in the morning and come in to a job you hate?'

I expected the response to be, "Well, I'm sorry; go talk to your manager; Blah, blah." His comment was: "If you hate your job, quit. It is ridiculous to spend your life doing something that you hate." That kind of attitude, to me, is part of what has filtered throughout this change from old to new.

◆ THE FEBRUARY 1994 LEARNING CONVENTION

The first of OilCo's annual three-day learning conventions took place in February, 1994. Its sessions introduced many concepts that would become fundamental to OilCo's transformation work: the need for financial literacy throughout the organization (and a set of methods for developing it), the notion of leadership as a competence that people could develop and improve, and the "mission, vision, and values." The audience was relatively elite—about 100 of the top-level managers.

The first day of the conference was information-rich. A half-day lecture, commissioned by the Executive Council and delivered by internal and external consultants, introduced the need for urgency, the importance of shareholder value (even within the organization) and the basic principles of financial literacy (see Box 3-1, page 44); then, one by one, Executive Council members presented the mission, vision, and values from the podium. The quotes of people reflecting upon this session illustrate new values that were being emphasized by OilCo's leaders.

MANAGER, OILCO: I remember the buzz that was there in February of 1994 when everybody got together for the first time. The electricity and energy of having the whole group at the Doubletree. You could just feel it was in the air. I believe that helped fuel a lot of us. There is real power in the opportunity of getting together, working together.

What might have produced the feeling of openness and candor that people recall about this session?

MANAGER, E&P: The conference gave all the senior leaders at OilCo a chance to sit in one room. People stood up and took some personal risk, to say what they felt in front of a fairly big and important audience.

I remember talking about the problems of E&P culture, where people never wanted to tell anything except the positive side of the story. People in other businesses stood up and said, "Let me tell you what really is going wrong, right now today." To listen to that kind of talk in a room with the CEO up there at the front of the table represented a big change.

MANAGER, OILCO REFINING & RETAIL: I thought it was going to be one of these typical cascade things where your bosses tell you the message, and then you are expected to go tell your people, and then they are expected to go tell their people and so forth. There was a little flavor of that.

Many of the attendees were seeing the members of the Executive Council speak frankly about their concerns for the first time.

But then the leadership got up and talked as individuals and sincerely asked for input. A couple of them actually said that they had made mistakes. I didn't recall ever hearing any of them ever admit to making a mistake before.

I had never realized how angry I personally had been about the fact that the guys at the top, who had gotten us in trouble, were still there. It did not appear that much pain had happened in their lives. But the pain in the rest of the organization was immense.

There was power in being able to express vulnerability and authenticity.

I had always felt a tremendous amount of autonomy and responsibility. But I had seen my responsibilities as relatively definable and narrow. In other words, if I were the business manager for business X, I would do what needed to be done there. But it never occurred to me that I had responsibilities beyond the boundaries of business X. In that meeting, for the first time, I saw that this was bigger than just the piece I was assigned. I would have to contribute to the fabric of the whole.

Three comments show the range of reactions to the vision of OilCo being "the premier" company.

MANAGER, OILCO: When they used the word "premier," it was very unOilCo-like. OilCo had always struck me as this company not willing to go out on a limb. We would put about 25 qualifiers on something. Now here we were going to be the premier company in the United States.

MANAGER, OILCO: When I heard "premier company," I laughed at it. To think that an oil company would really aspire to be the best! Maybe you can be the prettiest leper in the colony; but how are you going to be able to be the best?

MEMBER, EXECUTIVE COUNCIL: As we look at the OilCo vision, the only words most people remember are: "the premier company." I think those three words really matter. I hear people say, as we're trying to make a decision, "Wait a minute—would the premier company do it this way?" I don't think any other words in that vision affect the conduct of too many people. In fact, even the Executive Council would have a hard time reciting all the issues covered there.

If you were seated at this traditional OilCo presentation, what would need to be communicated in order to allow you to challenge ideas and engage with the presenter?

MEMBER, EXECUTIVE COUNCIL: I presented the mission. I saw it as a quick presentation that did not need much preparation. After all, everyone knew our mission: We were in the oil business, and we would operate in the United States.

But then, all of a sudden, I was intensely involved in trying to defend myself. Why was shareholder value more important than customers? "But employees are awfully valuable also; what about that?" We went through the circular kind of debate that you get into on these subjects around stakeholders.

I'd never done this before—to step before a group of supposed followers and be vulnerable.

APPLIED LEARNING CONSULTANT: There were a lot of open displays of cynicism at the first Learning Convention. "Are you for real, [CEO]?" And a lot of "gotcha" behavior. People tried to ask passive-aggressive questions to trip him up, like a press corps: "Some people say you don't really mean this, [CEO]. What would you say to them?"

MANAGER, OILCO: We were asked to shoot short videos: skits representing the "old OilCo," followed by representations of the "new OilCo." In my group, we portrayed the old culture as "knowing every answer to every question." In the new OilCo, the questions were as important as the answers.

Already, a kind of "glass house" attitude about leadership was emerging at OilCo; see page 99. Was it a reaction to the old norm of not criticizing one another?

APPLIED LEARNING CONSULTANT: One video made fun of the fact that when managers were scheduled to eat in the executive dining room, they were afraid that the former CEO might ask them a question. If you didn't know the answer, you could be fired. So, they spent a lot of time preparing—for lunch.

The videos were a lot of fun, and people began to feel that [CEO] was really going to be serious.

These stories reflect the use of humor in creating a distance between old and new behaviors.

MEMBER, CORPORATE EXECUTIVE TEAM: The only person at our location who attended the Learning Convention was the site manager. He came back and spent an hour talking to us about the mission, vision, and values. We were supposed to review them.

This was obviously a style change: getting the leaders together and having a dialogue about these things. In the previous era, the site manager would have lectured us and left. Our views ranged from skepticism to endorse-

This comment, and the next comment, suggest that a new role of leadership was implicitly proposed at the 1994 Learning Convention—and immediately understood.

Is it the right role? And if so, are the leaders at OilCo prepared to take it on?

ment, but everybody ended up feeling positive. We sensed the potential to move in the right direction.

MEMBER, EXECUTIVE COUNCIL: For the first time a large community cross-sectionally in OilCo was coming together. This felt different. For a privileged group of people, it was an early sign of hope, a sign that stuff was happening.

But then those privileged people were meant to go back and get engaged with other people around the bandwagon, with these documents: Mission, vision, values, and the new employee relationship.

The pains of transformation started to become apparent. It was different from the pains of the cut-and-survive era. Now people said: "What's happening? What new 'wisdom' is coming down from these guys at the top? What are they going to force on us now? What do I say 'yes, sir' to today? It looks different from what I had to say 'yes, sir' to yesterday." Hope, uncertainty, fear, confusion, and anger all started to emerge.

CHAPTER 3

THE QUEST
FOR FINANCIAL LITERACY

The OilCo "Improving Our Economic Value" project is probably one of the largest-scale "open-book management" projects in history. [See Box 3-1, page 44.] It spearheaded the implementation of OilCo's two newly defined goals of business survival (10 percent annual return on investment) and growth (10 percent annual revenue growth). A set of consultants (first external, then internal) translated those goals into operations throughout the company, working with managers to specify critical indicators and metrics that would help each part of the business keep on track. Training in financial literacy was meant to give people a visceral sense of the links between their own day-to-day choices and the performance of the enterprise as a whole.

It was understood that it would take time to achieve a high level of competence; OilCo's managers were technologically gifted, but had rarely been required to bring bottom-line consideration to their decisions and implementations, especially in terms of boosting the company's share price. Yet the company's future depended on this new kind of awareness. This meant, in effect, that OilCo's people had embarked upon a quest: a journey toward a necessary but difficult result. Some saw the result as unattainable; others thought it could be reached. Clearly, the journey would be significant in itself.

The fundamental function of any quest is the development of the quester. Encounters and experiences inevitably change people, in unexpected and unalterable ways. As people move closer to their goals, their sophistication grows. Their understanding of the goals is altered, and they move into phases that they never planned or expected at the outset.

◆ **THE ORIGINS OF THE QUEST**

Concern about the lack of business knowledge among OilCo's engineers and executives was already building in the early 1990s.

> FORMER SENIOR ADMINISTRATION EXECUTIVE: I recall having big auditorium sessions in the early 1990s about the idea of running OilCo Administration as a business. Quite honestly, I got a lot of stares. Even though most of these people had business and graduate degrees, they couldn't visualize what was meant.
>
> About a year later, when I was making another set of presentations on the same theme, I was extremely impressed. People had become fluent with the idea. They might not have fully internalized what it would mean to them personally, but at least they were on board conceptually.
>
> We were pretty naive about how to go about communicating [this new idea]. We thought we were fairly progressive just to get out in front of everyone in an auditorium. We gradually found out, through feedback, that we needed small-group sessions where we could have real dialogue and interaction.

Early in 1994, the Head Applied Learning Consultant suggested articulating the critical financial ramifications of work done throughout OilCo. [Head Applied Learning Consultant] had written a book about General Electric, crediting its articulation of financial goals as one of the key elements of a successful transformation. When GE's CEO, Jack Welch, talked about "every business being #1 or #2 in its category," this measure provided a guide for businesses throughout GE. With a team of external consultants, he helped OilCo begin the development of its financial literacy project.[1]

What are the advantages of initiating financial literacy outside of the conventional finance structure?

CEO: The idea of financial literacy was very attractive to me. It offered a fundamental way to describe how a business has to be run, and it began to lead people to understand the financial implications of what they did. The idea of running your individual job as a business was completely off most radar screens around here.

Thus, in the fall of 1993, a group of people in corporate worked very hard to introduce financial literacy and see if we could use it as a mechanism.

MEMBER, CORPORATE EXECUTIVE TEAM: External consultants and corporate planning worked very closely in the early stages to develop the initial concepts around the "Improving Our Economic Value" project. This injected thinking into this company that was not here before. It was a prime catalyst to begin shifting engineers and scientists to become more like business people.

Some interviewees have the impression that the Applied Learning consultation was "not successful." Others credit it with making a dramatic, vital difference throughout the company.

MEMBER, CORPORATE EXECUTIVE TEAM: We worked up examples—one each in E&P, Refining & Retail, and Chemical—and developed what a managerial profit and loss statement might look like, as well as some very high-level ideas about key profit factors, financial leverage, and other elements of the "Improving Our Economic Value" project. We played that back to the Executive Council and others in the organization and got a lot of positive suction: "Yeah, this is stuff that we need and can use.

MANAGER, HUMAN RESOURCES: The idea came across, through the presentations on financial literacy, that our business approach was crap. We didn't understand our own profitability. This was expressed credibly enough to be convincing. People at OilCo might not like hearing it, and they might not like [Head Applied Learning Consultant], but they damn sure got a lot out of that one-and-a-half years.

One interviewee noted in passing that the idea of being the "premier company" had little tangibility. The scoreboards and indicators of the "Improving Our Economic Value" project provided a standard to which some people could relate more easily. It represented the first time they understood: "Here's the purpose of my job!"

MANAGER, OILCO: Interest in financial literacy developed by pull-through. The early days showed us that an idea can be put out without the classic OilCo approaches of videos, brochures, or program mandate: "This is the way you do it, now go comply." Some people out there saw the benefit, picked it up, and used it without it being "rolled out" or officially sanctioned.

The most significant part of the "Improving Our Economic Value" project was its highlight of corporate value as a goal—not just return on investment. ROI and growth together are required for corporate value. A high-ROI company that shrinks is not creating value. Whereas in the old model, we were shrinking OilCo in order to improve ROI.

MANAGER, SOUTHERN COMPANY: With the "Improving Our Economic Value" project we finally said, "Here's what we have to achieve, and here's the timeline." That was a watershed event. For so many years, I had been part of plans that we achieved—but they didn't win. There would be this weird logic. Everybody felt okay because they

---

Box 3-1:

FINANCIAL LITERACY AT OILCO

OilCo's "Improving Our Economic Value" project represented an effort to bring "bottom-line" and "top-line" awareness to every level of the company. People throughout OilCo were offered training, not just in the financial goals of their businesses, but in the meaning behind those goals. The training began with an introduction to the financial significance of the crisis of the 1980s and 1990s. Trainers (primarily drawn from external consultants, then members of OilCo's internal Corporate Transformation Group) described the financial history of the company. In the mid-1980s, at the height of oil prices, return on investment had hovered above 10 percent. This showed it was possible. But it had not happened since. Why was that target valuable? How could OilCo achieve it again? And was it possible to surpass it?

The next step would involve devising a kind of scoreboard for each part of the business. OilCo people were trained to identify "pivotal operational numbers:" measurements that managers could recognize their effect upon, and which could in turn be traced for their impacts on profitability and growth. Examples might include amount of scrap and waste, weekly numbers of orders, percentage of on-time shipments, hours

were meeting their targets, but the company was a loser.

I think people rallied around the new goals as a case for action: why we had to do it. That had been absent before.

MANAGER, HUMAN RESOURCES: To me, this financial literacy stuff was Business 101; it was something you took in your freshman year in college. But to many people, it was new and fascinating.

We had never assigned our costs in such a way that we understood what we were doing. Instead, we had had a kind of barter system. If I wanted my PC fixed, I picked up the phone and called someone. They came here and said, "You kicked the plug in the floor and it came unplugged. Anything else I can do for you?" And they went away.

In many corners of the company, there is still great resistance to the financial literacy concepts. Only the people who found the initiative compelling tended to talk about it in interviews.

worked per week per function, budget variances, customer satisfaction, departmental cash flow, and revenue per employee. The critical point was not just establishing metrics, but making clear that everyone understood why these particular metrics were significant.

In short, instead of using arcane financial terms, the "scoreboard" was deliberately designed in accessible language that "made sense," even to people without accounting training. Every activity by every manager was recognized for its contribution to revenue growth, cash flow, and shareholder value for the company. Products and services could be bolstered, cut back, or adapted accordingly, so they did not just meet technical and market specifications, but contributed to growth and profitability. Managers and employees thus took on accountability for the profitability of their part of the company.

The OilCo financial literacy program represented a comprehensive company-wide approach to open-book management, although it was never referred to by that name. The term "open-book," coined by business journalist John Case, refers to a management movement that first appeared in small businesses, where executives spell out financial goals so that employees see their contribution to the enterprise as a whole. Open-book management requires often-unprecedented degrees of openness, candor, and training, but it pays the company back in a broader base of capable decision makers. In OilCo's story, we see how the principles of open-book management can be applied to large-scale enterprises.[2]

I never knew what it cost to call them, but OilCo had just paid $150, or whatever it was. If I had been home and my PC didn't work, you damn well know I'd have checked the plug before writing a $150 check to a repairman. The "Improving Our Economic Value" project helped people begin to understand that.

The powerful impact of financial literacy, in some circles at least, led some observers to hope that it could be "rolled out" to more people. This led to the creation of the Corporate Transformation Group, a corporate-wide internal consultant's team with about twenty members.

Other people also delivered "Improving Our Economic Value" training: externals with Applied Learning, internals on E&P's "Quality & Performance Improvement" team, and Human Resources staff members. This meant that there would be a large variety of experiences with the "Improving Our Economic Value" project. All of these groups put forth their interpretations of the practice. At the same time, since all of this diffusion took place in small groups and workshops, only a small fraction of OilCo's people were directly engaged.

MEMBER, PLANNING INITIATIVE TEAM: At the 1995 Learning Convention, our team recommended extending the financial literacy work into a "boot camp," a series of intensive workshops. It would require a significant amount of staff to help carry that through. This eventually became the Corporate Transformation Group.

There was a fair amount of resistance to the boot camp idea. Everybody thought that they were already putting in 110 percent effort. So, the Conference attendees decided that the appropriate way would be to let each business adopt the "Improving Our Economic Value" project in the way that they decided would be best. The Corporate Transformation Group would help them.

Each business did it differently. OilCo Chemical basically did go through a boot camp process. Some businesses focused on strategy first, and only then followed the elements of financial literacy. Other businesses focused on financial literacy first and then followed the strategy.

◆ Hard knowledge leads to "soft" communication needs

The financial targets of any business are hard and measurable. People can talk about them clearly, even if they do not agree on how to achieve them. But by 1996, people found the financial literacy work leading them into "softer" issues, where it is difficult to maintain the same sharp clarity. To boost quality or achieve a rate of return, people would have to learn to bring others on board, or rise above OilCo's habits of competitiveness. They had to start thinking about leadership and attitude change.

MEMBER, EXECUTIVE COUNCIL: Early on, we talked about transformation as being a journey, not an event. It sounded pretty good, but as I look back, I appreciate how naive I was. I did not see the fear, turmoil, and uncertainty that transformation creates.

We had made hundreds of millions of dollars in 1993. People balancing their checkbooks, making $40,000-$50,000 a year, think this amount is pretty good. But it represented an ROI of less than 5 percent. How could we make the link to show how this result represented bad performance?

In the past nobody would have argued this question. We would have said, "We'll tell people to meet 10 percent ROI." We would have saluted and set it down on paper. We would not have admitted to ourselves that we could not get the message across.

But now, some of us started to say, "We can't just go out and tell people that 10 percent ROI is the target."

FORMER MEMBER, CORPORATE STAFF: I watched some businesses go through their financial literacy report-outs. It became painfully obvious that the human issues, and not the business issues, were getting in their way.

We started seeing organization after organization hitting these brick walls. They had done their numbers and strategy. But they hadn't addressed the human side and, therefore, they were making no progress.

MEMBER, CORPORATE TRANSFORMATION GROUP: The planning team had promoted, and the Corporate Transformation Group taught, month-by-month tracking of business decisions. If a business has made a recent investment, then instead of giving back some high-level, esoteric report next September on "Expectations from last year's investment," they should ask questions about it every month.

But to do this, we needed to be less polite; to accept an environment of constructive challenge and debate. We needed to invite inquiry instead of squashing it, based on old political or position power.

This led us to work a lot of the behavioral components into our workshops. We especially hit hard on teaching line leaders to coach other people, so that there wouldn't be too much dependency on us.

We had quite a few blowups after those exercises. People would get personal. They would say, "Jim did this to me a half hour ago, and I'm still mad about it." Bantering that has taken place for years below the surface comes out into the open. We hold it together with a lot of inquiry. We let people say what they want to say; even if there's conflict, we don't shut down the conversation. We allow them to get through it.

MANAGER, E&P: In 1991, when OilCo made only a very small net income, I didn't really understand net on net. I just knew that if I had had my money in the bank on that kind of return, I'd change banks!

Since that time, I have found that financial literacy, as an agent of personal transformation, has a lot of great places to grab a handhold.

In our old culture, I might be the only guy in the whole place with some vision of where the company was going. I would delegate tasks: "Jerry, you go do this. Ann, you go do that." Jerry's or Ann's results would be measured by how well they accomplished my demand. Whether I had the right vision or not wasn't part of the equation.

In the new culture, the strategy development process involved everybody in the company—121 people in my group. There was an incredible level of challenge, debate, energy and real feeling as we argued about how to pull ourselves out of a performance slump. By engaging people who normally weren't asked to think in that realm, we came up with a strategy that people could understand and get their teeth into.

The strategy became a filter for every opportunity that came our way. In the old OilCo, Exploration could often develop a dynamite prospect story—only to discover that the associated costs were prohibitive. Our total costs had been far above the industry's best cost of $6.50 per barrel. Now we focus on benchmark life-cycle costs, and aspire to be the best in the industry.

There's a lot of data involved in this strategy development. In the past it would all have been shared at management levels, but it never would have been taken down into the organization. We took it there. A lot of people said, "Wait a minute, I don't understand that. What is this 'life-cycle cost'?" The dialogue that ensued got everybody far more aligned than we had ever been in the past.

Today, if you walked down the hall and asked the first person you saw about strategy, they'd say, "Cost leadership and first to production." And they could also tell you what that meant to them.

◆ SOPHISTICATION: CAN THE METRICS BE QUESTIONED?

The "Improving Our Economic Value" project, by creating a tremendous expectation for success, has established a new framework for achievement at OilCo. There is an implicit message: If you are really good at financial literacy implementation, then your endeavor will succeed.

But some people at OilCo see this as an authoritarian prescription. They perceive that they will be held accountable for results, whether or not the results are possible. They argue that the "Improving Our Economic Value" project is not relevant to their type of work. Or they say that external business conditions prevent them from increasing the business value of their work. In other cases, people value financial literacy but have not been able to develop meaningful measurements for themselves or for individuals in their departments.

Others are already assuming that, as much as the financial literacy initiative influences OilCo's experience, OilCo's experience should influence the design of future work on financial literacy. They say that the "Improving Our Economic Value" project gave some people the power and capability to move beyond its prescriptions. By pursuing the "quest," people grow in sophistication and awareness. They can now question the measurements and the financial goals on their own terms and suggest ways to change the company's overall financial direction.

MEMBER, CORPORATE EXECUTIVE TEAM: A lot of people still don't really understand the financial literacy material. They run into a wall, trying to identify the key measurements related to their own human activities.

I've run into the same wall. I'm having trouble developing these measurements. Which activities are the most important to be doing?

It's relatively easy to find the key factors of the shop floor. You can measure, for instance, the run time of a machine. It gets harder when you talk about knowledge workers: Geophysical interpreters, geologists, and engineers, for instance, have a harder time determining what to measure. And it gets even harder at the level of leadership. What is leadership? How do you measure the value in that?

I get questions from my people at the end of the day. They really want to know: "Do we really need a manager in your executive position ? What is your real value?"

I feel dumbfounded that I can't answer it. I think I add value, for instance, by breaking down barriers to make it easier for people to do their work. But when I try to quantify my work, people perceive me as being defensive. "Well, yeah," they can say, "but maybe somebody else broke down that barrier. You just created a coalition and got other people involved. That's not very much for your value to the organization."

In today's world, people ask very tough questions. I think we're all better for it. We're talking about things today that we never would have talked about in the past.

Intuitively, everybody "knows" what they should be doing. But research has shown that our intuitions can be wrong. That's very powerful; and if there's some way to restore some portion of that misplaced intuition, then this would create value.

MANAGER, HEALTH, SAFETY, AND ENVIRONMENT: Financial literacy has been tough for us. If one of our guys had a tremendous success today, that would probably mean we don't have to spend $50 million four years from now. It's hard to take a financial-literacy approach to that kind of work, because what did we do today to make this success? Was it the three meetings we held with the regulator? Or the particularly persuasive letter we wrote, after poring through the regulatory records?

The things that have the greatest benefit may not be things that can be done efficiently. Even if they could be, you never know which of the five things you did was the most important in achieving your result.

MEMBER, CORPORATE EXECUTIVE TEAM: The 10 percent ROI figure is based on OilCo's average cost of capital—which varies a bit, from business to business, but overall is about 10 percent. Thus, one would expect that the shareholders, at least, should get a return, over time, of about 10 percent per year. The idea of 10 percent ROI thus represents a hurdle rate.

Of course, in a business driven by significant investment, the ROI for an individual project starts out very low. It creeps up, hits a peak, and then declines again as you depreciate the asset. So your ROI depends on your life cycle, and it's not as good a measurement as: "What improvement do you have in value—based on projected free cash flow?"

I don't think anybody worried about issues like these before the "Improving Our Economic Value" project. OilCo needed something to get people focused, so they chose 10 percent ROI. That's okay, but it's only part of the story.

MEMBER, CORPORATE EXECUTIVE TEAM: The most productive work that came out of financial literacy took place when people had a train wreck with their strategy development. "I've done my financial analysis. I think I've determined the absolute operational best I can get—and holy mackerel, I can't improve the numbers at all!" That created fertile ground for a strategy discussion.

Since then, we've continued to drill down into the more specific details of the financial numbers. And that's where the attraction begins to drop off a bit. "Gee whiz, is there really a benefit to go a lot deeper into this thing?"

Nobody has a perfect package developed yet, and I'm concerned that some business units are waiting for someone else to demonstrate what the perfect package looks like and to prove that it's all worth while.

Of course, the financial literacy initiative is an evolving, dynamic process. There are elements of good work in various places in the company. We have not done a good job at communicating and sharing those. People have to see what's been done and working in other areas and take the best practice elements and start applying them to their own businesses.

◆ GROWTH AND FINANCIAL LITERACY

Does a financial literacy initiative promote, or inhibit, the ability of OilCo ventures to begin and grow to fruition? We have heard both points of view argued.

For more about growth, see page 77, where we look at the attitudes about risk and growth that emerge in new ventures.

MANAGER, OILCO: If you look at the official statements and planning documents of the late 1980s and early 1990s, growth clearly wasn't a driving priority. "We need to get the ROI right, and then if we can grow," they said, "we will."

But between the "Improving Our Economic Value" project and the Future Imperatives projects, people began to have some processes and tools to work on growth. I'd guess we probably have hundreds of people across the company working actively on growth, who were working on something else before.

The formation of OffShore Gas, getting into the natural gas business; a series of specialized new enterprises, bringing together exploration and refining ventures; and OilCo Trading Company are all discrete business moves that were a direct outcropping of the workshop discussions we have held.

MEMBER, GROWTH INITIATIVE TEAM: Recently, some of us on the Growth Initiative Team interviewed a number of general managers and high-graded people. It didn't make your heart proud; there weren't a lot of stories of growth initiatives.

The responses show that we're confused as a company. People use the 10 percent ROI figure as an excuse not to grow. We didn't hear much talk about the value of growth in revenues. And to grow new ventures, people said, will require some investment. "I may not see a return for some period of time. In that case, my short-term ROI may be impeded. So what are we trying to do?"

I think the people were looking for more leadership. People said, "[CEO] needs to say 'growth' more often." It was disturbing to me that we laid the blame on [CEO], because in other companies, that isn't required. No one at 3M would blame their boss for not growing their unit. They would have been expected to grow it themselves!

At heart, it's a cultural problem. We just don't see people at OilCo grabbing us by the throat and saying "I'm going to go out and make rain." To be honest, I don't know whether the 10 percent ROI is an impediment, but people set it up as one.

On the Growth Initiative Team, we had thought we could solve the cultural issue with simple directives, encouragement from senior management, and processes to bring ideas to fruition. That's just not working. We had hoped that within a year to a year-and-a-half, new ventures would start to happen, but there have been only a few isolated examples.

◆ RESISTING FINANCIAL LITERACY (THE FLOORBOARDS DILEMMA)

Imagine that you are about to sell your house. You have nagging fears that, under the floorboards, the frame may be rotting away. But if you lift the floorboards to find out, you will be responsible to fix the rot before you sell.

You can't afford the $30,000 to $50,000 cost. So you don't look. Perhaps the house is fine, perhaps not; but you'll never know. Legally, you have performed sufficient diligence. But the problem, if you care about the results, goes beyond the letter of the law.

A prospective buyer comes to see the house. Instead of taking pleasure in showing your home, you worry: What if they ask about the foundations? Have you really protected yourself from liability? Why should you have to take the blame for a problem that wasn't your fault? Any conversation you have is tainted with uncertainty and anxiety.

In this segment, we look at the reluctance of managers to embrace financial literacy. The practice may be resisted because it asks people to "look under the floorboards" of their businesses.

If weaknesses are exposed, can managers work the problems out with others in the organization? Or will they simply be blamed and left responsible to fix the problems? These pervasive but unvoiced concerns may erode some people's enthusiasm and effectiveness. Does this "floorboards dilemma" dynamic apply more to some businesses than to others?

MEMBER, CORPORATE STAFF: Many of the leaders of refineries and chemical plants did not embrace the "Improving Our Economic Value" project. Instead of beginning to fundamentally rethink how they prioritized their work, they would hand it off to a local manager or team. "Do this."

At one refinery, for instance, the leaders created a sub-team made up of some high-level engineers and financial types to "be the financial literacy team." This subteam was supposed to figure out a good set of metrics for the refinery. They did their best, but they did not hit the mark at all. I don't think they knew how to push back, on the leadership of the refinery, and say, "Guys. What do you really want?"

Rarely have I heard Corporate Executive Team members articulate their vision with their employees. They rarely talk about the "premier" company. Which makes me seriously doubt that they own the concept. I have heard them express doubt about the appropriateness and value of financial literacy. They said they had struggled to try to implement it and to understand the jargon.

My assessment is: there has been a fear, unspoken and undiscussable, around drilling down with financial literacy. The fear is that it will expose some things about the operation that would suggest we haven't been managing those facilities well—because we have been working on the wrong things.

What kinds of things are managers afraid of revealing? That their organizational structures may be antiquated. They may have way too much overhead, in supervision and managerial staff. They may have people working on "crown jewels" that don't affect the bottom line.

They may also feel that they really don't want to expose what's going on in their own "sandbox." They can manage it themselves—instead of viewing it as a bigger sandbox that is trying to make money. The reward system has not rewarded us for exposing what's under the floorboards. Looking in dangerous places is not an inherent part of our pedigree.

CHAPTER 4

SOUTHERN COMPANY

In 1994, the decision was made to spin off one set of OilCo's exploration production assets into a stand-alone company, accountable functionally for its own results. Wholly owned by OilCo, Southern Company Inc. has its own financial imperatives, its own metrics for success and failure, and its own system of risks and rewards.

Southern Company is in the midst of a dramatic "quest" of its own. Its mandate is to become a self-contained, profitable, low-cost producer, operating in a business with a great many structural liabilities and obstacles. The story told here describes the phases of a shift from conventional "old OilCo" culture to the attitudes of an entrepreneurial enterprise.

◆ ORIGINS OF THE SEPARATION

Before becoming a stand-alone business in January 1995, this business unit was a somewhat underperforming asset of E&P. With a huge investment base and very poor performance, this neworganization faced difficult structural challenges.

FORMER HIGH-LEVEL EXECUTIVE, E&P: In the early 1990s, the upstream production assets in Southern Company's territory were singled out as an area of deep concern. Their financial performance was extremely poor. They were fraught with structural problems. They had a huge investment base. This territory is a very tough environment to operate in, with lots of strict environmental rules. The

This story is incomplete. Time and space constraints prevented us from including interviews with a wider variety of people, at more levels throughout Southern Company.

However, enough of the story is told to give a flavor of the situation, in a way that will hopefully be useful to other segments of OilCo going through similar full-scale shifts.

crude produced out there is a heavy, thick crude, which has relatively low value and high cost to bring out of the ground. A lot of it is steam-flooded, which means a high energy cost; so its margin was extremely small.

The challenge was: What do we do there? Do we sell it? Do we try to improve it? And how do we improve it?

PRESIDENT, SOUTHERN COMPANY: I got a chance to come out here and took it. This place was sick. Production was dropping 15 percent to 18 percent per year. We were just meeting targets that had been laid out for us; but, as we learned later, they were not winning targets. Even making those targets did not allow us to win as a company.

Our people had been told at one time, wrongfully in my opinion: "We're just going to cash you out and send all the money for development elsewhere." You can imagine how people reacted to that: "They don't love us. They don't care about us."

For more on the evolution of the governance model, see page 67.

CEO, OILCO: The idea of creating a separate subsidiary was consistent with the governance model, but not driven by the governance model. It came up in E&P when President, E&P and his group were looking at the situation in what is now Southern's territory. They had overpaid for some properties; they had enormous assets on the books; and they were in a money-losing business there. Many of the people felt, "My God, they're going to fire us and sell all the fields to somebody else."

From the point of view of business logic, this decision represents a leap of faith.

So President, E&P and his people looked long and hard at options for fixing that business. Finally they decided to bet on the ability of the people there to make their own destiny.

Once made, that leap of faith found resonance with the aspirations of the leadership in Southern's territory.

FORMER HIGH-LEVEL EXECUTIVE, E&P: Growth, in those years, was an unspoken word. But the momentum built around the idea. Local management got highly enthused about it, and it became the option of choice on our team.

We engaged people in a visioning meeting with the leadership of Southern's territory, and the leadership of

E&P in Los Angeles. The Southern leaders could see that it was being taken seriously by the head office E&P leaders. They became very excited about what it could become.

PRESIDENT, SOUTHERN COMPANY: We had outside financial people come in to look at our local operations here. They liked our property and they liked what we had to say about what we believed we could do. They believed the potential was there. Maybe the balls and chains we hauled around and blamed for preventing us from performing well really weren't there. Maybe it was just an attitude.

The spirit of the emerging enterprise becomes a critical part of Southern Company's portfolio.

We became Southern Company in January 1995. It was really the first entity under the roof of the new governance structure of OilCo.

◆ OPERATING ALONE

Autonomy rapidly led to a kind of culture shock, as the realization took hold: Southern Company would be responsible for its own future, and no safety net from OilCo was guaranteed.

MEMBER OF EXECUTIVE TEAM, SOUTHERN COMPANY: Before 1995, E&P might say they wanted to shift more money to other sites; they'd cut our budget. Or they'd decide that oil production was sliding, and even though we had a plan in place, they didn't like the plan. At the end of the year when results came in, there was very little ownership because we had someone else calling the shots and setting the premises.

But now it's different. The CEO of OilCo was out here when we started up Southern Company. He said, "We're going to give you the two-and-a-half billion dollar asset of this company. You're running it. We're not going to charge you a penny for it. But, there will be no excuse for failure. We'll have different people out here running this company if you fail."

OFFICE ASSISTANT, SOUTHERN COMPANY: "There will be no excuse for failure." That's about the last word we've heard out of the CEO of OilCo. Everybody remembers that; it was a call to action.

After that, no one would sit around and say, "Oh my gosh, what are we going to do?"

MEMBER OF EXECUTIVE TEAM, SOUTHERN COMPANY: As President, Southern Company said to us, "That first bullet that comes from Los Angeles is going to have the center of my forehead on it. But before I hit the ground, I'm going to take a bunch of you with me."

I haven't seen public lynchings in OilCo yet, so there isn't that big sense that if you fail you get fired. But it could come pretty close. A lot more close recently than it ever has before.

A number of people, including some people at Southern's location, said that at first they had little confidence that the Southern Company endeavor would succeed well enough to survive.

The reactions described here should be seen in that context.

TECHNICAL MANAGER, SOUTHERN COMPANY: I'm an optimist, so I never looked at the downside. Maybe I should have.

There were different types of people in this deal. There were people like me; I wanted to stay in here. We liked the new challenge and opportunities. I think we accepted this from day one and went forward. We were seen, a bit, as Pollyanna types.

Another group felt worried about their jobs. They didn't have any other place to go to, because of the "sink or swim" way in which we had set Southern Company going. If something bad happened here, people couldn't count on being transferred out to new jobs elsewhere.

And then there was a third group in the middle. They didn't mind staying here, but were worried about the business. They were committed, but they worried: "How the heck can we get the results that we need?"

MANAGER, SOUTHERN COMPANY: When we formed Southern Company, I went through quite a separation anxiety. I had ten and a half years with OilCo. I always thought, "If there was ever a separation between me and OilCo, I would initiate it." I didn't expect it to come the other way around.

I know we keep talking about how independent we are and how we will do different things than OilCo. That's how we talk and speak, but I'm not so sure that I have seen real concrete examples, yet. It doesn't mean that we aren't; it's just that I'm not so sure that I've seen the examples that really test the separateness.

Does it matter if the "way we do things" is different or not?
If it does matter, how would you effectively test the degree of autonomy of a Southern Company or any other independent spin-off?

PRESIDENT, SOUTHERN COMPANY: I'm just like all the other people here. I'm a Southern Company employee, not an OilCo employee. I don't have a string to pull me back to OilCo. I realize that if this thing doesn't work, I could be iced in this deal. I'll say good-bye and go do something else for a living. I had to accept that I could live without this job and it would not be the end of the world if I got fired.

But I was sick and tired of being at the end of the food chain. I really saw it as my and the leadership's responsibility to set in place what it would take to make this company work. I would listen and try and take advice, but at the end of the day, I personally would step up and take the risk. My neck was on the line.

◆ THE IMPACT OF FINANCIAL LITERACY

Southern Company was suddenly a semi-autonomous system, with new levels of risk. Its survival depended on how well people could internalize the principles and practices of financial literacy. Focused on improving the overall profitability of their business, the Southern managers began to realize how much they had to learn.

PRESIDENT, SOUTHERN COMPANY: We felt pretty confident that we were on the right plane. We had every person in the company involving financial literacy training. We had all spent countless hours working on this. But when the results came in, we realized that we were trying real hard, but we didn't have it right yet.

People in other parts of OilCo have expressed skepticism about the financial literacy work, but not at Southern Company. There seemed to be less reluctance to implement it, less sense of a "floorboards dilemma."

If this perception is accurate, then what was it about the Southern Company situation that made the financial literacy work effective?

OFFICE ASSISTANT: Unfortunately, in this huge corporation, nobody knew how to run a business. Our early work on financial literacy made us painfully aware of that. People just had been playing around with these millions and billions of bucks, and all this oil coming out of the ground, and seeing if they could balance the books. All of a sudden somebody said, "You're supposed to be increasing your value; you're supposed to be making a profit; you're supposed to be growing."

PRESIDENT, SOUTHERN COMPANY: We didn't have an in-depth understanding of what we were trying to do. We were doing our best with the data we had, but that data wasn't measuring the things that we really needed to know about.

So, we set out to create a more in-depth set of measurements for ourselves to give us that data. At first we called it a "managerial profitability project," but we realized that it was really for everyone, including the person operating in the field.

Leadership is a vital part of the entire Southern Company story, but particularly in this section. What kind of leadership is necessary to succeed in the challenging environment of a new entity like Southern Company?

We found that it was a lot more complicated to create this "operational profitability project" than we could have dreamed. Our data was in lousy shape; our processes weren't well defined. We had to get the management teams and operating people together to attack this thing collectively from ground zero.

We had to set a financial performance stake in the ground that would allow us to win, without completely knowing how we would meet the promise. We looked at 1,000 businesses in the U.S. and determined that to win we would have to perform in the top 20 to 33 percent of all companies in terms of delta economic value added, in 1999. This performance would get us up to 10 to 11 percent ROI, which was way over the 1 percent that was projected for us just before we formed Southern Company.

This new winning stake caused a major-league change in how we looked at things. We started with our leadership team and took a vow that we would all do this. We conducted only one test: Were the goals we set impossible? If someone demonstrated they were, then we worked out another target, and said: "Can you get there?"

TECHNICAL MANAGER: The teams—engineers and operations guys—got to say how much production they could make, how much money they would spend on drilling, and what their operating costs would be.

Previously, we might have gotten people to work on a plan; but everyone would have known that senior management would take the spreadsheet and change it, based on information that nobody else had. This time, senior management said, "Give me the spreadsheet, and let's review it. Consider these changes, and give me a new spreadsheet, and let's see if there are any more changes to come."

In previous years the teams had only watched production and operating expense. Now we were looking at our cash flow, our economic value improvement, and our net income. It's a whole different way of looking at things. Of course, the financial bottom line flows mainly from the production and the operating costs, but there are a bunch of other factors that we had never messed with before.

MANAGER, SOUTHERN COMPANY: I am sure we got our money's worth out of the financial literacy initiative. It forced us to think out-of-the-box. We started to establish measurement systems; all the way down to the operator and engineer.

Every two weeks, our unit area teams meet. We have three or four union operators on all of our teams. They have responsibility and are participating. They like the involvement. They're really good at what they do, but it's amazing when I think about it. A few years ago, we would never have thought about putting them on a team.

Results are more important than they've ever been. I'm more accountable for them. I've got the leeway to go out and make my own decisions and secure the proper resources. But I've got to deliver the results.

The same is true for my foremen, engineers, and operators. They used to finish a day feeling, "If nothing

This quote illustrates the power of financial disclosure within an organization. This comment and the next comment show how participative management may be systematically interrelated with autonomous governance structures.

happens wrong, I've done my job." Now, that's not an expectation any more. If they don't improve all the time, then they aren't adding value to the entity.

It also made the operations side more critical and demanding of the support and service groups. The attitude used to be: "We'll wait and see what we can get." Now it's: "What have you done for me lately and what did it cost me?"

OFFICE ASSISTANT: An individual from one of the Head Office staff organizations came out to introduce himself. He wanted to know if several of our managers could take Wednesday afternoon off and go golfing. He had made arrangements at a country club out of town!

I thought, "Dear god, why haven't they trained you about the way we do business out here?" Here we were, busting our butts, watching every penny and analyzing every action and expenditure. Along comes this person who was supposed to be customer-oriented, and he says, "Can you go golfing?"

I think not.

◆ EVOLVING COMMITMENT

The new Southern Company structure demanded an unprecedented degree of commitment from people. They began to recognize that everyone had accountability for the success of the unit, not just the leaders. This, in turn, produced a change in atmosphere that the people we interviewed applauded.

PRESIDENT, SOUTHERN COMPANY: I think it was this commitment, desire and sense of ownership that made the difference to us. We believed that we were going to make this company work.

You're sitting on the bottom of the heap. You keep telling yourself you aren't a doormat, and some start to believe it. Then you see little successes. And those little-successes drive other successes. Then people say, "Geez, I did that. Maybe I can do this." Once you start getting that feeling, then you start growing exponentially.

MANAGER, SOUTHERN COMPANY: I've seen a marked change in atmosphere. It's gone from very cynical to almost euphoric.

The main reason is that we are doing a lot better. In the past, when I talked to my OilCo compatriots, we were seen as the underdogs—as a nonperforming asset. "What is OilCo doing in this territory in the first place?" was the reaction.

Now, I get phone calls like, "What are you guys doing out there?" We've increased our net income from losing to earning hundreds of millions in two years!!

What does the Southern Company example offer to other segments of oil companies that seek to build the same level of commitment?

MANAGER, SOUTHERN COMPANY: We still don't know whether we're going to survive. Our goal is to have a 10 percent ROI. From January 1996 to now we have gone from 3 percent ROI to 8 percent. What was it that made it possible for us to do this? Whatever it was, it makes us think that we'll be able to make it.

This comment shows the momentum that stems from results. Even if the goals are not yet met, sustainable results build commitment, which leads in turn to better results.

DATA ANALYST, SOUTHERN COMPANY: At first I did not feel comfortable with the idea of branching off from OilCo. I wasn't sure that the partitioning of Southern Company was truly an effort to make it on our own, as opposed to making it easier to sell off pieces of our operation. Now, I feel much more comfortable.

MANAGER, SOUTHERN COMPANY: We've got to have growth here to survive. Our focus is on getting to be the best operating place hasn't given us much time to go out and look for growth opportunities. Southern Company has been separate for several years and the honeymoon's over on that. And now it's results that are most important. A lot of results depend on growth and so we have to really go after that. We're starting to look a little bit more out of the box.

This comment looks ahead to the next step beyond survival.

Are transformational shifts irreversible? Once they reach a certain point, is it impossible to turn back?

MEMBER, EXECUTIVE COUNCIL: A good beginning for our governance saga would be the first Executive Council session at Key West, in August 1993 [see page 28], a month or so after [CEO] became CEO of OilCo. Several initiatives came out of that; one was to look at governance, which we called "roles and responsibilities."

Box 5-1:

FEDERALISM AND SUBSIDIARITY

The concepts underlying the governance structure were deeply influenced by the original "balance of power" approach of the United States Constitution. British management writer Charles Handy, in the early 1990s, articulated the paradoxical capability of a "federalist" system, like that of the U.S. government, to balance authority between a central management and disparate, autonomous substructures.

Federalism, Handy insisted, was not just a "classy word for restructuring" (or for decentralization); it meant an ongoing balance of power between the center and the periphery, and it could not work unless people acted with good intentions, information, and education—and an eye for their own self-interest as well as the common interest.

A federalist organization is not simply a holding company with subsidiaries, but a group of autonomous enterprises linked by common purpose, culture, leadership, and resources. They need the flexibility of being small, with the ability to make decisions quickly—and the effectiveness of being large, with the ability to take advantage of their common resources and economies of scale.

The center of a federalist organization is "small to the point of minimalist," Handy wrote. "They exist to coordinate, not to control."

Handy argued that the most important governing principle of a federalist organization was subsidiarity. Power would belong to the lowest possible point in the organizational hierarchy. This approach had long been part of the doctrine of the Catholic church; another way to put it was: Stealing the decisions of a subordinate is wrong. Power is assumed to exist naturally at low points in the organization, and can only be taken away by agreement.

The OilCo governance structure represented a deliberate effort to make these principles manifest.[1]

We had never used the word "governance" in-house, to my knowledge. But the business heads were trying to understand if, in a transformed company, the real authority would still be vested in the head person. In the past, the business heads had not had much wiggle room. Now, under [CEO's] new presidency, how were things going to be governed?

I left the Executive Council session with an assignment to coordinate some work around roles and responsibilities. Thinking about it over the next few weeks, I gradually realized that the Executive Council had really been asking: "What is a governance model for us?"

Around that time, we picked up an article by Charles Handy on federalism in organizations (see Box 5-1).

One of the Council members later recalled, "I didn't think we were going to get into a big deal. We were just going to get clear on a few roles and responsibilities. It might take a couple-hour meeting and we'd be through it." But then we started to think: maybe this is bigger. It may mean redefining how we would govern the company in the future.

We looked at governance from various dimensions, and also benchmarked the governance models of companies that had turned themselves around from poor performance—Compaq, Tenneco, and General Electric under Jack Welch.

MEMBER, CORPORATE EXECUTIVE: In February 1994, the Executive Council met to talk about how the "new OilCo" could be governed. We had the Executive Council, a few McKinsey consultants, and me, from Planning, in the meeting. I presented a framework that Planning had developed with McKinsey. The framework was a 2 x 2 matrix. The horizontal axis measured business determinants like how volatile was our business, how tough was the competition, and how integrated was our business. The vertical axis measured our philosophy of how much involvement the corporate center should have in running the business. The framework indicated that since we were

Was there an expectation, already, that the CEO's regime would be less hierarchical than previous regimes?

Would a more transformation-oriented CEO automatically be more willing to shift patterns of power and accountability?

Why is subsidiarity so rare in corporations?

Could it be because of the subtle influence of consulting firms like McKinsey, which in turn derive their knowledge and position from supporting centralized power?

in a volatile business, with a fairly narrow range of business activity, then an active, more control-oriented corporate center might be appropriate.

When [CEO] saw that model, he knew where OilCo was going to plot. "I don't really believe the premise here," he said. "What data supports the idea that business determinants and leadership philosophy are equally important?"

Basically, all we could say was that a lot of management theory said that the best practice was to balance them. "I give much more weight to leadership philosophy," he said, "and how we want to run the company."

The Executive Council supported [CEO's] position. They talked about the way to improve performance was to devolve responsibility, dismantle the corporate center, and have more of a holding company approach.

"What is the value of the corporate center, anyway?" one of the Council members said. "I can run my business. Just give me a chance."

The consensus around the governance structure spread rapidly, in part because of the strong support that it had from members of the Executive Council.

This meeting struck me as being a fairly defining moment for OilCo. It was clear there was consensus about shifting governance to devolve accountability and responsibility. I have to admit, at the time I felt I had screwed up; I didn't get the model right. McKinsey came out thinking we were making a mistake.

But [CEO] and the rest of the Council were very upbeat. Several of them mentioned to me that it was one of the best conversations they had had as a newly formed Council.

MEMBER, EXECUTIVE COUNCIL: Was [CEO] going to continue to be the heavy corporate-centered type of person that former chief executives were? Or was he going to be different? Now we had an answer.

APPLIED LEARNING CONSULTANT: By early 1994, [CEO] was talking openly about how he wanted to go to a different governance model. He thought that OilCo, at his level, should almost become a holding company. The business units would function as autonomous groups. Each group would have a Board running the group, made up of people on the Executive Council. It was a complicated model, but [CEO] thought it would drive accountability into the businesses.

MEMBER, EXECUTIVE COUNCIL: In August 1994, the Executive Council held another governance meeting at Old Mill Pond. We knew that we had to define the structure; the names would go on the boxes. That's what people were looking for.

[CEO] and I had talked ahead of time, and the concept of four "independent business units"—E&P, Chemical, Refining & Retail, and OilCo Consulting—was pretty much in his mind. It was consistent with most of the other diagrams in the room; there wasn't much sense of conflict. The three main businesses would want to be independent anyway.

But this picture also defined OilCo Consulting as an independent business unit. That was a bold new concept that few, if any, companies had ever done. The CEO had talked for a long time about running Consulting as a business. But saying that, and going to the extreme we went to, are two different things.

The governance structure was perceived by staff and by senior managers as a critical, tangible shift. It was also remarked upon by newly spun off subsidiaries, like Southern Company. But lower-level people in the hierarchy in Los Angeles did not tend to identify it as often as one of their most significant changes.

ADVISER, EXECUTIVE COUNCIL: The picture that [CEO] drew at Old Mill Pond also showed the firm structures: The HR organization, for instance, now became the HR firm. Wow! Each of the firms would have to be run as a business, instead of a cost center.

He said something else at that meeting that I'll never forget. "Our new governance structure will be successful to the degree that we can establish quality relationships among ourselves."

A new governance implied emphasis on relationships, rather than positions.

MEMBER, EXECUTIVE COUNCIL: From the beginning we had the question of how many "big rules" we would put in

The new governance structure placed a great deal of pressure on the company's culture to tie the company together. Thus we see a sense of relief in comments like this one: implicitly expressing relief at the realization that both the "head" (Central Office) and the "hands" (branches) of the organization could continue to act with alignment, even if the Central Office no longer maintained the same kind of control.

place that all the businesses would follow. A "big rule," in Charles Handy's term, is a reserve power held by the corporate center. We have a big rule, for example, that the independent business units cannot do their own financing. Financing is done through the corporate center. OilCo can borrow money at a much better rate, so it makes good sense.

Another big rule is: we'll all adhere to a common Mission, Vision, and Values system. We also said that we wanted the entire company to adopt financial literacy as a practice.

But [CEO] strongly resisted putting other big rules in place. He has not required, for example, that the entire company run under a common financial information system. He seems concerned that any time he exposed the organization to big rules, it was as if he were reverting back to the hierarchy.

ADVISER, EXECUTIVE COUNCIL: It took several months for the Executive Council members to internalize the new structure. In effect, [CEO] became the investment banker for the companies. The titles of the leaders changed from Vice President of OilCo to President and CEO of their particular businesses. They had to take full responsibility for business success. As they needed to fund capital projects, they had to come to [CEO], their investment banker, and say what they wanted to do. Once they got that money, they had to make a return on that investment.

What should the role of staff functions be in a shifted governance environment? Has this transition been made effectively by staff?

MANAGER, HUMAN RESOURCES: The governance structure changed my life. Before, my basic job was to police and enforce the structure. Now I can contribute in a much different way. I don't have to maintain the status quo or defend it. I can be out there trying to shake it up.

When this started, about a year and a half ago, I started keeping track of my time on a computer program. I realized that I was spending half my time doing work that I thought was important, but I had no customer for it. If I had to get somebody to write a check to support that work, I would be out of luck.

I feel fairly empowered by all this stuff and I'm having a lot more fun than I used to. But it is scary. It never crossed my mind that I might be out there, over 50 years old, looking for work. Now it crosses my mind pretty often. I'm getting to be an old guy; it's going to be hard to find a job. If I'm not doing well around here, it's going to be a problem.

◆ **WHERE DOES POWER FALL?**

The independence of the various spun-off units is only beginning to be tested. Some of the individual businesses that were formerly components of a whole now find themselves in the roles of suppliers-customers, or in some cases, even as competitors. In these positions, they feel compelled to try to get a good deal for themselves, sometimes at the expense of their former partners within OilCo. Conversely, some of the newly independent "businesses" within OilCo find themselves drawn to more cooperation and information sharing than they did before.

As Charles Handy notes, people in federalist systems must always deal with the ambiguity of power structures. Are the mission, vision, and values—or the business priorities—of the "spun off" companies consistent with those of the larger, formerly vertically integrated company? Do people work for their unit or for OilCo? Where should loyalties rest if there is a conflict?

This segment describes how these ambiguities were recognized, and how specific measures, such as the formation of the Corporate Executive Team, were instituted.

MEMBER, EXECUTIVE COUNCIL: Some people wanted the responsibility and authority, but when they heard the word "accountability," it meant, "Oh, that means you're going to fire me." So there was a bit of push-back at first. Now people have seen that this governance system has not only empowered people—putting the decisions down at a level where the knowledge is. It has also given groups, whether they be firms or businesses, the right to set up their own rules.

OilCo Chemical can decide to have a compensation system different from that of E&P. This change is big, because we tried to do that in 1982. E&P was a big money maker, and they wanted their own compensation system so they could keep people from going to the competition. The answer came back from the General Executive Office: "Oh, no, everybody has to be treated the same; we can't treat people differently."

In the past, the business people made all the decisions through the General Executive Office. Now, with people from Tax, Legal, Finance, and HR on the boards of the subsidiaries, each with a different viewpoint, it sends the message that this is more than a change of form. It's a change of substance and behavior.

This comment provides a candid overview of the inconsistencies of the governance structure.

The concern about the makeup of boards was expressed by several people. (The members of all the boards, currently, tend to be members of the Executive Council.)

The concern about inconsistent levels of autonomy has also been raised several times.

Are these transitional concerns? Will OilCo evolve further in its governance structure?

What conversations could help the evolution of OilCo's governance structure move forward effectively?

MANAGER, OILCO CHEMICAL: Have we really created independent companies? Sure. But how much is "paper"?

The Boards have similar personnel—kind of strange, isn't it, if you want independent thought? If you want governance, then you need to have new thoughts.

Let me give you an example. We were planning a cut-back, and the OilCo Chemical managers came up with an approach that was different from previous cut-backs. The plan went to the Board and was rejected. The implicit message was: "You have to do it our old way." This kind of situation can send wrong signals and destroy faith and trust.

As an organization, we need to be sensitive to this type of situation. It becomes difficult to lead your staff when visible things that seem contrary leak out without logical explanations. If not careful, you create an atmosphere that governance and other initiatives are "lip service," used when convenient. Inconsistencies without valid explanation rupture our ability to gain faith and trust from our employees.

Recently, I have seen a number of these types of inconsistencies. This has caused me to question, for the first time, whether I can retain credibility with my people. If I can't be sure that we do as we say, then it hurts my effectiveness.

APPLIED LEARNING CONSULTANT: [CEO] kept saying, "The Executive Council, as a group, should be looking closely at the businesses." At the same time, he was saying, "You guys are independent. You're responsible for your results." There was a conflict in the message.

In retrospect, I think that he was a little bit early with governance. While he was trying to change the culture, he changed the structure at the same time. People immediately jumped on the structural changes, not the cultural change needed. The question became: "Why do we need an OilCo culture if we're each going to have our own businesses? What has to be common?"

External consultants also mentioned inconsistent messages from the top—sometimes promoting autonomous action, and sometimes reining people in.

What systemic forces might be operating to produce this dynamic?

PRESIDENT, E&P: We, the Executive Council, don't make decisions about running the corporation. We had a big learning to go through to understand that. Most of our time is spent dealing with the transformation process in OilCo.

This differs from the way the E&P leadership team functions. In the E&P leadership team we are more into the decision-making mode than the Executive Council for OilCo is.

This view, from the Executive Council, shows a very different perception of the same ambiguities.

MEMBER, IT TEAM: In the Information Technology team, we backed off on the concept of appointing a Corporate Information Officer. The big issue was: Is strategy created at the OilCo level? If it's not, then do you need a Corporate Information Officer at that level?

And yet there is a clear best practice, that we have seen over and over again, about centralization in information technology: You get costs down by buying one type of equipment off the shelf and forcing everybody to use it.

This quote describes a specific autonomy-related dilemma, common to many segments.

How will learning—for example, technology transfer—occur among the businesses?

Is it enough to have OilCo Consulting, the firms, and internal resources like the Corporate Transformation Group, pollinating and cross-fertilizing?

The governance structure has been a problem in making that work. Essentially, the refining companies want to go off and do their own thing.

This tension between "what's good for your business unit" and "what's good for the whole" is everywhere, not just in IT.

What does governance mean to the average OilCo person?

Is there a conflict between identifying with a component of the business and identifying with OilCo as a whole?

MANAGER, OILCO CHEMICAL: Until recently, when you heard about the governance model at OilCo Chemical, you heard that "From now on, OilCo Chemical's going to be responsible for its own debt."

But I didn't know what that means, and I'm a mid-level manager. I didn't know where the debt was held before. What would it do to my department's books? Most of us have no clue what it really means, so we ignore it.

"Governance" then means, "We do different things than Refining & Retail." And most people see that in people terms: "Refining & Retail manages people one way and we manage them another way."

The creation of the Corporate Executive Team was a response to the pressures and requirements of the new governance structure.

Its role as a group of "agents of change" emerged out of the requirements of the new governance structure.

MEMBER, HR FUTURE IMPERATIVES TEAM: When we first thought about the governance structure, I wondered how we would keep from throwing the baby out with the bathwater. If we lost all our integration, that would not be good. We needed some unifying glue.

That was why the Human Resources Future Imperatives Team, of which I was a member, suggested forming the Corporate Executive Team as a formal body.

MEMBER, HR FUTURE IMPERATIVES TEAM: Most of the companies we benchmarked had some kind of senior leadership group, akin to the Corporate Executive Team, that was important to the success of the enterprise. But we put in one other feature: We envisioned the Corporate Executive Team as agents of change, rather than just recipients of extra compensation. They had a role in the transformation, as opposed to being just bystanders.

CEO: Many people questioned the governance model at first, saying, "You're creating enormous silos. You're isolating people. Do you think you are going to break the company up?"

Obviously, that's not the intention. So we have to institute other mechanisms that become the glue in the fabric that weaves across these vertical structures.

I think in the long term, the Corporate Executive Team is becoming a much more interlocked group. There are many common experiences, at the Corporate Training Center and in other activities, that are creating communication ties between people.

Interestingly, only a few members of the Corporate Executive Team whom we interviewed pointed to the Corporate Executive Team's formation as a significant event for them. Does this suggest that their interests are still focused on their own parts of the business?

◆ Enforced risk, accountability, and blame

Governance sets up a way of life that compels people to take risks. But risks imply that failure is not only possible, but likely at times—if only because, statistically, most entrepreneurial ventures fail. Failure, in many organizations, means that someone will be blamed. The fear of being blamed paralyzes people's willingness to take risks. Which in turn undermines the intended effect of the governance policies.

How can this self-defeating pattern of behavior be understood better? Perhaps by understanding the attitudes that underlie it.

Member, Corporate Executive Team: There's still a question in a lot of our minds: Do we really hold people accountable?

What happens when people fail to produce results? The jury is still out. That's a piece of undone business.

In some companies, they can tell you exactly what it means to be accountable. You have a certain period of time to meet your targets. If you don't meet your targets, there are clear consequences and penalties. There are also very clear rewards for meeting or exceeding targets.

In OilCo, there is lack of clarity around what happens if you miss targets. It's almost an undiscussable question right now because I don't think we know how to address the problem.

There is an implicit assumption in the governance structure that people create their own results.

But some interviewees believe that they do not create their results. To them, the results are created by outside forces (like commodities prices) over which they have no influence.

Here is the other point of view: We all contribute to the improvement of each others' results.

This cultural attitude about risk can be a brake upon growth of the company in general.

Does OilCo's culture unintentionally undermine efforts to grow?

MEMBER, CORPORATE STAFF: The vast majority of people think there is no effective way to correlate their performance to the financial results—even after exposure to the financial literacy initiative. For example, a refinery is tied to Refining & Retail's financial results. Refining & Retail includes refining, marketing, transportation, commercial products. So a person at that refinery will wonder, "How do I influence those financial results? They're so far away that they're not even a line of sight on my radar screen. And yet, my pay is tied to them."

CUSTOMER SERVICE, OILCO CHEMICAL: Some people feel that no matter how hard they try, there's not much they can do to improve the total performance of the company. That's probably why we're number four—because so many people feel that way. We all have to take ownership and realize that we are a part and we can make a difference.

I'm not saying I can go out there and influence pricing and market trends, but there are things I can do internally that might help somebody's attitude who deals with pricing that would maybe change something within OilCo that would force something somewhere else to have an impact. I don't care how small your job is. I think everyone can influence.

MEMBER, GROWTH INITIATIVE TEAM: There have been any number of attempts to generate ideas for new businesses over the past six or seven years. People work and work, and then try to hi-grade the ideas up through the organization. They look for somebody to support them from higher up, and it kind of falls apart. If you look for examples of success, you come up with two or three. That actually might be a pretty good success rate.

But then the failure of the project becomes a personal matter. Maybe there was a very good reason why it didn't work, but they invested time in it, and they feel personally damaged by the fact that they got rebuffed. "I tried something, and it didn't work. So, screw you, guys, you're really not committed to this growth effort."

Everybody feels they have to be a winner.

CONSULTANT, HOLISTIC LEADERSHIP ASSOCIATES: The entrepreneurial ideas of the new business structure don't quite match the managers' capabilities. They misjudge themselves; they think they're more capable than they are. When push comes to shove, their instincts are not yet attuned to the cut and thrust of the marketplace.

Or are there missing skills and capabilities needed for growth, as this external view suggests

These skills have developed dramatically in recent months, as a result of new alliances, negotiations, and other external interactions.

Nonetheless, OilCo managers are buffered by the huge structures and resources floating around in the OilCo System. You don't see the ingrained, embedded frugality that you find in a small business. OilCo managers work with a 10 percent margin. That's a nice margin. Stockbrokers work with a 2 percent margin.

◆   THE JOY OF OPPORTUNITY: RUGBY VERSUS RELAY

A small, but apparently increasing number of OilCo people feel the visceral excitement that comes from new levels of opportunity. Their confidence in themselves has been tempered and/or strengthened by their experiences.

MEMBER, PLANNING TEAM: The typical OilCo culture was: "We're going to do something, and we're going to study it and lay out the plan thoroughly." So one person does Step A, the development step, and then hands it off to another person, who does step B, and so on, like a relay race. The sequence is all laid out in advance: "A, B, C, D, E . . ." and it takes a long time to make things happen. The mindset becomes very rigid in the process, plus it usually involves a big first step at the initial launch point.

Does a "growth" sensibility require a new day-to-day management style? One member of the Planning Team argued that it does.

But the new approach is more like a rugby team. They can't tell you exactly what sequence of passes they're going to use to get to the goal. They're going to

We present one story at length here, to show the evolution of thinking in someone who gets involved in an entrepreneurial, self-governing, startup venture within OilCo—in this case, within E&P.

These attitudes are sometimes regarded as unusually optimistic for OilCo. But our interviews suggest that they are more prevalent within OilCo, today, than many insiders recognize.

go where the defense isn't and, adjusting their plans as conditions change, take advantage of opportunities as they unfold. They can do this because they all have a clear vision of where the goal is. This metaphor helps a lot in developing new ideas.

MANAGER, E&P: In the middle of 1993, I was exploration manager of a division of E&P that had been torn completely asunder. We had laid off 250 people, cut the budget by one-third, and gotten rid of most of our acreage. I worked very hard, but in December 1994 I came to the conclusion that it wasn't going to work.

Close associates accused me of having given up. I suspected that I might be giving up the coveted leadership position that I'd fought so hard to get. But I felt that, as the current senior leader out there, I owed the company an honest assessment. It would never return cost of capital to the shareholders.

So I went to President, E&P and asked for the opportunity to look for something different. Lo and behold, he said: "Go ahead and take some time. Take a small team, get your thoughts together, and tell us what kinds of opportunities are out there that we're not currently looking at."

Around August 1995, we came up with an emerging theme. OilCo has a long history of excellence in research and development. Unfortunately, during the downsizing period, true seminal research was cut back intensely. A lot of research ideas were tucked away in desk drawers. We stumbled across a treasure trove of potential new business opportunities that, by and large, were the intellectual property of OilCo. We could make some new markets with them.

We went to the Board of Directors with an out-of-the-box notion that we should start a new environmental remediation company, called OilCo Technology Ventures. We found that when we could back up our ideas with some logic and fact, people had a lot of time to listen. In fact, people got excited about the idea, and pretty soon—rather than having to fight my way as a lone ranger through the system—there were people helping me open doors. At the same time, nobody had said, "That's a great idea, let me show you the right way to do it." They made us prove it ourselves.

Starting the new company changed my life. It meant a lot of responsibility; this thing will only go where my team and I take it. It means our career path and potential are undefined, and will only be what we define them to be, by and large. It's made a lot of opportunities for people who were afraid that there weren't any opportunities. And every senior manager that I've talked to since we've been through this process has commented that it could not have happened in OilCo in 1990.

Someone making a new venture in OilCo today is actually testing three things at once:

1. Their own capabilities

2. The perceptivity of their business plan (the market, costs, etc.)

3. The capacity of OilCo to make use of their venture and experience.

How well (or poorly) does the OilCo system recognize these three separate components?

CHAPTER 6

NOBLE PURPOSE: THE OILCO CONSULTING GOVERNANCE STORY

Changes in governance put groups in new relationships with one another. Traditional ways of doing business and servicing customers rapidly disappeared, as internal units had more freedom to build relationships with outside entities.

This story, based at OilCo Consulting, shows how internal service provider units faced an immediate challenge: dealing with the breakdown of old relationships and the challenge of being "merely" a supplier.

◆ LEARNING THE NEW ROLE

The story begins in January 1995. A change in governance structure was announced. OilCo Consulting would become a separate entity, responsible for its own bottom line, with only a two-year "grace period" in which current contracts inside OilCo would be guaranteed. After that, OilCo Consulting would be completely dependent on its ability to keep customers—customers inside OilCo and elsewhere.

MANAGER, OILCO CONSULTING: It wasn't just a matter of business performance. It was our life line. Either we turned ourselves from a cost mentality into a profitable business, or we'd probably go away.

I still hear people from the rest of OilCo saying, "Oh, poor you, that must be awful to work there. You all will never make it, will you?"

Several interviewees noted that there had been grave doubts, at first, about OilCo Consulting's ability to find a niche as a profitable business.

MANAGER, OILCO CONSULTING: The initial reaction, when the announcement first came down, and the sustaining reaction for the longest period of time, was panic. We would have to compete on the open market with established mainstream consulting firms, including some whose names were household words.

MANAGER, OILCO CONSULTING: In the first year of this transition, our first priority became to hold the current customers and start transforming our relationship from a cost basis to a market basis. Holding them was more important than how much we did, or didn't, make on them. We did almost anything to hold them.

◆ THE PAY SHIFT AT OILCO CONSULTING

As part of its new autonomy, OilCo Consulting's managers were forced to reorient the pay scales of the company. Instead of being tagged to OilCo salaries, salaries would now be competitive with competitors in the services and consulting industries

Would most employees of OilCo Consulting agree that this episode was handled equitably? We did not conduct enough interviews to be ertain of an answer.

The people we interviewed tended to agree that this difficult transition had been handled well—although some still argued, as you see here, that it should never have happened at all.

MANAGER, OILCO CONSULTING: When we benchmarked our costs, they were too high—in part because our people costs were high. So we went out and got market pay data. This was not an HR project; the business line managers did it. Then we compared every one of our employees against the market, saying, "Is this person in the range for what their job is generally paying? Are they high or are they low?"

In June, we went to every single person in our organization and told them where they were on the pay comparison. We took money away from some people, and gave others increases. The dollars probably played out to where we took money out of the system, but gave more people increases.

Over the course of six months, we had lots of meetings with the group of forty leaders, talking about how to work through this. There were a lot of very emotional conversations; we had to face up to telling people that we couldn't justify paying them what they had been paid all these years.

MANAGER, OILCO CONSULTING: It's really difficult to look into the eyes of people who were the big boys when you started, and tell them, "You don't have the skills to make it any more."

EMPLOYEE, OILCO CONSULTING: For twenty years we were paid like oil companies. Now, we're paid like a service company. As one girl in my office said, "Oh, great. We are going to be paid like the garbage man now."

I think it's not only the cut in the money. OilCo always had the best salaries and the best benefits. We are no longer OilCo. We are OilCo Consulting. So we no longer have that level of payment, even though we do the same job.

What can the rest of OilCo learn from the Consulting experience?

MANAGER, OILCO CONSULTING: I'm not convinced the pay shift was worth the pain that we went through. We've been given the burden of fixing problems that have existed for years. For years, for instance, we've promoted people who have not stayed marketable enough to stay competitive. We went through and tried to fix all this in one deal.

MANAGER, OILCO CONSULTING: The pay process was dialogued openly from the start. "We are going to have a reorganization. We don't know yet what effect it will have." Then, as it got closer, we heard, "This is the top-level overview. We will tell you more as things progress."

It's very nice to be able to know things ahead of time. By the time it was happening, we understood why. Then each of us was individually counseled on where we fell out. I think that's an openness that we haven't seen in the past. In the past, we wouldn't have known about it until the result was there.

◆ A SHOCK TO THE SYSTEM

One year after the governance shift, the loyalty of relationships within OilCo was tested. A group of managers at Refining & Retail decided to seek other bidders for work that had been traditionally conducted by OilCo Consulting.

MANAGER, OILCO CONSULTING: In February 1996, our world got rocked. A large customer within OilCo Refining & Retail indicated that it would be bidding out a significant amount of the products and services that we ordinarily sold them.

In the next several comments, different descriptions indicate how the same events can be seen differently from different perspectives. A competitive strategy for one group is a life-threatening challenge to another.

MANAGER, OILCO CONSULTING: One group of customers was pushing extremely hard for lowest conceivable cost. Often, I think their view of an achievable low cost was below what we thought could be done—not just by us, but by anybody.

But we were barely out of the blocks. We didn't have a market-based understanding of the true cost of providing some of the services, because our old accounting systems and approaches were still in place. We couldn't prove the costs were what we believed them to be.

It caused us to mature faster than we otherwise would have. But we did feel squeezed.

What forces have led both groups to their different views of the same situation?

MANAGER, OILCO REFINING & RETAIL: By mid-1995, we recognized that we needed to change our legacy financial systems and the business processes around core financials. All of these systems had the "year 2000 problem." In our recent large IT projects, we had spent a lot more money connecting to these older legacy systems than on the new software we needed for business.

We were open to a variety of approaches: Install an all-new system, or simply remain customers for the existing service, as long as it could evolve with us and meet our strategic cost requirements. We couldn't afford a high-cost system. We approached OilCo Consulting in fall of

1995, with our view of the way forward, which would include an RFI [Request for Information] early in 1996. We gave them our word that they could preempt any RFP by making us a proposal that would meet our costs.

From our perspective, this conveyed the spirit of preserving our long-standing relationship with them, while making the case for change.

MANAGER, OILCO: One of the architects of that decision had talked with me about it. I thought it made a lot of sense. He said there were a number of IT and accounting-related areas that simply were not creating significant value for them. Some of those areas were operated by OilCo Consulting, and some were not. They had concluded, "Gee, let's get rid of all these areas, and have somebody else worry about our IT needs."

MANAGER, OILCO CONSULTING: I remember being extremely disturbed about the way our client chose to execute this— by taking it to the open market before talking to us. From an OilCo shareholders' standpoint, it seemed to be the wrong approach. Why wouldn't Refining & Retail come to us and say, "We'd like someone else—presumably you, OilCo Consulting—to operate all this for us, and let's talk about how." If those discussions broke down, then they could do an RFI.

But those kinds of dialogues don't seem to happen.

According to some participants, the type of conversation desired here had taken place ahead of time. The perception persisted, however, that the two companies remained isolated from each other.

MANAGER, OILCO CONSULTING: At first, we felt betrayal. We knew the OilCo Refining & Retail customers well, from the Corporate Executive Team and elsewhere. We had talked about OilCo as a whole with them, and about supporting each other. Some of us who were more directly involved felt that we would have to carry the burden of these types of losses for all of OilCo Consulting.

But other people poured out an unbelievable amount of support and concern for us. In at least one meeting, it brought tears to my eyes; I realized that I didn't have to carry all of this myself. For the first time at OilCo,

The relationship between supplier and customer is traditionally fierce. The relationship between collaborators is traditionally mutually supportive.

Now, a new type of relationship would have to be forged.

This comment is from a staff person who was not directly involved in that part of OilCo Refining & Retail.

Does it faithfully represent the attitude of the customers?

I openly showed an emotion other than anger. I think that's when personal transformation began to take place for me.

MANAGER, OILCO REFINING & RETAIL: OilCo Consulting is in a situation where the current environment is no longer viable. Their competitors can offer some of the same kinds of services, and they are faced with the harsh reality of going toe to toe with them in the bidding process. The customers in other parts of OilCo will make their choice on the basis of service and cost.

Moreover, I think we are going into an era in which the pace of change is so great and so continuous that the value that OilCo Consulting people used to provide—continuity and "teaching you the ropes"—can actually become an impediment. Frequently, the person who has been immersed in a technology and the OilCo way of doing it has the hardest time letting go and adopting a new way.

This is very hard to come to grips with. But it's going to happen whether they like it or not.

◆ LEARNING FROM NEW ROLES

To cope with this "shock to the system," managers at OilCo Consulting discovered that they had to do more than rethink their operational practices. They were being thrust into a new set of attitudes about each other... and about their customers.

MANAGER, OILCO CONSULTING: The week after we heard the news, we brought the thirty people in OilCo Consulting who would be impacted by this event into a dialogue. Each of us saw the threat differently. Some said, "It's not a threat. Let them do it." Others said, "No way can we let this happen."

In three hours, we took our thirty diverse opinions and perspectives and gained consensus to act: How much to spend, what resources to dedicate, and what we would do. The year before, we would never have gotten that many people in a room to agree on a common direction and approach.

I've come away from this event with a sense of renewed purpose—not just about this project, but around OilCo Consulting, my family, and the purpose of my life. I spent more time in reflection; and that helped me become centered. I recognized that part of my success would depend upon the individuals whom I felt had betrayed me. So those relationships began to be repaired.

I have found the thing that works best for me, in dealing with all this, is to carve the time out to sit down and think about the week's events: why they happened, and what could have happened better. Could I have taken the conversation to a different level? Could I have been more supportive? Could I have said what I felt? It is very helpful to analyze the levels of events versus patterns versus systemic structure.

When we changed the governance design, people's behavior changed as a result. When I saw those behaviors change, I thought, "Well, they must not like us at OilCo Consulting." But that wasn't the problem.

I saw this when I attended a leadership meeting in their part of OilCo Refining & Retail. They talked about all the things that we had talked about: What was their competitive advantage? Did they have the right skills? I heard operations people telling marketing people: "I'm not sure I can afford to pay for that from you any more." I realized they were doing everything we were doing. Just as it had with us, the new structure had given them a new set of challenges to deal with.

MANAGER, OILCO REFINING & RETAIL: Initially OilCo Consulting had promised to have their proposal completed by late February. By early March, however, they had reached the conclusion that outside partners would be required to meet OilCo Refining & Retail's needs and to really build a business for themselves, developing their work for us into a service for other customers as well.

To deal with a hard business issue, the group would have to reframe their "soft" system of interrelationships.

The notion of "events versus patterns versus systemic structures" derives from system dynamics and the work of the MIT-related consultants. It refers to concerted, educated efforts to see the underlying chains of causal interrelationship that link seemingly unrelated events.

If learning comes from adversity, is adversity necessary for learning?

Bit by bit, a transition to a more collaborative relationship became apparent.

This quote, made in August, shows that mistrust and tension still exist across the system.

What forces might contribute to these problems lingering?

What would be the most effective way to continue resolving them?

While we were impatient, we continued to delay the RFP and to work with them. By July, they had produced a proposal that we could support for our future direction.

The overall process created some tension. Certainly there was a lot of learning on both sides. We had to get our act together at OilCo Refining & Retail, and so did OilCo Consulting.

MANAGER, OILCO CONSULTING: Later, in a major meeting, a key customer at OilCo Refining & Retail spoke of OilCo Consulting as their preferred provider. This was significant because he had let us know that he had not been happy with some of our past practices. That was a very positive result.

There was a negative side—we were saddled with very low rates—but it also put us in a position where we have much better knowledge of what it takes to provide these services.

MANAGER, OILCO CONSULTING: More recently, in another series of events, we had another meeting between my OilCo Consulting team and an OilCo Refining & Retail team. We had agreed to go forward with a joint venture. We had identified objectives, deliverables, and deadlines.

Then my counterparts in OilCo Refining & Retail changed their mind. The conversation went something like, "We don't trust you. All the cards aren't on the table, and we're not going to put all the cards on the table." They were explicit and honest about that, but it meant that a handshake agreement was violated and a great deal of business might be lost.

I said, "I understand that we work for two different companies, but we also both work for OilCo. We need to find a way to work through this distrust that's developed between our companies." They said that they didn't think we ever could.

That's an example of the tension that the new governance system creates. I feel it as a sense of alienation from the rest of the company. People make jokes about First

Avenue (where many OilCo Consulting offices are located). One manager told me, "I'm not meeting you on First Avenue. I will not walk on First Avenue. We're giving someone else the project, and I don't want to be near the people who didn't get the job."

I look at my peers within OilCo Consulting and I see mistrust there, too. I notice that many people are considering leaving. That's something they never would have thought of before.

MANAGER, OILCO REFINING & RETAIL: In the end, we reached a cost-effective solution that offered them opportunities to grow this piece of the business and that gave us a much more near-real-time system with a more integrated view of our own data. This collaboration ultimately led to a new approach for the design of our future systems. I wonder whether either OilCo Refining & Retail or OilCo Consulting would have been able to make the same progress over the same time period under the old system.

MANAGER, OILCO CONSULTING: As OilCo Refining & Retail and OilCo Consulting progressed through the process, we both realized that our mutual interest would be served by clearly understanding each others' objectives and motivations, and working collaboratively.

The story as a whole suggests that, although governance changes will have unintended conse-quences, OilCo people may possess the ability to address those consequences.

By now, after moving through each step of our long journey, our relationship has strengthened. I now feel we are forging more of a win-win relationship. We've learned not to jump to be defensive, and they seem to have learned not to jump to attack. This journey has been painful and difficult, but it has produced significant opportunities for organizational learning and my own personal growth.

What does it take to move forward from a governance-related impasse?

◆ OILCO CONSULTING'S "NOBLE PURPOSE"

As OilCo Consulting managers continued to ponder their new roles, they deliberately initiated a voyage of discovery into the organization's purpose and identity. Everything was up for grabs. If OilCo Consulting would move from being a cost center to a profit center, from being a part of OilCo to a supplier, then perhaps its purpose should also shift, some said: To include reshaping the role of the oil industry in society.

OilCo Consulting people described their own lack of experience in "thinking like business people." How does a cost-center organization learn to make the shift to a profit-driven business?

One critical component was a shift in pay structure: See page 131.

MANAGER, OILCO CONSULTING: President, OilCo Consulting had to form an organization for the new consulting and services company. So early in 1996, he took the leaders of the old functional organizations: procurement, business processing, administrative services, information technology, etc. We started meeting as a "leadership team" of ten people, to think about a longer-term strategy and vision for this new company.

We asked ourselves what was going to be required, to make this a successful company? What did it really mean to move from running a cost center to running a business?

What strategy would get all the people of the new company engaged and committed and would win in the marketplace?

Can a company purpose be developed by ten people in a post-transformation organization of several thousand people?

Can it be developed by forty people?

Here, an organization balances the need to move forward quickly with the emerging recognition that each member of the company has something to contribute to its sense of purpose. But how can all those contributions be brought together effectively?

MANAGER, OILCO CONSULTING: Then in September we put a new "Executive Council" in place: forty senior people who would be responsible for successfully executing the strategy.

You can imagine the first time that this group of forty tried to come together and have a conversation. Each one of them was fighting for survival within their narrow domain. Few were looking at OilCo Consulting as a system.

We met in December, in a three-day off-site "Learning Convention" at Georgia Pines.

As one of the ten people who had worked so hard to develop the new strategy, I sat there thinking, "Surely, these 40 people will see the wisdom, vision, and power of what we've put together."

Of course, the minute we got there, the questions began. Why that? Why not this? Facilitated by Holistic Leadership consultants, we went through the exercise again: We looked at current reality. We defined where we wanted to go. The conversations that began to come out were very powerful. Some things were said that heretofore would probably not have been said in front of some of the more senior people in the organization.

We sat around the campfire at night and talked to each other personally about who we were—our backgrounds, experiences, and beliefs. Every day we had a better, deeper, more meaningful conversation than the day before. We kept asking why we were in business. Would it be enough to simply make money? Or did we want to create something that would live long after we weren't here any more?

On the third day we had a defining moment. In about an hour, we articulated a noble purpose collectively that went much further than any we had posted individually. To this day, it bonds many of the people who were in the room. "We would provide solutions that revolutionized the energy industry."

PRESIDENT, OILCO CONSULTING: For us, this purpose was pretty revolutionary. The purpose concept goes beyond the vision that we want to be the premier company. It considers why we want to be the premier company.

MANAGER, OILCO CONSULTING: What would it mean to revolutionize the energy industry? Well, OilCo E&P, for example, had revolutionized the offshore energy business. They were out drilling where people had never drilled before, and had revitalized an industry in the process. We felt that, with information technologies, seismic processing applications, knowledge of the oil, gas, petro and chemical business, process control systems, and other competencies, we could have a similar impact. We could bring the energy business into new frontiers—because if it didn't continue to evolve and change, then it would become a dinosaur.

Why had the poor reputation persisted for so long? Was it related to the long-standing culture in which people did not look at their business as a business?

It also meant that OilCo Consulting's existence would continue to depend upon the energy industry as customers.

The first thing that popped into my mind was: "People will laugh." OilCo Consulting was not viewed as terribly innovative; we had a reputation for poor customer satisfaction. Did we really have what it took to revolutionize the energy situation?

We didn't get to an answer that day, but we did identify the gaps that existed and developed action plans, on the spot, to start addressing those gaps. We assigned resources and developed timelines for our highest priority items and then set out on our new journey. We weren't sure how to do it yet. But we knew what we were trying to do and, to this day, you hear it in almost every conversation we have. "Will that help us revolutionize the energy industry? If not, then why do it?"

Would the noble purpose enroll lower-level employees as much as it enrolled senior managers?

CONSULTANT, HOLISTIC LEADERSHIP ASSOCIATES: There was something special about OilCo Consulting's noble purpose. At first, it looked like just a bunch of words. But as people talked about it, they became more and more enthusiastic about it. They were taking a transformational role for their industry, and that lifted it above their daily work. The noble purpose enrolled people as they spoke about it.

◆ "WHAT DOES THE WORD 'NOBLE' MEAN?"

PRESIDENT, OILCO CONSULTING: In May 1996, we had a company-wide meeting using closed-circuit TV to link everyone. Five or six people who report to me stood up, and with great conviction and passion, talked about the company and their roles. I told the audience that, to me, this is a great sign of change: That senior managers in the company can stand up and do that.

Then Employee "A" challenged me from a remote site. He is a fairly junior individual; so far from me in the hierarchy that I had never talked with him before.

"I thought about the noble purpose," he said. "I like the idea. But I don't think it's noble enough. What do you have to say about that?"

EMPLOYEE "A", OILCO CONSULTING: The noble purpose had come through, in our organization, in a series of meetings where they had explained it to us. "This is your vision," they said. "We want everybody to buy in."

In every meeting, I had said, "I don't understand what 'noble' means. Tell me." The response I got bothered me: "If you don't like the word 'noble,' just ignore it. Write in another word."

But the word meant something to me. There is an opportunity, when you write a noble purpose for a company, to really engage thousands of people. Our current "noble purpose" said that we were interested in profits only; the mother company wanted us to return a certain amount of profit, and we would—one way or another. We would use Senge's five disciplines, or another consultant's leadership principles, or keep calling in consultants until we could figure out some way to get people lined up to produce profits.

But a noble purpose, to me, would address concerns that were much larger than profits. It would allow me, as an individual, to get up and say, "I'm going to work today because I feel good about it. I know that OilCo is contributing to the world, the nation, and the community, and it cares about people. It's taking care of the environment. I know, deep in my heart, that nothing like the Exxon Valdez would ever happen to us. And if it did, we wouldn't respond in the same way that Exxon did."

So, at this teleconference, I finally asked President, OilCo Consulting about it. That was a somewhat frighten

The leader describes the phrasing of the challenge as much more extreme, in tone, than the version remembered by Employee "A", who made the remark. No matter how it was phrased, the question was deeply challenging.

All "noble purposes" face deep challenges, because everyone has a different perception of what "nobility" should mean.

Does this fact of life imply that we should hunker down and avoid "noble purposes?" Especially in a business?

Or does it suggest that OilCo Consulting, and other for-profit businesses, have an opportunity to set examples of "nobility" without defining the limits of the term?

Why hadn't questions about the noble purpose come up earlier?

How should people who play "outspoken" roles be recognized or cultivated by the company? Is it necessary to be outspoken to be heard?

ing thing to do. To speak on closed-circuit TV, they have you go in a room with a telephone. You can hear what's been said, but you can't see anything, so you don't know exactly what's going on.

I said that I appreciated the opportunity to speak. I very much appreciate the openness that our company has moved towards. But I told them that I didn't see the nobility in our noble purpose. "What does the word `noble' mean?" I asked.

"I don't know," he said. "To tell you the truth, I haven't thought much about it."

PRESIDENT, OILCO CONSULTING: I thought about his question for a minute, and then I said, "I'm going to have to be honest with you. I just hadn't thought about it that deeply."

I was caught right there, with no other answer to give.

He had asked a great question. The truth was, I had been at the meeting where we had worked that noble purpose. I had accepted it. I had endorsed it. But I had not thought enough about it.

Some people who had been in the audience disagreed about the "remarkable catharsis": "This was not that profound an 'a-ha' turning point."

Yet observers also agreed that they saw the leader's shift as genuine.

CONSULTANT, HOLISTIC LEADERSHIP ASSOCIATES: There was a remarkable catharsis in that moment, because President, OilCo Consulting did not react, as everybody had feared, in the old punitive way. He simply listened. And empathized.

That incident caused a quantum shift upward in his leadership credibility, a sense of alignment among everyone there.

EMPLOYEE "A" OILCO CONSULTING: I never heard the end of the conversation, because they disconnected me before the leaders were finished replying. The operation of the phone didn't work very well.

Remember, I was in a closed-off room with a telephone. When I came back out, they told me that people had cheered and clapped, and they were still discussing the noble purpose.

I didn't feel like much of a hero. I wasn't the first one to ever notice that there was no definition behind "noble." I was just the first one to say it out loud.

For weeks thereafter, people I didn't know would stop me and shake my hand. That made me feel like I had done the right thing.

EMPLOYEE, OILCO CHEMICAL: I believe that OilCo can be a very strong company, but can we meet all of the criteria of a "Premier Company" and still be profitable? I believe that we should follow the letter of the law with our operations. But if you go overboard on something like being a good neighbor, your cost of manufacturing could go up. Who is going to care if you were a good neighbor when you have to close your doors?

Although the recounting of this story concludes here, the OilCo Consulting's effort to develop a "noble purpose" is still unfolding.

How much did this episode open up possibilities for OilCo Consulting? Where does the sense of purpose evolve from here?

This quote, from someone at approximately the same level as Employee "A", represents a counter view: the down side of "noble purpose." Net profit is the most measurable goal. Does that make it the best goal? Are we here primarily to make money? If so, is OilCo the best place to work?

CHAPTER 7

THE GLASS HOUSE OF LEADERSHIP

When people come out of a strict hierarchical system, they tend to look to their immediate bosses for direction—even when it comes to implementing the new behaviors of transformation.

At OilCo, however, the bosses are themselves wandering in uncharted territory. They are seeking answers to the question, "What is effective leadership?" But there are no prescriptions for success.

This theme provides insight into the dilemmas people face as they strive to become more effective leaders. It's complex because every leader now works in a "glass house" since transformation. Not just the leader's actions, but his or her attitudes and conversations, are fully in view and open to critique, in a way that is unprecedented for this company.

◆ THE EXECUTIVE COUNCIL: EVOLVING EXAMPLE

In any organization undergoing transformation, the senior leadership group will find themselves called upon—if only by themselves—to provide credible examples of the new kinds of leadership behavior they are calling for. If they want genuine information passed up to them, they must pass it on to others. If they want collaboration across organizational boundaries, they must find ways to collaborate themselves. And if they see benefit in learning how others think and feel, they must find ways to express their own thoughts and feelings, without retreating behind the old OilCo "mask."

Thus, beginning in 1995, the members of the Executive Council examined their own relationships and leadership styles.

All of these quotes, from separate interviews, show a preoccupation with the human aspects of leadership that became increasingly strong after 1995.

MEMBER, EXECUTIVE COUNCIL: Leadership in this company is not like it used to be. Twenty years ago, E&P was an organization of "good ol' boys": A crusty bunch, hanging around on drilling rigs, drilling those wildcats. Any sense of emotion was uncalled for. It was a sign of weakness, and certainly not something you would expect to see from leaders.

The leaders of this company were probably good people, but seen from below, they weren't really human. They were just somebody with a senior executive position in a corner office.

Without better human capability, these quotes suggest, business results cannot be improved.

MEMBER, EXECUTIVE COUNCIL: In 1995, when the new organizational governance model came along, it meant that I had to involve a much broader cross section of people in my firm in common decision-making.

Others on the Executive Council did the same. That's when we started to stumble on the fact that the way that we were interacting, from a human perspective, was less than ideal.

MEMBER, EXECUTIVE COUNCIL: Our agenda began to include the idea of lifting the model of what was expected of leadership. Leadership was more about listening to people than telling people. There was a much greater sense of inclusion and creation.

MEMBER, EXECUTIVE COUNCIL: We recognized that we needed to improve the way we were thinking and practicing. Our human systems needed much more attention than our business tools.

In mid-1995, the Executive Council called the Holistic Leadership Associates as ongoing leadership coaches for themselves and some other senior managers. Holistic Leadership Associates was a new consulting firm, co-founded by four associates of MIT Consultant, with an approach that built upon the "learning disciplines" of systems thinking, personal mastery, and team learning. Some Holistic Leadership Associates consultants were long-standing consultants to OilCo.

This consultation was explicitly geared to personal transformation, in a way that other efforts at OilCo (including most of the Applied Learning and financial literacy work) had avoided.

CONSULTANT "A," HOLISTIC LEADERSHIP ASSOCIATES: One of our first encounters with the Executive Council took place in a meeting around April 1995.

CONSULTANT "B," HOLISTIC LEADERSHIP ASSOCIATES: My general impression was of a great deal of individual advocacy and not as much listening as I might hope for. And there was not much in the way of personal revelations. It looked like [CEO] was in charge, and the rest were a group of individuals looking to him. They did not act as a council.

These two external consultants were interviewed together. They described this event as a way of showing the kinds of indicators of leadership authenticity. It is evident not in the words spoken, but in the way that things are done and the tone of conversation.

CONSULTANT "A," HOLISTIC LEADERSHIP ASSOCIATES: But then the Council began talking about some candidates for positions they wanted to fill, and all of a sudden the quality of the meeting significantly changed. Real engagement, and real risk-taking, began to unfold. For about ten minutes, it felt like we were watching a group of people who deeply cared about OilCo and its success.

MEMBER, EXECUTIVE COUNCIL: As far as our credibility was concerned, we began to receive a lot of feedback in 1995. Consultants, Holistic Leadership Associates went around conducting a series of interviews. They learned about our organization, and they helped us to understand the system of OilCo: why it worked the way it did, and how all the pieces fit together—the culture, the results, the systems, the people.

What would determine which consultants' approach will be favored in a transformation?

CONSULTANT "B," HOLISTIC LEADERSHIP ASSOCIATES: First, we asked for interviews with people who were not at the top, but who were informal leaders in the system, with great knowledge of what was going on—and who could be frank. Ultimately we knew we were going to see the Executive Council members. And we did see them. . . but not immediately.

Some people said that they have recognized that transformation begins with individual personal change. For some of the ramifications of this point, see "Who Am I?," page 183.

The journey of transformation takes time. Will the 'transformed' remember that others may not be at the same place on the journey?

What is the safest way to give and receive this type of in-depth feedback?

Can this type of consultation and feedback be extended? To how wide a group of people? Can it be done safely by internal OilCo staff?

One Executive Council member noted that while the feedback had been effective, the same results were possible through other types of consultation or reflection.

The interviews we conducted lasted for three hours, at minimum. They were a way of entering into deep dialogue with people and setting a kind of field for the entire project. The way in is through deep listening. There is a shift that occurs at a certain moment when you are listening to someone, and they feel listened to, that you perceive a deep, palpable connection. The relationship shifts and there is no separation there.

Nothing will happen at the larger, organizational sense, without also happening at the personal level. Personal transformation is, in essence, a journey that an individual takes. And you can also describe the transformation of a company as a hero's journey. We did not explicitly explain this at the time. We just. . . listened to people.

Then we gave them very specific feedback about their own behavior. We tried to do this with the deepest kind of respect for the individual. This can be done over a whole series of meetings and you don't give them all the feedback at once. You're very respectful and careful. You might feed back a little bit and then do a lot of listening again, walking them through this type of learning. It takes a long time.

MEMBER, EXECUTIVE COUNCIL: As part of that effort, they gathered quite a bit of information on all of us in the Executive Council, and they fed that back to us directly. Some of it was pretty doggone powerful feedback. Of course it was confidential. You didn't know exactly who said what, and so on. But it was all from people whom I respect, talking about how I had impacted them in the past, and I had never heard much of it before. That was threatening, but it also caused me to give some serious thought to things.

My first reaction was defensive. "Gee, that's not really the way that happened, was it?" But then, as you think about it, maybe it was the way it happened. Times were different. You think, "Well, I didn't mean it that way." But

I don't think I would ever have seen it without going through this kind of process.

Meanwhile, throughout 1995, the Executive Council members began to redefine their own role vis-à-vis transformation—moving from a relatively passive role to a more active orientation as designers.

MEMBER, EXECUTIVE COUNCIL: Initially, the Executive Council had little control over the agenda of our meetings. We would not know, when we walked in, what we were going to do. The perception was: "The consultants are in charge, and you're here to do basically as you're told." Our dissatisfaction with this situation continued to build until a meeting we held at Wintergreen, Virginia, in October 1995.

This meeting was later recalled as a "defining moment" in the corporate transformation and personal changes of leaders.
What conditions might have contributed to the shifts in thinking and behavior that came from this event?

We ended up with frank and candid discussions about two issues. First, who was in charge of the transformation? Was it the Executive Council, or [CEO] with the support of the consultants? [CEO] was open to this point and made it clear to the consultants that they were there to serve the Council. He was not the client. Typically, now we end our meetings by planning the agenda for the next meeting. This is not somebody else's agenda; this is our agenda.

Second, what was the role of the Council? There was almost total disagreement about this at first. [CEO] saw the Council as a deliberative body, not a decision-making body. His concern was that we would become some sort of super-body, imposed on the governance process, making decisions that would be better decided by the individual company boards.

We agreed that we would not make business decisions as the Executive Council.

CEO: Wintergreen was a very good meeting. Now I could hear the difference from our earlier meetings: the quality in the conversations, the depth of understanding, and the willingness to expose our thoughts and honestly listen to others. We were not perfect; we were still stumbling around like children; but there was a marked difference.

These themes from Wintergreen became the basis of what was later called the Agenda for Corporate Transformation.

We settled in on three basic themes that we wanted to emphasize—originally for the year 1996. But it has become clear that these are enduring or ongoing themes: Leadership, Commitment, and extending the financial literacy initiative.

Are these sorts of dialogues a model for other leadership groups throughout the company?

MEMBER, EXECUTIVE COUNCIL: I feel more comfortable in the Executive Council meetings that we can talk about any item that we want to talk about. I don't think that there's any subject that would be considered taboo. Certainly there's no subject that I would be reluctant to raise.

As the dialoguing practice evolves, will there continue to be a need for rules that set what can and cannot be discussed?

In addition, the discussion and the dialogue are much more open and candid. Opportunities for true dialogue are valued. We've started to meet for dinner once every six to eight weeks, with no outsiders and no consultants. One of the ground rules is that we won't talk about operational problems, or the state of our progress toward 10 percent ROI. We just talk about issues related to transformation.

◆ RETHINKING THE COMPANY'S CORE VALUES

One of the first efforts of transformation had been the definition of five core values: belief in people, trustworthiness, excellence, innovation, and a sense of urgency. Beginning in 1995, as part of an effort by a corporate team to create a model of leadership, the core values have begun to be revisited.

How were the values seen when they were first presented? As a mandate for the way people "ought to act"? As a springboard for reflecting on one's own values? In this account, they are seen as a vehicle for the judgment of leaders.

MEMBER, EXECUTIVE COUNCIL: When we first developed our mission, vision, and values, back in 1993-1994 (see page 31), we realized that we wanted to make it an evergreen process, that we would come back and revisit.

Over the period of almost three years since, we have done a lot of thinking about the original values. So has the organization. In the values survey we took in 1995, in the focus groups we conducted, and in the thousands of flip charts we've filled out, people have told us repeatedly:

We weren't being truthful or courageous. We weren't risk takers. We were lacking in our moral courage, moral imperatives, moral excellence. The organization saw that.

I guess they were talking about the leaders, but also, perhaps, talking about each other.

MEMBER, EXECUTIVE COUNCIL: Our initial model on core values was that we had to get something out quickly. We had a series of cascading workshops in the organization. Maybe we had to do it that way just to get something out. But that was a very shallow exercise with something so important as core values. It was as if we were still old OilCo, telling people: "Okay, you've got three hours. Now, go internalize the core values."

I think several thousand people went through those workshops, but I bet most people couldn't recite the values today. I don't fault them. The cascading model just doesn't work, in my opinion, but it was the only way we knew how to communicate.

The good news is, I don't think we're stuck with those values. I don't think a "sense of urgency" is needed as a corporate value today. We needed it then. We needed a sense of urgency.

With the transformational triangle, we're talking once again about aligning individual and organizational values. So maybe we've got a golden opportunity here to reopen those questions around corporate values and what they should be. Plus, we're about to initiate dialogue on a new leadership model.

CEO: We on the Executive Council know we missed the mark at first in terms of vision and values. We have been missing a process to help get better alignment between people's personal values and aspirations and the values and aspirations that have been articulated for the company. Alignment had once primarily been enforced through discipline. We needed to try to transform that into an alignment based on commitment, and peoples' understanding.

For some, they became a safe vehicle for talking about leadership and behavior in a company where the "soft side" was always taken for granted.

Does a leadership model or a set of core values allow for diverse styles? How can a leadership model or core values be communicated (and useful) in a diverse organization?

Despite the considerable effort made to develop a shared set of core values, few people mentioned the values explicitly in interviews.

On the other hand, implicitly, the conversations in this report refer constantly to questions about values. Does that indicate a subtle effect of this work?

When a CEO admits "missing the mark," what does that suggest about this individual's leadership? About leadership in general?

What does "personal and organizational alignment" mean, in day-to-day terms? Is it the ability to trust one another? How long would it take for the heart of the triangle to be "real"?

We developed a diagram, at the Wintergreen meeting, which we labeled the Agenda for Corporate Transformation, to represent the three activities that we think are involved in rolling out the transformation: Leadership, Commitment, and extending the financial literacy initiative. In subsequent discussions, we've added the phrase "personal and organizational alignment" at the heart of the triangle (Figure 7-1).

A lot of people hate sports analogies and I don't think of it necessarily as a sports analogy, but it does have reflection in various teams that we have been members of. If you had any military experience, if you were in small elite units, you would have found that kind of fundamental personal alignment between individuals is there. It's part mutual confidence and part reliance on each other. That's what we're hoping and trying to build. It's just a slogan right now but it represents the ongoing essence of what we're trying to do.

MEMBER, EXECUTIVE COUNCIL: We've begun another project to define the role of leadership at OilCo. I've been with OilCo for twenty-five years and no one had ever told me

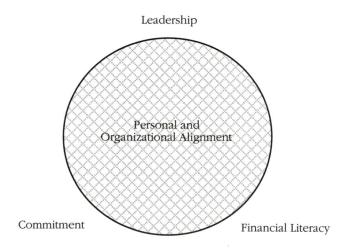

FIGURE 7-1 *Agenda for corporate transformation*

what leadership means. So now I've dug in and said, this is how I think leaders should be in OilCo.

Working with a team of about ten people, we have begun to develop conversations and dialogues on leadership throughout the organization, in town-hall meetings and work group sessions, to talk about the shared commitments that represent our core values.

Consider trust, for example. In the past, we have almost beat ourselves to death over the concept of trust in this company. In our work group sessions on leadership, that's the first thing that went on everybody's flip chart. "People do not trust you, as leaders. They don't trust each other." Everyone said, "Yeah, we've got to get the trust back." But no one ever knew how to do it.

Humility is a lightning rod. People cannot get their mind around the idea of a leader being humble. They say, "What about George Patton? What about MacArthur, Churchill, and Vince Lombardi?" This brings on a conversation that leaders come in all sizes and shapes. Humility is not a requirement for leadership, "but it is a quality that you have told us you want in leaders."

The first time I rolled this (see Figure 7-2) out to a group of Corporate Executive Team members, a refinery manager—a very passionate guy—pushed back. "I just can't see how you can be a great leader and not be a little arrogant," he said. I challenged that. I said that humility was not weakness. It was a strength. If you're arrogant, you believe that nobody can beat you; and you won't worry about getting any better. If you are humble, you will always be strong enough to continue trying to improve.

He didn't buy in, and we went on to some other subjects. About ten minutes later, another manager said, "Look, I want to go back to humility and arrogance. What about the L.A. Lakers? [a professional basketball team]— what about Magic Johnson [a star player on the team]? Or Pat Riley [the head coach]? They demonstrate all of those virtues, including humility."

Developing a model like this is very meaningful. But when it is handed to other people, will this model repeat the "cascade" style of engagement of the original core values?

What would you want to see included, if you were articulating a model of leadership?

Our interviews turned up divergent attitudes about humility. Some said, in effect: "Humility is subtle, yet very powerful. People rally around people who acknowledge their flat spots and limitations."

Other people felt that humility is a sign of weakness: inappropriate as a corporate value because it leads people to lack confidence in their leaders.

It may be an asset to have a leadership model which is presented with acknowledged disagreement about specific elements, so that core values are conversation starters, instead of "the last word."

The key to rolling out the transformation, I think, is to be able to have these conversations and this type of reflection—not just on what we do, but on who we are as leaders. And how we behave as role models.

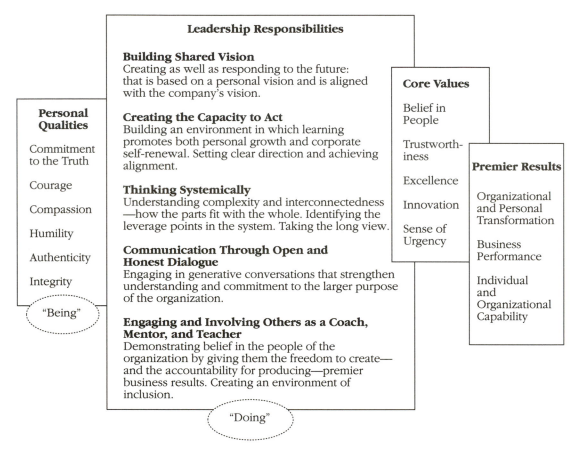

FIGURE 7-2 *The emerging OilCo leadership model*

◆ EXAMPLES OF LEADERSHIP IN ACTION

Many interviewees described their efforts as leaders—or their observations of other leaders. These are some of the most compelling examples.

MEMBER, EXECUTIVE COUNCIL: In the past, my job was to go fix problems. I am a good problem solver. If you brought a problem to me, I loved it. "Put it on the table; get out of the way, I'll fix it."

Which means I had just taken accountability away from you. I've stolen your work, without you even knowing it.

SENIOR MANAGER, E&P: If something is said which I vigorously oppose, instead of jumping out of my seat and saying, "That's the dumbest idea I've ever heard," I stop myself. We don't have dumb people working for us. I still have to grab my chair handles sometimes, but I am getting better at respecting and valuing diversity of thought. My target is to listen 66 percent of the time, two ears, one mouth.

Based on what I see happening up and down these halls, that one behavioral change in me is having an exponential effect on the willingness people have to speak up and to be heard.

People would say to me, "You wouldn't understand my problems. You've got a three-window office and an underground parking space." So I decided that the underground parking didn't really mean that much, and I'd give it up. My wife suggested, "Why don't you give it to someone, and let them give it to someone else, and keep them passing it along?"

So I started in February, giving it to my secretary, who's handling all the secretarial work now for three offices. I said, "I really appreciate all the efforts you put in. I want you to park in my space for the week, with this caveat: on Thursday, you tell me whom you'd like to take it for the following week, and why." It kept going after that, with everyone's name posted on the bulletin board when they were chosen to take the spot.

Personal recognition by peers is probably the most important form of recognition, and this approach takes it completely out of the management ranks.

OPERATIONS FOREMAN, SOUTHERN COMPANY: We were going to shut down a dehydration facility that was pumping 1,500 barrels per day. I had an operator who refused to go

People in management positions learned to step out of those roles so that others could emerge as leaders.

This memorable anecdote suggests that there is a lot of leverage in using the conventional perks of privilege in unconventional, creative ways...

... and a lot of leverage in taking risks on behalf of peoples' ability.

What would have happened if the operator hadn't found a solution?

These leaders are experimenting with power and relationship.

People have not, in our interviews, drawn "principles of leadership" out of their experience. The stories speak for themselves. But are there principles of leadership to be drawn forth here?

The next two quotes shift gears, to show the impact of "humility-based" leadership on people nearby.

along. "You're doing it all wrong," she said, "I can keep you on-line and running." I had thought that physically there was no way to do this.

It was almost funny. She'd known a long time that we didn't have to do it the way we were doing it. But she had always done what she was told until the accountability here had changed. Now she said, "I can't afford to lose production."

She had a bunch of us red-faced and angry at her, but she refused to budge. We showed her diagrams from the engineer. But she stood her ground.

Finally I scratched my head and said, "Figure out how to do it. It's all yours, take care of it."

Three years ago, I'd have said, "The engineer says this is what you do because he's an engineer and you're an operator." Instead, I let her hold up the project a few days to solve the problem, and six to eight weeks to implement her solution. There would be times when I would go out there and she would be sitting on a brick cement wall, motionless. I was thinking, "Damn, she's sitting on a brick wall. What are we doing here?" She was thinking about the problem. I had to force myself, personally, to say, "I'm willing to allow you to do this."

In the end, I give her all the accolades. She came up with a process whereby I never lost a barrel of oil! What she did was very, very intelligent—a simple procedure that let us bypass the treater that was causing the problem. She was determined that she was not shutting down.

ADMINISTRATIVE ASSISTANT, CORPORATE: As one of the support staff at one of the learning conventions, I had a delightful experience. We had a large work room that we called our "command central." It was filled with laptops, props, and materials.

One day, one of OilCo's most senior executives came in between sessions for a break. He was very relaxed, and sat visiting with us. The phone beside him rang and he picked it up and said, "Hello. No, he's not here. May I take a message?" He took a message for one of the mid-level managers at the session. Nobody said anything, and he may not have realized the impact that had on us, but it was very refreshing!

In the past, management at any level would have let it ring until a support person answered, even if we had to trip over them to get to the phone. We were all amazed at this executive's humility and willingness to do that simple task as if he were "one of us."

MANAGER, OILCO CONSULTING: After each quarter, or when some significant event happens, [CEO] leaves a phone message for everyone in the company. It says, "We're doing a great job," or "These are things we're working on." It's nice to hear feedback from the president of a company. It makes me feel more a part of the whole, and part of the effort to make things better.

INTERNAL CONSULTANT: I remember an off-site meeting where my boss talked a lot and didn't listen. He was one of the most senior executives in the room, and the other people shut down. I ended up giving him feedback. "Have you noticed that you're doing all the talking and nobody else is? Have you noticed the body language in the room?" This was not welcome. He was pretty mad about it.

For a period of time, we had a lot of these conversations. I would try to coach him, and he would get angry. Finally I told him I didn't want to work for him anymore. He could find somebody with better chemistry for him. He may never have had anybody tell him that before. He called me into his office and lost his temper at me.

I stayed working for him, but for the next several months there was a lot of tension. I remembered some ince advice that I'd been given regarding change management: "If a customer doesn't want you, don't try to push up hill." So I worked harder at developing other

Is this an example of a leader "walking the talk?"

Increasingly, technology will be taken for granted as a vehicle for expressing leadership to broad populations of employees.

In these next two quotes, we hear from an internal consultant and the consultant's boss—who was once considered "difficult" and is now reframing his behavior.

Is this type of coaching and confrontation a key part of the job of internal consultants at OilCo?

What confidence does it take to play this role?

coaching relationships.

I got through it because I was not willing to give up. An external consultant gave me one valuable piece of advice: "You probably have a list of fifty criticisms you

want to give your boss feedback about. Talk to him about two, and then talk about ten things he did well." I changed my approach and started doing that.

My boss, meanwhile, was going through his own personal development. Lo and behold, he started noticing that I was doing good work. All of a sudden, things picked up. That was almost a year ago, and now we have a wonderful working relationship. He is a model of leadership for the rest of the organization.

Part of the change came from my changing my approach. But honestly, most of it came from him. For whatever reason, he decided that he wanted to be a more effective leader—a different kind of leader—and it shows.

Who knows what is going on behind the public faces that senior managers have learned to adopt?

THE SAME BOSS AS IN THE PREVIOUS STORY: Are you familiar with Danah Zohar? She's a quantum physicist who talked to us at the last Learning Convention. She said that people over time become wired in a certain way, and to start changing those circuits is very difficult.

I had never done much reflecting, but I started to do more. I realized that I wasn't going to be like my old way of behavior any more. If that meant I had to leave the company, that was fine. I was going to be the person I wanted to be—the person I was.

Does the evolution to leadership require the willingness to "chuck it all" in the name of authenticity? If so, is that a limiting factor?

That was a tough decision, because I was sitting there with a reasonable degree of success. It is still an uncomfortable transition.

◆ The "glass house": A paradox of leadership

Every leader at OilCo lives in a glass house. They are public figures, subject to new forms of scrutiny, in a way that leaders never were before.

This has created a new leadership dynamic at OilCo, a dynamic that will influence the evolution of OilCo's governance system and its corporate culture.

MANAGER, HUMAN RESOURCES: [Member, Executive Council] has said, "The old hand of OilCo just reaches out and grabs you and tries to pull you back." So your behavior slides, and you go back to the old style on occasion.

But once you go back you lose so much credibility. You just reinforce the idea that transformation is just another program of the day. Which means that the next change process is going to be more difficult to accomplish.

How much latitude do leaders have to make mistakes? Or to let old authoritarian behavior slip through?

MANAGER, HUMAN RESOURCES: I think that there are one or more very senior managers whose behavior is widely recognized and perceived as being inconsistent with our values. They are tolerated because results are there.

[CEO's] getting a black eye because he's not dealing with it. It challenges our credibility. It says one more time that, if I get the numbers right, it buys me wide latitude for behavior that is not aligned with the transformation.

It's not a game breaker. We'll deal with it. All of us, including [CEO], need permission to make mistakes.

But there is a certain amount of "glass house" in OilCo today: The more senior you are, the more visible you are, and the more leverage that you have in modeling behavior.

Everybody, from the highest to the lowest levels of the company, is vulnerable to the accusation of "not walking the talk." Fingers point up, down, and across the hierarchy as people search for answers.

Also see "Coach, coach, coach," page 149.

EXTERNAL CONSULTANT: There were a number of members of the Executive Council who, in my own judgment, I thought were walking the walk. But everybody told me, "No, he's not. He's just talking well." They were doing things like: keeping tight control. Expecting people to bow and scrape. Working toward agendas that weren't open and up front. Not being direct in their communications. Trying to please [CEO] to a fault.

Not being able to see this myself was really unusual for me. Sometimes being at OilCo was like being Alice in Wonderland. Things are not always what they seem.

This "glass house" phenomenon seems to represent a significant shift from the old "silent house" management culture, which held a norm of not openly criticizing leaders, past or present.

What are appropriate standards for a "transformational" manager?

There's a history of focusing on appearances and looking like it's a gentleman's club, while all sorts of things happen beneath the surface.

MANAGER, OILCO: I think typically in OilCo, people are critical, but not openly critical. You might not think much of your bossbut you aren't going to tell him so. On the other hand, one group who reported to me was a set of early adopters of the transformation. They were pretty vocal critics. It felt almost like a feeding frenzy. It was clear that I was not doing the things that they wanted from a leader. I was too directive. I was not in the office enough, in part because my job included dealing with our outside clients, and so I was not stroking them enough.

Are people just asked to "act" in new ways? How can people discern differences between good acting and genuine changes?

I felt like I was doing the best I could and that they were holding me up to an unfair standard: "You're a transformational leader, and therefore you should be perfect. But you're not perfect, so I'm questioning this whole arrangement." I never did figure out a way to make it work, and eventually I moved on to another assignment.

I think this is endemic in the OilCo culture. On the one hand, there is a lot of deference to leadership—but also a lot of cynical feeling about leadership. Those two sentiments clash and it becomes very difficult for groups that I have been in and that I have observed. It is very difficult to accept a leader as just another human being, trying to contribute to the effort.

These two comments imply that authoritarianism lingers as a deeply ingrained mental model at OilCo. Is the "glass house" phenomenon simply a flip side of the old authoritarian culture?

Does OilCo oscillate between these extremes?

SENIOR MANAGER, OILCO CONSULTING: We are still a very deeply rooted hierarchical company. Hierarchy matters. If you don't believe that, try to get a parking place at the main OilCo headquarters lot.

It matters how many people work for you. It matters what your title or grade level is. It matters if you're on the Corporate Executive Team. I'm not sure we'll ever get that out of our system. It won't be during my career. It's hard for the big guys to let that go, even if they intellectually want to, and even if they are inspired by the idea. You are reminded, when you see them, that they are the boss.

MEMBER, EXECUTIVE COUNCIL: The OilCo system created a group of people who still look for the old style of leadership. Whenever there is a question, all eyes in the room immediately focus on the senior leader. They look for that person to have all the answers. I don't think that's good, because the senior leader can't always be there any more when decisions have to be made.

How will leaders be remembered? What stories will be told?

Is the same true for people at all levels?

ADVISER, EXECUTIVE COUNCIL: I've come to realize that the leadership ability of senior management is not defined by their intention. Their leadership is defined by the stories that prevail—the stories that are told by others who interact with them. It doesn't matter if the stories are true or false. Those stories represent the legacy they will leave behind.

What might be unanticipated side-effects of pushing people to be more open or communicative than their natural tendencies would support?

◆ SUSTAINING TRANSFORMATION IN THE FACE OF CHANGING LEADERSHIP

People are worried about the sustainability of the transformation. They want to know, "Who will lead when the CEO is gone?"

We offer here only the comments that, instead of speculation, offer insights about the legacy of OilCo's transformation to date. These comments raise the question, "Once a transformation and change in governance is initiated, is there any turning back?"

MEMBER, CORPORATE EXECUTIVE TEAM: I don't think any of us, including [CEO], expect that a CEO clone will come in after him. He would even say that would be inappropriate. So then who is the successor? What might that successor want to do? In other companies, you hear about successors coming in and dismantling the prior three or four years. My God. Can that happen here?

Once you begin to let the genie out of the bottle, it's hard to put back in. For instance, we've been talking about putting together a team of nearly thirty people to

Do sentiments like this, however worthwhile, set up an organization to be dependent on a "charismatic" hero-leader?

have a say in how the benefits at OilCo are reshaped. Now imagine that a successor came in and said, "This is just a waste of time. These people have work to do. Let's go back to basics."

Whoo! I think it would create more dissatisfaction than the dissatisfaction that we currently have from some of the downsizing events.

Maybe it's the natural order of things for "something else to become the big deal." Or perhaps that would mean that transformation didn't "take."

EMPLOYEE, OILCO CHEMICAL: When I first started at OilCo, quality was a big thing, but no one talks about it now.

I'm sure in a few years something else will be the big deal instead of transformation. I don't have a problem with the change, it's just a matter of the conviction of that change. Let me know if this is going to be forever, a ten-year plan, a three-year plan, or the plan du jour. I can live with whatever is decided.

What are the challenges to senior leadership when external factors cause business results to decline, and handicap their abilities to invest in and financially justify improvement programs?

CEO: People have said to me, in public and private: "Well, this is your deal, it's going to last as long as you last and then we'll go on to something else." That's probably right. Somebody else can have this job and they will do things differently.

But if the transformation is going to be successful, it will be the creation and the product of an awful lot of people.

I can't create it, but I can stop it—either intentionally or unintentionally—any time. All I have to do is send out one message or get up in front of one audience and say or act in certain ways and I can bring it all to a close. I guess I view myself as representing more threat than anything else.

Moreover, if people attribute the elements of the transformation to me, then they never commit to it personally. This has already been a very significant barrier. First of all, they're skeptical of me. "He says this now, but let the oil prices go down and results turn bad, and he'll revert back to the old command and control ways like they always do." That's the serious test. In the board room or with security analysts, the questions get a lot more pointed when profits are going down.

Second, they may accept that I will stay with it, but perhaps my successor won't. I think that's a very counterproductive attitude for the whole process.

I would steer away from the idea of personalizing the process. Whatever we've done, we have done collectively. I think we recognize we can't do it without a whole lot of people.

CONSULTANT, HOLISTIC LEADERSHIP ASSOCIATES: For this effort to be truly evaluated we would have to look at it ten to fifteen years from now. These are the extreme early stages.

If this thing is truly working it won't just show up in financial results. It will also show up in the quality of life for the people working here.

What would an "improvement in quality of life" look like? Has it "shown up"? If not, how long would you reasonably wait?

CHAPTER 8

BUXTON FALLS' HIGH-PERFORMANCE TEAMS

The Buxton Falls refinery in Ohio was one of the precursors to transformation. Sparked by an innovative group of managers, it developed an operating environment with high-performance, self-managing teams and a series of innovative union-management partnerships focused around improving safety, environmental, and (later) financial performance. For most of this period, the innovations continued despite continued financial difficulties at the refinery.

◆ BUXTON FALLS' CASE FOR ACTION

As with other precursors, the changes at Buxton Falls began in response to severe economic downturns.

SENIOR MANAGER, OILCO: Why did Buxton Falls go to self-managed teams so early? To reduce cost. This was the highest-cost refinery in the OilCo system, and pretty much in the industry. If it kept going the way it was, it would not survive.

Businesses that were most economically challenged had the greatest incentive to change.

FORMER MANAGER, BUXTON FALLS: In the early 1990s, margins started to drop precipitously: from $6.00 per barrel to $2.00. Buxton Falls went from making millions per year to losing millions per year.

The plant had a culture of eleven unions. In general, there was more employee loyalty to the union than to the

The first two comments offhandedly describe the work of bringing together a collaborative senior management team with a case for action. This, in itself, is a difficult thing to do—but at Buxton Falls, as at many locations, it was only the first step.

company. If you asked someone whom they worked for, you'd hear, "Well, I work for the operating engineers local," or "I'm a pipefitter in our local." Many were second- or third-generation OilCo workers.

Buxton Falls also had OilCo's overall worst safety performance, four times worse than any other OilCo refinery. In the 1980s they had a major emissions discharge; and several noticeable oil spills.

A new plant manager arrived in November 1989. He was one of the most outstanding transformational leaders that OilCo has ever enjoyed. I joined him at Buxton Falls in January 1990. We found a culture that hadn't had a lot of change, hadn't had a lot of financial information, and hadn't had a lot of financial pressure placed on them. The workers had, of course, heard of refinery closings, but it had never happened at OilCo. Now, because of the financial pressure, they were really hurting.

So we began building a shared vision of what Buxton Falls needed to become. We started with the senior team, spending time in workshops, talking about premier performance. We wanted to really excel in the refining business. As we got to know each other, we discovered that we shared a lot of common core values—dignity, respect for the individual, trust, and empowerment.

FORMER MANAGER, BUXTON FALLS: We developed the Buxton Falls mission, vision, and operating principles document in 1990. I'm proud to say we never put it on a card or hung it on a wall. It was more of a living document. Everybody had a copy with scratch-outs and changes; people could personalize their own copy in a way that made more sense to them.

◆ INITIATING SELF-DIRECTION

A ten-year plan for moving to high-performance teams was initiated at Buxton Falls in 1990, propelled by the interest of the plant manager and other senior managers at the plant. An organizational effectiveness manager at Buxton Falls, who had experience with high-performance team management at another company, designed the plan and the initial training.

Self-directed work teams achieve high performance by managing all of their processes collaboratively, with training but not much external supervision. They take care of all the positions, deciding how to divide the work, keeping the statistics that help them improve themselves, and acting together to be accountable for their collective results.

It's important to note that other initiatives were also going on at Buxton Falls—collaborative work between union and management on improvements in safety, environmental quality, and ultimately financial performance.

FORMER MANAGER, BUXTON FALLS: At first, few people seemed to buy into the concept of self-managing teams. Some people said, "Not on my shift; you'll never do that." Their favorite term was: "You're handing the asylum over to the crazies."

Shifting from the traditional supervisory structure to the team model would involve a change in thinking for everyone. It would also involve a significant investment.

The start of any good team concept is being sure that everyone in the organization has a good handle on the fundamentals of running their business. The first training sessions also included material on how to run a meeting and coaching, and on the manufacturing system as an open system, in which all the pieces interrelate and affect each other. And we started taking seventy-five people a year—out of the 1,800 people in the plant at that time—through five-and-one-half-day workshops.

By the time 1993 came, we really had a significant number of people who understood how a self-managing process could work. We were three years into our ten-year plan for moving to self-managing teams, a plan that I had thought was aggressive.

That year, we were asked to downsize big time. We lost half the first-line supervisors—not by layoffs, but by voluntary packages. They decided to take the seven years left in our plan and compress them to eighteen months.

UNION SHOP STEWARD, BUXTON FALLS: Our union bought into self-directed teams from the beginning, simply because they knew that for us to survive, we needed to abandon the way we were. As workers, we needed to cooperate as much as we could with minimal resistance, as long as things stayed within certain parameters.

One of the reasons, I think, that our department made the transition so smoothly was the fact that we had a manager who was willing to meet with the union on a regular, almost a scheduled basis. A lot of times we would just throw a bunch of stuff on the table. Or, if there were concerns, we'd address them. But he always let us know where we were going, so we were in the loop. There is nothing worse than being blind-sided by some big change.

If something's gonna come up, you might not agree with it, you might not like it, but you have time to prepare yourself for it.

Any major shift in team-level governance involves a disenfranchised element. How might this transition have been managed more effectively?

OPERATOR, BUXTON FALLS: I was an hourly foreman. All I knew was: We were going to have self-directed work teams and our department was going to be one of the first to switch. I was just told that all of the shift teams were going to go to an eight-hour class and we're going to play with tinker toys and hula hoops. We were going to come away from there one big happy family and the next day when we got back to work we wouldn't have a foreman.

That's exactly what happened. I was in the foreman's job on Monday and I was working an operator's job on Thursday.

FORMER MANAGER, BUXTON FALLS: The most threatened group was foremen, because their jobs were to go away. When we set up self-managing teams, we created a whole bunch of disenfranchised folks.

Ironically, for twenty years we had stressed the importance of first-line supervision in manufacturing. "A foreman is the key to everything."

Then one day, I walked in and said we didn't need foremen anymore. To make this work, I had to acknowledge—and this is the most important aspect of transformation—that my own fundamental beliefs had to change.

I too had gotten a lot of value out of building foremen as strong leaders. I had to convince the people that the new approach was right. "Look," I said to them, "trust me and give it a chance. You will be heavily involved in the design of the process. It won't be done to you."

Note two different perspectives on the same event. One person says, "The shift was done to me." The other person says, "We tried to involve them in the design of the process."

OPERATOR, BUXTON FALLS: The first thing was they pulled all our front-line supervisors away from us. We went from having near-blow-by-blow direction and having our paperwork laid out to: "Okay, starting September 1, you will no longer have shift foremen."

There was a real feeling of abandonment at first. They had taken people away whom we needed in a crisis. We quickly found out how to work together better, how to delegate work among ourselves, and we weeded out a lot of trivia quickly.

We learned to survive. I couldn't remember everything that needed to be done on that unit, but another person knew what I didn't. And that person might ask me how to bring something up on the computer and I'd help him. We needed to rely on everybody because there was so much responsibility to take on.

Workers talked of a feeling of abandonment, yet needing to learn to work together to keep the plant running and survive. The foremen's presence, in the past, had covered up for lack of cooperation.

OPERATOR, BUXTON FALLS: "Chaotic" is not the word for it; it was beyond chaos. "Clicking in" is not the word either, because a few folks took to it like ducks to water. They didn't have a problem with it, and those were, for the most part, the more experienced people who had a lot of confidence in themselves and their abilities. They felt, "I don't need a foreman anyway. I know what I'm supposed to be doing. I know what to fix."

Those with lesser experience, less knowledge, struggled more. Some of the teammates with experience didn't

Or, from another perspective, the foremen had kept the plant from drifting into chaos.

How do the "people who took to it like ducks to water" compare with the people who are "taking to corporate transformation"?

mind being the helping hand. Others felt that it wasn't their job. "I take care of my section in the world over here and what happens, happens. I didn't ask for this. I hired on as an operator. I don't want to be a foreman, I don't want to make decisions."

◆ ADDRESSING BEHAVIORAL ISSUES

Finding ways to change the culture of the refinery was a bigger challenge than changing the structure.

Moving from foreman to operator meant a significant shift in relationship with the other operators

FORMER FOREMAN, BUXTON FALLS: A couple of weeks after we switched to self-directed work teams, we had a classic case of grief and agony from the troops. One night, I was working the board job. The board has three computer screens, where we can monitor and run the unit.

On this night, the department that feeds us hydrogen was having problems at 2 AM. There were two operators plus myself working that night, both of them outside. I called in one of them, someone with much more experience on the board than I had, and he said we might have to crash the unit. The other operator didn't agree, and he came flying into that control room yelling and screaming, ranting and raving, calling me every name he could think of. I lost it after a while, and the yelling was mutual.

This was one of his ways of saying, "You're not my boss any more."

The other former foremen experienced similar things.

FORMER MANAGER, BUXTON FALLS: The easy part was taking the foreman's supervisory duties—calling overtime, working with maintenance—and dividing them among the troops. The hard part involved inappropriate work-group behaviors: Abusive language and treatment. Or how do you deal with the white guy who won't work in an intimate team setting with a black pipefitter?

We discovered that, in many cases, these problems had never been dealt with effectively by foremen. Their job was to keep that stuff under control, and not to let management hear about it.

At that point we had to teach the teams to do that themselves. Now, if you were an abusive person, you'd have a session with three or four of your co-workers. "We're gonna give you some 360-degree feedback," they'd say, "and you're not going to like it. We want to hear your issues, but we've got to get this dealt with."

That's powerful.

Are there other "old systems" at OilCo which, in one way or another, had kept abusive problems "under control" without ever looking at the fundamental causes of the problem?

FORMER OE MANAGER, BUXTON FALLS: Within eighteen months we had all but one of the departments go through the training. Now we could see the changes in the teams. Externally, there was not as much bitching, moaning, complaining, and whining. It was more proactive: "How do we get this done?"

There's always a whiner in every group. You don't ever do away with them but the team manages them in a way that they're not destructive. One of the whiners would start, they'd listen to them, they'd see if there was anything valid, and then they'd say, "Thanks for sharing," and move on. Well, they probably weren't that polite.

I'd get calls in the middle of the night from the team that a manager was out there ranting and raving, trying to throw his weight around. "Would you come out and help us coach him?" At 2 AM, there I would be, heading back to the refinery, to ask, "OK, what's going on here?"

And there was never any right or wrong. It was usually a clash between the old way and the new way.

FORMER MANAGER, BUXTON FALLS: I had to let people make mistakes. I had to let them do things that I didn't think of and I had to change too.

Very early on, one of the managers said, "I want to put the union steward on my management team."

Trying to apply these concepts became a challenge because they meant taking on long-standing systems, such as HR approaches, that had been built to support an old style of management.

I said, "You want to do what?" But I thought about it, and agreed. It was a good way of bringing the union into feeling like they had an active involvement in this process. Later, it dawned on me: I need to do that too. Before I left, I was probably the only superintendent in OilCo with a union leader as a member of my management team.

◆ How are the teams doing?

Self-directed teams are well established at Buxton Falls now. Different people have different perspectives on the effect that they have had, or the degree to which they are successful.

If benefits do result, does it take several years for those impacts to reach the bottom line?

OPERATOR, BUXTON FALLS: Now everyone is totally self-directed except for one department on the far southwest corner that is part self-directed and part not.

OPERATOR, BUXTON FALLS: The bosses have been gone three or four years now. We're a team as far as keeping everybody trained and working together. The bottom line is that these barges and tank cars come in and we load 'em and ship 'em.

OilCo is relying heavily on peer pressure. If an individual makes an effort, then everybody bends over backward for him. But if someone is not trying, they're slacking off and putting more work on everybody else. There's a little bit of bitterness to it.

With such a span of responsibility, what can a supervisor accomplish? Does this form of supervision match the intended design of the team system?

OPERATOR, BUXTON FALLS: We have one supervisor of operations and maintenance. He's responsible for about 140 people, some who work twenty-four hours per day, seven days a week. He is the only one, outside of the manager, who has supervisory authority.

I wish that we had more supervision, but that's against the company's direction on self-directed work teams. All the supervisor can do is put information in the daily plan. He spends his day going from meeting to meeting. He doesn't have any time to interact with the people. With what little bit he sees, and what little bit he hears, he has a good feel for what's going on. If people are to be more accountable, then you've got to be able to hold them accountable. Even when they do something wrong. One person cannot supervise 140 people.

I don't believe that the self direction is as far along as a lot of people in high places think it is. When you have a culture whose attitude is to do just enough to get by and this has been allowed by management to exist for years, change is not going to happen quickly.

OPERATOR, BUXTON FALLS: There used to be a lot of distrust between unit operators. You would think, "They run their unit. We run ours. We don't even affect them over there."

One group would say, "You're shooting us too much feed!" And the other would say, "Oh, we'll slow it down in a minute." But now they would say, "Look, let me cut it down immediately."

It's not that we know them any better. We have the attitude that "I affect my brother." It comes from the meetings. People are starting to believe it: "My job is important and I am affecting somebody and I'm going to do the best job I can."

If somebody tells me that they're getting too much feed, it's not just your individual idea that you're going to turn it down. You do it because he tries to keep his yard clean, and I'm going to keep mine clean. That keeps the whole neighborhood better.

OPERATOR, BUXTON FALLS: It's been three years since I and others became extinct as foremen. Slowly people are realizing that the foremen are not coming back. I think the teams have gotten better.

Gradually you see some people take on more responsibility. One person in our department came from the warehouse. She's excellent at ordering, so on her shift she

Note the amount of time it takes for people to "try out their wings" and build self-confidence.

does a lot of the ordering and helps others learn how to do it too. Gradually people are starting to rely on the strengths of others on the team. It's coming around, but it's been a rather slow process.

SENIOR MANAGER, BUXTON FALLS: We have much stronger operators today than we had in the past, because they don't have supervisors to rely on. They've got to rely on themselves and on each other. I think that is one of the main reasons our performance has improved.

The concept has permeated into other groups. We've got some craft groups now that are basically high-performance work teams.

At first, I was skeptical of the concept myself. Two things convinced me. One was in talking to other companies and discovering how prevalent it was in the work place. And secondly, I dug deep within myself. If I really believe in people—and we really do have good people out her—why can't this group of people manage their own affairs?

For the most part, people like high-performance work teams. They now understand that they are in fact capable of making decisions. They're capable of controlling their own actions on their jobs.

There are still some people who say, "It's not my job. I'd rather have a foreman and let him tell me what to do and I'd go do it." But if you took a poll, you'd find that probably 80 percent of the people feel very good about it. And if we tried to go back, they would fight us. Not that we have any intention of going back.

OPERATOR, OILCO REFINING & RETAIL: In our church, we've got people who shirk, and people who shouldn't have been trusted. And we've got people whom you thought you shouldn't trust, but who turned out to be the most honest people you could meet. After you've worked together, you know these people. You know what they can do.

That's the way that [Manager, OilCo, Buxton Falls] and [President, Buxton Falls] have been. For the past year,

Although "self-managed" and "high-performance" are not synonyms by definition, in practice they refer to the same type of collaboratively organized, mutually responsible work group.

These teams raise a significant question that applies to all work-place environments. To what extent can "subsidiarity" and autonomy operate on the department level? On the team level?

we've heard the message: "We know you people at Buxton Falls can do this." It sounds more sincere than the "rah, rah, boom boom" of a few years ago, where they were just pulling my chain to get me to do more work. Now they say, "We know we have some good craftsmen and good operators here."

Their attitude sounds more sincere than before. But they still need to do more about trust. Don't make me "team-conscious" with just my peers. Make me be able to talk to [President, Buxton Falls], just like I'd talk to the guy across the control room—and in a respectful manner. When I tell you something, it's important. Appreciate it. Don't put me off because I never went to MIT. See that you're working with a good crew, and they've got good ideas, and they're not just talking to be heard.

When [President, Buxton Falls] comes down to my control room, they don't come with the deep voices: "What's going on here?" Instead, they just say, "Hey, how are you doing? My name is [President, Buxton Falls]. I'm just looking around. If you've got any questions, I can answer them. And maybe I can ask you some. . ." Just low-key.

That's the way I feel people who want to go places in a corporation should act. It should be just like me talking to my kids. The only time we need to get "parental" is when somebody's not heading toward the goal. At other times, we can be comfortable talking to each other. If we're working toward the goal, and there's a cooperation and respect, then you and I are working for the same money. You just make more of it.

The team effectiveness also depends on the relationship between operators and the senior management. Do they trust each other? Do they communicate with humility and clarity?

◆ FACING THE NEW CHALLENGE OF AUTONOMY

In 1996, the Buxton Falls facility became the OilCo Buxton Falls Refinery Company, accountable for profitability and growth, a subsidiary company like the other refineries in OilCo. With so much change behind the people of Buxton Falls, might this newest challenge be easier for them than for other organizations within OilCo that are also learning independence?

Cautious optimism characterizes the attitude of Buxton Falls people these days. They're not ready to claim success, and yet they point to major improvements across the operation.

This comment is typical of plants with self-managing teams. Some operators often feel responsible for the plant as a whole—for its modernization and capability.

OPERATOR, OILCO REFINING & RETAIL: They talk about state-of-the-art attitudes. "We're going to be the forefront, the leader. And, you're the crew." You walk out and feel like you'll be working on a brand new Star Trek Enterprise.

Then you look out there and it's an 1862 sailing vessel. You've got pulley ropes and you think you're supposed to be able to push a button. And it doesn't jell.

If you've got ideas, then sink the money into the company, because that's what motivates you. If you're going to tell me I'm riding into the future, and we're going to be high-tech and number one, then we're not writing with pencils. We're writing with computers and laser disks. And show us that. Trust people by showing us the equipment and renovation.

But self-managing teams give them a vehicle for expressing their concerns, as if the state of the whole plant mattered to them.

To what extent will the success of such teams depend on instilling everyone with a financial understanding of the enterprise?

OPERATOR, BUXTON FALLS: If the company isn't making money then they don't have any need for us. If we're a burden, why should they keep throwing millions of dollars down the drain year after year? They can't do it very long, so I'm glad to see that we've got things turned around.

We're on an upward climb now. Are we near the top? No. Not even close, but we've bottomed out and we're starting up and that's good. That makes me want to keep trying. Hopefully, some of my positive attitude and ownership will rub off on others.

CHAPTER 9

THREE SIBLINGS
AND THE PACE OF CHANGE

In this theme, we look at the cultural responses to the roll-out of transformation throughout the organization, as it has occurred thus far.

Planned change is never monolithic, and the reactions to it are also always varied. What, then, do we know about the various ways in which OilCo people respond to transformation efforts, the forces that influence those responses, and the effects that those responses have upon each other?

◆ THE NEW EMPLOYEE CONTRACT

To consider these questions, we begin with one of the most familiar aspects of OilCo's recent history: the deliberate unraveling of the implicit employment contract of the past.

MANAGER, HUMAN RESOURCES: OilCo had never had a history of layoffs. In the past, when we closed facilities, we went through extraordinary efforts to help people stay with OilCo who wished to do so.

Did the company actively promote the old employment contract? Or just embody it?

CEO: In our initial work on values in late 1993, the Executive Council was trying to redefine the relationship between individual people and the company.

One of the things that we all had in common was a feeling about OilCo's unwritten employment contract.

What influence does an unwritten psychological contract have?

What influence does an unwritten psychological contract have?

What happens when such a contract is destroyed?

In breaking the old contract, is OilCo breaking a promise?

Is the company losing the authority that people felt under the previous contract?

There had basically been a belief that if you were hired into OilCo and did what you were told, you had a career in front of you: job security for you and your family, nice rich benefits, and all the rest of it. You may not rise to the position you wanted, but it would be okay.

That contract had been fundamentally altered during the preceding three years. We had ripped it up when we turned loose so many very good people. Now we had to try to redefine that relationship.

MANAGER, OILCO REFINING & RETAIL: Just after he became CEO, [CEO] was quoted in an OilCo News article, which was a significant emotional event for this company. It's still talked about.

How did people interpret the text? Some felt anger: they were being pushed out the door. Others felt encouragement to "try their wings" and take risks. One interviewee noted that the message presented "a real adult choice to not depend on OilCo, or blame it for future business decisions." The message also gave employees more responsibility for their own career choices.

"... without the old belief of lifetime employment, the Company takes on different obligations. The Company now has the responsibility to help employees develop their skill levels to a point where they could, if necessary, go to another place of employment with some assurance of finding a place in the market. In effect, employees will take more responsibility for their own financial security ..."

(From "A Conversation With [CEO]," *OilCo Inhouse Journal,* September 1993)

MANAGER, OILCO REFINING & RETAIL: As I saw it, he was just describing reality. But to many employees, it was a wrenching, emotional turning upside down of their understanding of their relationship with the company. They read it as being put on notice that the company would not be loyal to them. They felt anger and betrayal.

Senior management showed they were aware of this reaction many times. But they dealt with it by dismissing it. They labeled it as a sense of "entitlement," with the implication that people felt entitled to things they didn't deserve.

But that diagnosis missed the more fundamental, primal issue of betrayal. It's as if your spouse of twenty years said one day, "You ought to trim down and take a look at your wardrobe, because you might be back in the dating game again one of these days."

One interviewee recalled feeling resentment over these types of " entitlement" remarks. Another said, "Had we really tried to apply engagement skills, we'd be in a very different place today."

STAFF MEMBER, CORPORATE TRAINING CENTER: At the Corporate Training Center, we heard the stories and we saw the anger. OilCo hadn't taught people how to live this new way. And [CEO] was saying, in effect, "I'm only going to tell you what I need. You'll have to figure out how to do it. Or you won't make it. And we won't make it as a company."

This interpretation suggests one reason people might feel things are out of control.

There were some people steeped in anger and bitterness. They were like spitting cobras; they made personal attacks on people who said positive things. Someone would say, "I'm really excited because my Corporate Executive Team member showed me his mask." And another person would say, "Yeah, right. He just did that because he had to."

Some people involved in the roll-out of transformation, or who are positive about it, find themselves cast as the enemy, which hurts.

Others may perceive the proponents as smug. Or they may feel excluded. See "The Three Siblings," below.

And other people would chime in: "This is a waste of my time. They won't tell us what we're transforming to." And you could feel the anger; you could see it in their bodies. And then we would have a class on "winning spirit." It was like throwing a little gasoline on the fire of discontent.

But there were also a number of people who came in frustrated and went out feeling more charged and empowered. I got personal notes from people: "I came here to the Corporate Training Center wondering why I had to be here, since I have so many other things to do. And on the way home, I realized that learning how to create a winning spirit is more important to OilCo than whether I spent three days doing what I always do. Because if I can create a winning spirit in my organization, many of my day-to-day duties will disappear.

EMPLOYEE, OILCO CONSULTING: We had been lured by the old employment contract into a false sense of security: "This job is permanent. It is mine. I have been here for sixteen years, and nothing is going to change."

It was just kind of a mind set that we got into. And it was wrong. Things did change.

It is very painful when the change actually comes. Recently, I went to a Christmas party with all my friends from the office here, who retired before I did. It was just after we announced the outsourcing of benefits, and I was surrounded. "What is happening? What are they doing with the Provident Fund? Are they going to out-source pensions?" They suddenly couldn't get the same level of service. In the past, if you had a benefits question, you walked into an office where the secretaries knew you by name; now, you get a recording.

I felt like saying, "Please, don't ask me any more questions." The fact, is, they didn't live through the transformation. It was harder for them to accept that these changes are taking place. Just being with them was like being in another place and time.

Being more competitive is seen as requiring less emphasis on loyalty and stability. Are the two really mutually exclusive?

If you agree with this perspective, what are the implications for people's creativity and capabilities? Can non-competitive, non-assertive people be valued in the new OilCo?

MEMBER, CORPORATE EXECUTIVE TEAM: I don't think OilCo's going to win with the "employment for life" mentality that, in the past, employees have expected. We have to expect, and almost relish, a lot more employee turnover as employees seek other development opportunities and OilCo brings in new skills and capabilities.

New blood coming in, people going out to other opportunities, an environment with mobile benefits that allows this to happen: a more fluid, dynamic company. That's what I think we'll need to be competitive.

Of course, we need to retain critical skills and capabilities, but other very successful companies have found ways to manage this new environment. It's not a feel-good, Mom and Pop environment. It's much more competitive and aggressive. People want the results of this new environment, but they want the old paternalistic, "take care of me" environment too. You can't have it both ways.

◆ THE SHIFT IN HUMAN RESOURCES

OilCo's corporate and business staff members, particularly at Human Resources, found themselves challenged and changed by transformation. The shift in HR has implications for all staff members, whose primary clients have shifted from the "person at the top" to the company as a whole.

SENIOR LEADER, HUMAN RESOURCES: Our world has turned upside down. In the past, Human Resources had one customer, basically, and that was the CEO. We filled a policeman's role. We were an enforcer. We established and controlled policy.

Now, the businesses of OilCo are our customers. They pay the bills, and they set the requirements for what we do.

MANAGER, HUMAN RESOURCES: We were the corporate speed bump for years — a control system, designed to control the interaction of people. You can't have democracy in a control system. You can't have chaos. You have to slow down innovation, risk-taking, and differences. Keep things one-size-fits-all. Don't let any palace revolts crop up. We did that very well.

MANAGER, HUMAN RESOURCES: I can't deny that we were good at those kinds of oppressive, Dirty Harry jobs. We gloried in them. . . But that reputation was also a burden. I detested it.

Was this "controlling" aspect of the old HR undiscussable?

HR people, who had once been the controllers of the employment contract, now realized their role would change dramatically They would have to recast their role as a strategic business partner, helping "superintendents and process managers" implement change, instead of controlling it.

Many HR people, as these comments suggest, welcomed the change. Many had joined this profession precisely to take a transformational role. Now they had a chance, but ironically, they faced suspicion. Would they be allowed to contribute

Because of their past role, HR was marginalized by external consultants at the start of transformation.

This comment represents an outsider's view of internal "change agents" and "heretics." But perhaps it gives an unfair picture of the dynamic. How can people be loyal to their role as "change agents" and simultaneously, to their needs to make a living and maintain their relationships within the company?

MANAGER, HUMAN RESOURCES: Superintendents and process managers now have choices. But they're still pissed off at HR, because they remember us telling them what they couldn't do. "I wanted to have team-based compensation, or gain-sharing. They wouldn't let me do it."

And, guess what else they say? "I've got to transform my work group now, and I don't know how to do it. Why isn't HR telling me how? Why aren't they here with the tools and solutions and answers?"

APPLIED LEARNING CONSULTANT: In the first year of transformation, we external consultants didn't even talk to the leaders of HR.

Some HR people were on board with transformation and recognized that they could play a very key role. But they didn't know how to become empowered. The only way they knew how to get power was to build up power bases with individual clients at OilCo.

In one or two cases, a staff person would tell me that someone with power in the system was blocking progress in some way, either unwittingly or for political reasons.

I would say, "Why don't you tell him, why don't you speak up?" In short, why didn't they take more of a risk?

They would say, "That's easy for an outsider to say. You don't understand the culture." They would tell me it wouldn't be successful; they would just alienate the person.

And I would think, No, it's because you've got too big a mortgage. Kids in college. You've sold out, and you're not really a change agent. You're playing to preserve the system.

MANAGER, HUMAN RESOURCES: [Head Applied Learning Consultant] made it clear that he didn't want any support from internal organizational effectiveness or human resources consultants.

I said to him, "You don't know how good the HR people can be. They really are change agents. They can be helpful to you."

He finally agreed to meet with them. But the only time he had available was at 6 AM. When I put the word out to the HR people, people said, "The hell with him." But they all showed up. No exceptions. The ones who griped the loudest were there the earliest. It was a great meeting. [Head Applied Learning Consultant] told how management still sees them as part of the hierarchy: "If you're there, then the managers think they have an out. They can tolerate an outsider like me, knowing that they can just do it their way after I leave." The new approaches had to come from outsiders — who had enough of an ego to stand the heat.

In this anecdote, we see some HR people fighting to create a new role for themselves.

At least [Head Applied Learning Consultant] was honest. He told them that later, they would be needed. Now, they would have to help below the surface. "But you can't be visible."

Could an outside consultant charged with bringing about wide-spread changes afford to wait for internal "staff" people to become supportive of these efforts?

How might the larger "system" of expectations for who does what in a change process be functioning to produce these behaviors?

We arranged that two or three of the HR people would come to an Applied Learning workshop, so they'd have some taste of Applied Learning's process. Some of them resented that it had to be on this basis, but they did it.

Ultimately, we had [Head Applied Learning Consultant] back at a regular meeting in mid-1994, to ask: "What would you have done differently? What did you learn from OilCo?" To his credit, he came to a day-long meeting of internal change people—and not at six in the morning.

Does this story pertain only to the narrow function of Human Resources—or could its lessons apply to anyone who tries to be a change agent?

◆ NEW COMPENSATION: PAY AND PPP

The new reward system, Performance Pay Plan (PPP), was a frequently discussed "noticeable result"—generally unfavorably. Pay schemes always represent a translation of the values of the company into a "hard" measurement of dollars and cents: What behavior and competence are valued most? In the past, that translation was the job of compensation experts. Now, it is becoming a matter of open conversation.

MANAGER, HUMAN RESOURCES: I was on the corporate pay team that came up with the PPP design. The need for it

At least one interviewee said that this entitlement mentality was not characteristic of OilCo: "In my case, for instance, I was very thankful for the raises and promotions I got)."

was clear. With the entitlement mentality so ingrained, people thought they were owed automatic raises and promotions. People didn't appreciate the value of what they had.

When [CEO] became CEO, he decided to charter a pay team: mostly high-level line managers with only two HR people. We worked from fall 1993 to the spring of 1994. One of the givens in our charter was: developing a system of variable pay.

In our first design, we based variable pay on performance relative to other companies. But that recommendation didn't fly. [CEO] said: "I will not pay for being the best of a sorry lot." I loved that line, and I have brought it up many times since, because the idea of relativity is silly. Who cares that you're doing better than Exxon, if you're both losing?

The other thing that was changed—and I still believe it was a mistake—was to base the absolute segment on the same objective for every part of the company. The quote from [CEO] was: "It's 10 percent in '98 or out the gate." If we didn't make 10 percent ROI by 1998, we'd be in deep trouble. We fought pretty hard to have different paths for each business, but we lost.

The plan was implemented fully by mid-1994. We announced the bonus plan and sat on the staff ladder promotions. Boy, there was a hue and cry.

The pay system represented an opportunity for engagement with people throughout the company. Many observers say the opportunity was lost.

What could have been done better to explain the system?

MANAGER, HUMAN RESOURCES: Our overall goal was to make sure that our compensation was more closely linked to business performance. We did a first-class job on the design of the plan, and getting the information out. The brochure was descriptive, and easy to read. We had a well-designed package, and we took advantage of multimedia.

But we didn't do a reasonable job of explaining the mechanics of the system to employees—or of trying to get their commitment.

MEMBER, CORPORATE STAFF: When PPP was birthed, there was not enough case for change made. There was a one-time communication rolled out: "This is the system."

There was tremendous skepticism about it. There was never buy-in at the field level. The PPP premise said, for instance, that over time, people who could more greatly influence the company's direction should have a greater proportion of their money at risk—and thus corresponding opportunity as well.

But the reality was that everybody's base pay was frozen. From the field, it was viewed that the people in the upper tiers would gain more from this, and it wasn't fair.

CLERK, OILCO CHEMICAL: People say, "Those who are up there, get enough to buy a new car. Those who are down here, if we are lucky we get enough to make a car payment."

MANAGER, HUMAN RESOURCES: Today, what people say is this: "My pay has been frozen for three years." It's a very human reaction. They see their pay monthly. They know it hasn't changed. They get their bonus check once a year. They feel good for a week. The check gets spent on a car, put in the bank, or sent to the kid's school. And then they still feel: "My pay's been frozen for three years."

Whereas if you looked at their W-2, it would be equal or greater at the end of the year than it would have been under our former salary program.

MANAGER, OILCO CHEMICAL: Right now, with PPP, I go home and tell my wife, "It could be anywhere from $1,500 to $2,500." And she'll say, "What does it depend on?" It depends on my individual performance—how my boss perceives it.

I would rather have a formula. If you popped in the numbers, there would be no guesswork. It should include an amount above the PPP to give to exceptional contributors. The current approach feels like the bosses take a couple of hundred bucks off the top of everyone's check, and give it to the "exceptional contributors." We tried to explain that the PPP formula was just a forecast, and not a bucket that would be filled, but it comes across as robbing Peter to pay Paul.

Was the roll-out of PPP an illustration of the old style of top-down, one-way communication?

Would an appropriate pay system reward teams, individuals, or businesses?

This quote overlooks a sore point with some people we interviewed. Base pay is used in computing benefits; PPP is not. So even if the W-2 is the same, net benefits are not.

Systems that encourage managerial discretion are perceived as arbitrary and unfair.

However, systems that discourage managerial discretion might be perceived as rigid.

This type of diversity in pay plans was never possible in the past. Is it possible now?

MANAGER, OILCO CONSULTING: Ideally, you'd like to provide everyone a choice. On one dimension, let them choose between relative stability of income versus relative risk. Someone who chooses a more variable rate, with less of a steady stream of income, would be compensated more.

Can a pay system reasonably help individuals accurately discern the larger system effects of their own and others' behaviors?

MANAGER, OILCO CHEMICAL: The intent was to drive behavior change, and that failed. People had a hard time seeing how their individual performance impacted the number on which their PPP depended. "Some huge multimillion dollar decisions are made, then all of a sudden I cancel a meeting to save costs." It looks rather insignificant.

How valid is this point of view?

MANAGER, HUMAN RESOURCES: When I'm confronted with these kinds of complaints, I say: "Look around, check it out, see what you can get, and see how bad a deal you have around here. If it's that bad, you owe it to yourself and your family to go look somewhere else."

Does this resentment and perceived inequity represent a problem for OilCo as it builds accountability into its businesses?

To what extent is the problem rooted in poor communication? To what extent does it stem from the specific design of the PPP? And to what extent is it linked to deeper structural issues?

SENIOR MANAGER: We haven't communicated well, but we're going to try. We're looking at how much support there would be from the businesses to try to develop programs that would address some of these issues.

But even if we do that, pay at risk is not a real popular thing. If we the Executive Council and the Corporate Executive Team really believe in it, we have to do a better job of getting out and talking to people. We need to do a better job of defending it, explaining what we're doing and why.

Maybe, at the end of the day, we'll find that a segment of our population can't work in that kind of environment.

What kinds of communications and feedback sessions would help people move forward?

The good thing about the transformation is that we have a new vehicle for approaching this issue. We won't rely on the traditional approach: "Throw data at 'em, throw multimedia at 'em." This time, we're going to have to get the commitment of the leadership—get them on board, get their hearts and souls into this. And then start working with the employees in group sessions.

Who knows? In the process we might learn some things about how to do it better. People want to succeed themselves, and they want the company to succeed. There's got to be a way to get those thoughts together.

◆ FLEXTIME

Several human resources innovations, such as job posting, FlexTime, and a greater acceptance of part-time and flexible hours, have been singled out as valuable components of transformation. In each case, they are seen as recognition of the value of diverse human needs. The FlexTime system, in which people have every other Friday off by working eighty hours in nine working days, has acquired significance far beyond its scope.

SENIOR MANAGER, OILCO CHEMICAL: There was a series of focus groups that talked with a cross section of employees about balancing work life and personal life. Out of those groups came a list of things. FlexTime was selected as one that we could put in place, and quickly. The cycle time, from conceiving it to implementing it, was remarkably short.

FlexTime has been called "the most positively impactful sustained culture-changing event in twenty years."

This was a big difference for us, because we were a leader. We were the first major oil company out with something like this.

MANAGER, OILCO CHEMICAL: The story I heard was that in mid-1993 before the transformation began, E&P recommended an alternative work schedule to the head office. They were told no. Then I guess the Executive Council looked at it that fall and it was implemented within three months. They decided to do it in one meeting; they didn't take five meetings to debate the merits of it. It was a no-brainer: Morale was down, the employee relationship was changing, we had just had three consecutive years of layoffs and this was a benefit that cost the company nothing.

We heard several different stories about the origins of FlexTime, credited to various parts of the company. To us, this indicates the idea's success.

DATA ANALYST, OILCO: The interesting thing about the FlexTime work schedule was that it was proposed by field hands at our remote site. OilCo Corporate listened to a proposal from us; and it actually got done.

CUSTOMER SERVICE, OILCO CHEMICAL: I had an opportunity to consult, and make a lot more money. But I stayed at OilCo; and it always seemed like the FlexTime was the reason I thought of first. I hated the thought of giving that up. You're able to have a life outside of OilCo, and you're able to cut back.

I even considered going after an MBA. University of Dallas has an executive MBA program that takes place every other Friday, and one or two Saturdays a month. So, the FlexTime program suits that as well.

Some people told us that, in itself, FlexTime has convinced them to stay with OilCo.

Why is time flexibility such an important factorWhat makes it different from other, less persuasive, policies of transformation? What do those differences say about human nature or aspiration?

TECHNICAL STAFF, DUCK COVE: The shift to a FlexTime work schedule for crafts at Duck Cove was a hard sell, and passed by a narrow vote. There was a lot of concern and lack of trust about the reason the company wanted to do it.

We spent a lot of effort talking to people about the real reason. The employee gets every other Friday off, a win, and the company gets the hours that would have been spent in lunch, breaks, and cleanup on that day, a win. It turned out so well that—again, by a narrow vote —the crafts now work four-day/ten-hour weeks. They get every Friday off and the company has regained another day's worth of lunch, breaks, and cleanup time, a win.

A few interviewees expressed comments like these, more skeptical about FlexTime.

SENIOR MANAGER: "Isn't this wonderful, we have FlexTime?" Half the people work on their FlexTime day off. There's no balance any more between family and work life.

Member, Corporate Executive Team: I do not participate in the FlexTime program. There are other ways to balance home life and work life. I tell my colleagues, "Don't read into my behavior that I don't support the company policy. Take your FlexTime day off." But I don't think you can give up two days a month and competitively be premier. When I need time off, I go on vacation.

SENIOR MANAGER: As a leader, because I support the FlexTime program, I have to consciously resist the temptation to come in on my own FlexTime day off; and I have to resist scheduling or agreeing to attend meetings on Fridays. Thus, FlexTime has been helpful in thinking about leadership in a broader sense: in recognizing how important my behavior is when I interact with people.

Is there a fundamental problem in the demands that OilCo's work load places on people? Is this a problem with OilCo, or with business culture generally? Does OilCo have a case for action to deal with this problem of overload frustration?

◆ THE "THREE SIBLINGS"

In our interviews, we heard three different types of attitudes about the impact of transformation at OilCo. It's as if there were three different types of "siblings" in the OilCo family:

- The "first-born," regarding themselves as the most responsible, espousing commitment to the transformation (in part because it is the established order now), and feeling recognized and rewarded as achievers;

- The "middle" siblings, feeling unrecognized and unsupported, as if they don't "fit in" somehow with the transformation, despite their commitment and innovative thinking;

- The "last-born" siblings, not ready to make a commitment, relationship-oriented, and loyal to the values of the old, pretransformation OilCo.

These descriptions represent attitudes, not categories of people. They do not, for instance, represent chronological age or levels of the hierarchy. There are "first-born" attitudes among some young staff members, and "last-born" attitudes among senior people at the Corporate Executive Team and Executive Council levels. Indeed, all three "sibling" attitudes probably co-exist in every person at OilCo.

In our interviews, nobody talked about themselves as "first-born," "middle," or "last-born" siblings. The team that produced this report— seven OilCo people and five outside learning history people—developed the metaphor during our "distillation" process, after all the interviews were conducted. It's only a metaphor, but it rang true for us, and it seemed to highlight leverage that can help the engagement process take place more effectively.

This quote, from a refinery manager, describes one view of the three sibling attitudes: first the last-born,"then the first-born, and then the middlesiblings. Other views might disagree, finding the last-born more heroic— or might disagree that these three categories apply at all.

MANAGER, OILCO REFINING & RETAIL: There are a few folks in OilCo who don't get it and don't really want to make an effort. The best thing for them would be to find somewhere else to work.

Many folks can see where the transformation is going. They're excited to be a part of it, and they're going to be right there, providing leadership. Even if they're not in management, they'll provide leadership in other roles.

There's another group of folks who don't quite understand the transformation yet. They would like to be there, but don't quite know how to get there. I worry for that group, because I get the feeling that somehow they will be left behind. Some of those who get it might think they've got a corner on the knowledge, and that they know how to do it better than anybody else. This group will become the target of that feeling of superiority, which will split the company and really slow the transformation.

The First-Born Siblings: People with this attitude see themselves as a vanguard. Rewarded in both subtle and obvious ways, they know they will gain creative positions, new forms of teamwork, material rewards—and long hours. Transformation provides a long-awaited opportunity to shine.

There's a lot of competitiveness inherent in this point of view. People measure themselves against each other by the new rewards: bonuses, awards, recognition, appointment to committees. Some first-born-oriented people are accused of garnering rewards and recognition without "walking the talk" of transformation; others are regarded as genuine transformational leaders. But all of them live in the "glass house" of leadership (see page 99).

MANAGER, E & P: Transformation has offered an opportunity that I don't think had been attainable for me or any of my counterparts anywhere else in the industry. We have a unique opportunity here, and I'm grateful that it came along during my career, at a time when I have a chance to impact it.

MEMBER, CORPORATE STAFF: We're not moving fast enough. I'm not moving fast enough, in terms of my contributions. Indeed, there is enough effort, motion, and activity. But am I really trying to move faster on the most impactful areas? This is a question I lose sleep over.

Do I feel doubts about, "Can I really do this?" or, "Can we do this?" No. Not once. The only doubt is if we're moving fast enough. I don't think OilCo really understands—and I'm part of OilCo—how fast we have to move.

A number of interviews conveyed this attitude, which seems to us to be typical of the first-born sibling.

Does the first-born attitude create opportunities? Or does it emerge when people feel there are opportunities available to them?

MANAGER, OILCO CONSULTING: I can tell you about an adventure I had. We wanted to learn more about what it was like to win and keep business. So I worked at an external computer consulting company; OilCo paid my salary. They assigned me to several clients, including a four-month assignment to a media company in a major metropolitan area. I documented my "lessons learned" and shipped them back every couple of weeks.

I thought it was pretty gutsy of OilCo to say, "Yeah, we are going to invest in you." The umbilical cord was cut to the point where I wasn't allowed to use OilCo resources, even to make sales. "What you have in your head is yours, but everything else is off-limits." I learned the power of my own network, being out there on my own trying to make business happen.

And I learned a lot about long-term travel. Our current corporate travel policy says that we can't be reimbursed for health clubs or dog sitting. I have a dog, and a health club membership. As we get into new on-site situations, long distances away, management is being receptive to these kinds of requests that a normal consulting firm grants. Five years ago, I would never have made those requests. It's interesting to see us transforming in that way.

Sometimes, the perks and rewards granted to people with first-born attitudes seem remarkable and refreshing; the old OilCo culture would never have permitted anything like this....

First-born siblings respond to entrepreneurial opportunities—if the rewards are manifest and the recognition is evident. Does OilCo have room for (or would it even benefit from) a work force of thousands of people who are primarily entrepreneurial and aggressive?

The Middle Siblings: In their view, they are as much "on board" as any-one (albeit from within the confines of their positions), but they don't seem to "fit in." They receive neither the recognition they deserve, the protection that would make them feel safer, or the fast-track opportunities they want.

People with this attitude come across to others as "fence-sitters." Their behaviors shunt between compliance and commitment. They feel as though their work is a roller-coaster ride between triumphant heights and frustrating lows. One month they are ready to leave the company; the next, they are energized and excited. In their frustration, they compare themselves with the other siblings: "Mother OilCo always liked you best."

There is evidence in the interviews that some people feel subtly tracked into the middle sibling role. Others discover that they have been tracked later, when they are denied encouragement. They then face a dilemma: How can I choose my fate at OilCo, when people have already decided who I am?

MANAGER, OILCO CHEMICAL: I think I have a good vision. But ultimately, no amount of arguing or logic will con-vince other people. There's so much ego, and when one person initiates something there tends to be an immune reaction, so I give up. After a while, you tend to push less, because you don't get positive response.

There are a few other people I resonate with, people with creative ideas—and they're pushing less, too.

Here's a typical story in which someone's feeling of personal commitment is given the "cold-water" treatment.

What happens when personal engagement in change is met with a lack of tangible business results? What happens when it is met with skepticism or lack of recognition from more senior managers?

INDIVIDUAL CONTRIBUTOR, HR: Sometimes I get really down on OilCo. I had a plane trip in which I sat next to a per-son from another large oil company's chemical division and he said, "Oh, yeah, you guys are doing so much that we just shy away from."

I asked him what, and he started talking about the casual dress and the FlexTime days. And I started brag-ging about the transformation and all the stuff that's hap-pening—how you should push decisions closer to the customers and the effects of governance. Then I stopped and said, "I really thank you for this conversation because it's put me in touch with the fact that I do have passion for this. I thought I didn't. And I'm just about to cry." I get kind of puddly just thinking about it.

So I went back to my boss and told him how exciting the conversation was. "Yeah, it seems great," he said. "But we're still not making any money." It was like having cold water thrown in my face.

ADMINISTRATIVE ASSISTANT, CORPORATE: As a member of the support staff, it is hard to justify working such long, hard hours here. Senior management make at least three times our income, plus larger bonuses. I must reassess my priorities occasionally.

This comment from a support staff member also shows someone who feels tracked into being an outsider.

What attitude should a " transformational" company take toward its members who fall outside the conventional description of "success"? What types of appreciation and reward would be effective?

It has always been my work ethic to give 100 to 110 percent at whatever job I'm given, and I'm also not as interested in making overtime money as being home with my family. If I work overtime, however, then I do claim it, because it is one of the few "perks" nonexempt staff get.

I've noticed some exempt support staff who work regular hours and lack any sense of urgency in their work except when the boss is around. They do the minimum required. I can now relate to this attitude more as management is flattened and there's more work for fewer people. . . . It's a challenge to see how the transformation could benefit support staff.

MEMBER, EXECUTIVE COUNCIL: As one of the junior members of the Executive Council, at times I have felt unrecognized. I learned something from one of the coaches who worked with me. He said, "As long as you feel a victim, you're causing part of the tension that you feel. Stop doing that."

This comment, from a member of the Executive Council, shows that people at any level in the organization may be subject to the feeling of being an outsider in some respect.

Now, when those moments and feelings come back, I listen a bit longer, and take a bit more time to search for what has caused me to feel tense. But I don't jump to the conclusion that, "This isn't working because I'm an outsider," or that, "They're not listening to me."

The Last-Born Sibling: Many people still care deeply about the old OilCo. They mourn the loss of the old culture and feel responsible for the people who were let go, or for the human needs of the people who remain. They are the caretakers, eager for security and stability. In the past, protected by the implicit employment "contract," they never had to worry about the company as a whole, only doing their job. Yet they felt that the company depended upon them.

Now, the severance process has decimated the ranks of their colleagues; their work load has doubled. They are told, "You can leap ahead! Touch the stars!" But they feel paralyzed. They mistrust the rhetoric of transformation or haven't experienced its benefits firsthand.

People with the last-born attitude are frightened: Is there a place for them in this company? They know they can't have the security they once had, but they need to know what security they can assume.

Several people have talked about this attitude—"I need to get back, to clear up my desk. But transformation gets in the way."

Does this suggest the need for reorienting transformation, reorienting people, reorienting both... or neither?

CLERK, OILCO CHEMICAL: My boss knows what I do. But he doesn't know what's involved in it. I do my job. I come in on time. I put in my nine hours, and I don't rock the boat, but I believe I do a good job on my desk. It is a job that has to be done, and all these people who have all these computer skills—and they're whiz-bang smart people—are not going to do the kind of work I do. If an urgent fax comes in, I don't mind getting up and hand-carrying it to somebody's office. I do peon jobs and I don't mind doing them.

This group I work with—we basically get along, and we care about each other. We've had three employees, since the first of the year, who had their fathers die. We take up money for them. We buy food. We're kind of like family. We don't always agree with everything that's said every day of the week, but basically we're good, caring people. Nobody has to tend that family spirit as "part of their job." It just kind of happens. We've gone from fifty-two people down to thirty-eight, but we all still like each other, and work well together.

Meanwhile, if I had my way, I would never attend another meeting of any kind. While I'm out there, the filing work stacks up-up-up on my desk. And I keep thinking, "I need to get back, to clear up my desk."

MANAGER, OILCO CHEMICAL: OilCo recruited the conservative, analytical plodders. We specifically did not look for risk-takers or creative types.

When I hired on with OilCo, I had taken two graduate level and one undergraduate public speaking classes. But I had to go to another public speaking course just to learn OilCo's way of making presentations. Their argument was that I hadn't had the OilCo stamp of approval.

So I think that's what employees are wrestling with. Not, "Is my job safe?" but, "Is this my nature"? We are conservative by nature. We don't take risks. Now, all of a sudden, we get the sense that OilCo doesn't want that type of person.

People with last-born attitudes may need their concerns about security addressed explicitly, instead of being ignored or subtly scorned.

EMPLOYEE, OILCO CONSULTING: When I started working in my current location, there was one man who had been there a long time. William a pseudonym was my "answer person." I went to him whenever I needed to know something: "William, what is this? William, what year did that happen?"

All through the years, they had increased William's salary and responsibilities in our office. He was a rock, the one who remembered the lawsuits and the old deals, and why they were important. There is nothing written down. All you have is people who remember.

But then William didn't get along with a new manager, and she traded him down to another office. And the work was graded lower than his current salary, so he's had to decide whether to leave or take a pay cut. He's in his fifties; he has one or two kids.

What are they going to do when they get rid of the "Williams" and nobody else remembers what they know?

Many people with last-born attitudes are the kind of people who have traditionally filled the informal role of providing "institutional memory," as in the story here. Now they are leaving or being transferred, or retiring. In their absence, who or what fills that role? Is it filled by information systems?

◆ "COACH, COACH, COACH?" OR "COACH, COACH, CHANGE?"

Who really "belongs" to OilCo's transformation? And what, in turn, should be done with the people who do not seem to belong?

This question was raised in the earliest stages of transformation by the external consultants from Applied Learning who had worked with General Electric. And it continues to be raised. Should "resistant" people (at any level of the hierarchy) get a reasonable amount of time to shift attitudes—coach them once, coach them twice perhaps—but then if they don't come on board, "change" them (i.e., remove them)? Letting those people remain in place means that passive resistance will continue to hold back the transformation.

Or perhaps the "resistors" need continued coaching until they gradually join in the transformation full-heartedly. A "coach, coach, change" policy would deny the company the benefit of its accumulated experience and loyalty—and it would repudiate the deeply held attitude that, after all, people can learn.

There is no company-wide answer to this dilemma. People espoused both points of view, with well-honed arguments, in our interviews. The issue was first raised with the Executive Council itself. . . .

MEMBER, EXECUTIVE COUNCIL: [Head Applied Learning Consultant] said that the people who would not be good participants in corporate transformation should not be allowed to remain in leadership positions.

So we formed our own lines of communication to another company where he had consulted, where they had implemented his approach. It was true. They'd had terrific turmoil in their executive ranks. Rightly or wrongly, [Head Applied Learning Consultant] was tagged as having some connection with that turmoil.

And we still have not come to grips with this issue as a company. What are we going to do with people who are in leadership positions, who do a workmanlike, competent job from a business standpoint, but who frankly don't share the transformational thoughts and views? Even if they say what they're supposed to say about the transformation, they're not following through with action, and everyone knows it.

We have said that keeping such people in leadership positions is unacceptable. There's been a lot of discussion about it, and there's a lot of resolve: "Yes, we have to take action."

It's such a tough issue, for many reasons. We're still driven by business results. So what if we, in effect, replace a current leader with someone with greater transformational zeal but lesser business skills? Is that in the interest of the company?

Then there's the question of how it should be handled. If it's not dealt with at all, it places the credibility of the transformation in jeopardy. On the other hand, if you deal with it in a clumsy way, you may do serious damage to the company's business performance.

And finally, someone might have said the same thing about members of the Executive Council when we started transformation: "They're not really on board." At that time, you could have argued for the replacement of many of the Executive Council had you decided to act on that basis.

There has been real growth in some of these individuals—in fact, in all of us. And the same can be said of the Corporate Executive Team. It's not right to just pick a point in time and say, "We're going to measure your capabilities and commitment to the transformation. If you don't measure up, you're out of here." That can't work. Otherwise, you would end up with inequities.

People say, "How can you be serious about such-and-such group transforming, when Joe Jones is at the head of it?" But nobody has said anything to Joe. He may not have received the necessary counseling and advice.

Can we be candid with people in that situation? Can we point out the need to change and grow? What sorts of conversations ought to occur? What is a reasonable time to allow for change?

Individuals have opinions, but I don't think there's any collective or shared view of how to deal with this issue. I think it's part of the maturing of this transformation. And it has to be done in a way that's consistent with OilCo—not the way another company might do it, or the way a consultant feels we should do it.

MEMBER, EXECUTIVE COUNCIL: In the early 1990s, we had a number of people on my staff who didn't see that we had

There is an "undiscussable" quality to this conversation. Talk of "coach, coach, change" inevitably leads to talk about personalities. From the most senior levels of the company to the most junior levels, people pass judgment on each other. Who should be permitted to stay? Who should be forced to leave?

What effect does it have on the company to raise questions about the "transformational" value of specific people?

Are there different standards for people in leadership positions?

What are the "diversity" implications of selecting for people who change at a certain pace?

The next three comments make a case for "coach, coach, change." The case is based, in part, on people's experience with the effects of resistance.

a problem. "Be patient," they said, "and pretty soon things will be okay. Prices will go back up, and all we want to do is go back to our old ways." They were not interested in changing.

I think we were pretty patient. Some people just flat refused to change, and we had to have a mutual parting of the ways. There were twenty-four general managers and vice presidents on our leadership team at that point in time. And now we have eight.

SENIOR MANAGER, E&P: They say it a lot around here: "Coach, coach, change." But what we really do is: "Coach, coach, coach." This process of bringing people around is just so slow. [CEO's] got the patience of a saint. I'd have changed some of these people a long time ago. We're into multiple choruses of "Coach." Somebody needs to sing the refrain: "Change!" It's time!

Several very high-level executives made arguments like this one.

STAFF MEMBER, OILCO HEADQUARTERS: I've never been part of a transformation where somebody doesn't get sent home.

Now, you do it fairly. You do it compassionately. You don't do it ruthlessly. But if someone is not on board, there has to be a consequence. You can't say, "Gosh, if I really don't want to go along, I don't think I should have to." The stakes are too high.

This isn't a Sunday tea social. It's an economic war that we're trying to win for a host of constituencies. Retirees are looking toward their golden years based on our performance. Employees are investing their thirty years toward their aspirations. Shareholders have equity stakes. Companies can go out of business. The average lifespan of a company is less than forty years.

STRATEGIC PLANNER: The funny part about it is, while everyone says we are changing our management style for the better, I have seen a lot of managers with good techniques leave. Those guys could have been trained in the new style.

Instead, I see inexperienced people taking their places. Yeah, they have more rebel spirit. They like to scream and holler, rant and rave, when they are in front of an audience. If you catch them alone, they play it just as safe as can be.

For instance, if everybody feels that dressing more casually creates better communications among employees—and I think they have made that statement—then everybody ought to do it at all levels. But when Senior Leader shows up in his three-piece suit and tie, everyone who has a meeting with him that day will wear the same attire. And I still get a better reaction when I am dressed up than when I wear a pair of jeans.

They are not playing the game any differently. And they are making a lot more mistakes with the people.

MANAGER, HUMAN RESOURCES: Almost every organization of OilCo is much more willing to understand where behavior is out of line; or to see where skills and interests are mismatched with responsibilities and to deal with that.

I give us high marks. We haven't had a blood bath. I don't think we needed one. I don't think it would have worked in the OilCo culture. At the same time, there are people who can't and won't make the transition. We need to deal with both those groups.

I think we can move boldly in a way that quite fits with our kinder, gentler culture. It's a culture where compassion for people is fundamentally important—paternalistically driven, perhaps, but still: "Do you have to beat people quite so hard?"

CEO: I don't believe that people are permanently either "on the bus" or "off the bus." I think that fundamentally, almost everyone would agree that the characteristics of transformation are desirable: Disagreeing with someone who is higher in the hierarchy, showing the emotions that you may have had.

People have been conditioned over time that you don't do that kind of thing in the organization. These

The next two comments make the case for continuing to coach.

This person argues that the people who need coaching most are the people who espouse transformation the most.

Some argue that the coach, coach, change attitude creates a three siblings dynamic, by tracking people into the less-desired group arbitrarily.

In creating this learning history, the authors tried to avoid a bias toward either the case for coach, or the case for change. We think this is an issue where having a balance between these attitudes may serve OilCo best. In the end, the readers of

the report should think it through for themselves and with each other.

qualities were distilled out of us through a very powerful culture.

So the culture, not the people, has had to change.

◆ LEVERAGE IN ROLLING OUT TRANSFORMATION: HOW THE PIECES FIT TOGETHER

It's possible that only a few managers at OilCo have ever figured out how to lead the middle and last-born siblings effectively. How can OilCo's leaders hold together an appreciation of the whole organization, and the different people that make it up, while promoting and furthering individuals' leadership abilities in new ways?

The comments in this section represent a starting point for thinking about leverage—either in management structures (such as the pay system) or in human aspects of management, such as coaching and engaging.

MEMBER, EXECUTIVE COUNCIL: I'm not sure that we distinguished among people and their natural abilities. I think we had a one-size-fits-all transformation prescription.

I don't think, for instance, that we took the people who are naturally good at transformation and used them in a more constructive role. We treated them like everybody else.

Is this the dynamic that leads to a population of "middle siblings"?

We haven't, for example, placed them in leadership positions, where they could take part in the training of others. We haven't had those natural leaders going out and speaking in small groups to their colleagues, in any kind of organized or sanctioned way. They could easily be effective at the colleague level in talking about: "How does this affect you and me? Are there real benefits to the individual as a result of being involved in this process?"

MEMBER, R&R INITIATIVE TEAM: One message came out very clearly in the focus groups conducted by the R&R team in 1996: Nobody at OilCo felt valued. To be sure, the lower graded people didn't feel valued. But nobody else did, either.

All the "reward and recognition" issues—the inequities in pay, the working conditions, the ability to make a personal commitment—are related to this problem. Managers are not investing much in understanding this issue. But if you don't, you can't manage your part of the business because you're disconnected. And so you are probably working on the wrong things to get employee commitment, ownership, and all that.

We have to find a way to make people feel valued and still get the job done. But our approaches to valuing people are vague and related to formulas. OilCo likes a little booklet, where if you go through the seven steps and check them off, you have recognition and people who feel valued. But it just doesn't work that way. And it can't work unless people in leadership positions understand how to create a sense of valuing people in their little piece of the OilCo world.

The complexity of this issue, and the need for individual leaders to own it, means that this won't be a rapid fix in the organization. It will take several years to get there.

MEMBER, R&R INITIATIVE TEAM: We realized that we were looking at a holistic system. If you tinker with one aspect of the system, like the employment relationship, then something else gets out of synch. To be successful, all the reward and recognition systems must be aligned, and that means you must often dig into areas that are uncomfortable.

MEMBER, CORPORATE STAFF: Our job at the OilCo Corporate Training Center is to create a critical mass of revolutionaries—to the point where they can sustain the momentum of the transformation. How many people make up a critical mass? Clearly it requires commitment, and not just support, from the CEO, the Executive Council, and a majority of the top 200 people. Those people set the climate, and the cues and behaviors from their span of influence are enormous.

Does the resentment about pay exist because, in some way, PPP (the new pay plan, described on page 137), heightens the difference between the eldest child and the other two categories?

Or is it a simple case of lack of engagement?

Resistance breeds resistance: The slower the roll-out progresses, the more inbred resistance undermines the intentions for change.

This leads to less effective results, which in turn leads to more resistance and reinforces a slower pace.

But from the point of view of the organization, has the pace of change been too slow? Or has it been too tumultuous? Is there some critical path that would allow change to take place without destroying the trust and mutual respect that people cherished from the old OilCo culture?

How many more people than that? The opinion on that varies. We cannot touch everyone, and not everyone will be on board. So we go where we can make a difference. We try to develop the pockets of excellence to the point where the transformation can sustain itself, independent of personalities.

Quick feedback, new opportunities, and sustained coaching may or may not offer as much leverage as pay.

MANAGER, OILCO CHEMICAL: In groups and formal feedback, people have said, "It's not the money that matters; it's the other stuff." They want thank yous, appreciation, and to know that they have been valued. That's one thing that comes from my background in organizational development. Money does not motivate. People want to contribute because of whatever intrinsic reasons they have.

But when I talked to them honestly and got through all the layers, they said: "Yeah, it's the money. Talk is cheap. Back it up with something." They're tired of mementos, certificates, and pats on the back. Days off are nice and money is nicer, regardless of what Herzberg says.

MANAGER, OILCO CHEMICAL: I had dinner with a group of large chemical company people who were bench-marking OilCo.

This may be one of the most memorable comments in the entire document. "We just don't celebrate, even when we have reason to do so."

One thing that really confused them: "You, OilCo, had a record year this past year. All we heard was, 'We failed, here and here. We have to improve this.' We would expect to see a happy company, in celebration."

At OilCo, we don't talk about success. Rather, we focus on problems. This tendency to "beat ourselves up" gets burdensome and depressing after a span of too many years. I, personally, am not spending enough time being a cheerleader, celebrating the successes.

CHAPTER 10

DOWNSIZING DURING TRANSFORMATION: THE OILCO CHEMICAL STORY

OilCo Chemical's downsizing followed the mold of similar stories elsewhere at OilCo, but the Chemical story is unique because it took place after the transformation had begun. Thus, in addition to all the other issues involved in restructuring, the leaders of OilCo Chemical had to cope with the expectations and anxieties that transformation had raised, and the messages sent by a staff reduction program during a time when prior years' financial results had been quite strong. Finally, the senior-most executive of OilCo Chemical, [President, OilCo Chemical], was new to this company. He had previously been an executive in Europe, and he and his subordinates both expressed a sense that they misunderstood each other at times.

At the time these interviews were conducted, it was not clear how the Chemical story would unfold, and many events were still controversial within the company. We present the story here as we first presented it, with the final decision about direction still to be made. The questions and reflections raised by the Chemical story may be particularly useful to leaders during tough times.

◆ INITIATING A RESTRUCTURING EFFORT

As in the other branches of OilCo, transformation led to a case for action. In the case of OilCo Chemical, the case for action was announced: Although profitable, the company was not competitive enough to be assured of continued success.

The case for action depended on results, which led to a perception of people's aspirations and capabilities; somehow, according to this view, a group of admittedly ambitious people were not producing the desired results.

The managers we interviewed were divided. Some recognized the case for action (as in one comment below: "It was the right thing to do.") Others, as shown here, quietly questioned it.

PRESIDENT, OILCO CHEMICAL: When I arrived here, I had certain surprises that I didn't expect. I thought that, in this country, with all the competitive and dynamic pressures, it would be the best in the world. But I didn't find the kind of world-class performance or operational excellence that I thought I would. Did people want to be the best? Or did they want to stay the same? I found that there was a plan to move to world-class performance in our redesign efforts, but it was too slow to win in the world productivity race.

My second discovery came when I started to drill into the program: Why was their operational excellence not as good as it should be? We had a nice opportunity to make ourselves the best in the world.

That was the difficult side. On the positive side, I felt the ambition of the people. They were basically very ambitious here. They could think big. They could be flexible, practical, and pragmatic. That impressed me. You can read about it from afar, but then you come here and experience it yourself. . . .

MEMBER, CORPORATE EXECUTIVE TEAM: When the President came in, there was a severance episode at OilCo Chemical. People had a hard time understanding it. Over all, OilCo was recovering and making more money. Why did we need to lay people off? Why couldn't we find other ways of re-employing them, having them add value, or changing their jobs? When we are making more money each year, people have a hard time understanding why we need to lay people off. There was plenty to be done; most employees felt the pressure to work longer and harder. They felt that more was being asked of them.

EMPLOYEE, OILCO CHEMICAL: We just went through the layoffs at OilCo Chemical. But my group's ROI, as far as I can figure, was well above 10 percent. Our sales and revenue over the past five years have more than doubled.

So I question the need to cut back as much as we did. We have 25 percent fewer people doing much more work. The morale is really suffering.

I know President, OilCo Chemical had his study and said that for OilCo Chemical's size and output, we should have X people, and I can understand this. But in the meantime, we have less time to do the things suggested by the financial literacy work—things like, "I need an extra penny out of this deal," or "I need to use a different carrier because it's a better cost." Now it's: "Get it out the door. Move it, move it, move it. You just don't have time to sit down and think about the most economical way to conduct the business."

These comments show how the "Improving Our Economic Value" project has encouraged people at lower levels to feel competent raising similar questions. Do financial literacy skills, in themselves, provide enough information and guidance for people to make judgments about complicated issues that include, but go beyond, strict "economic value"" concerns? Can financial literacy be used to sub-optimize—to provide answers which don't fit the big picture of the company as a whole?

MANAGER, OILCO CHEMICAL: When President, OilCo Chemical came to the HR council with the program for staff reduction, it had been eagerly accepted. No one said, "Hold it. Let's really understand this. Do you really want to live with the implications"?

More than one manager made comments like this, which say, in effect, "I thought it was wrong, but I went along with it." What aspect of the system led to this dynamic?

◆ IMPLEMENTATION OF THE NEW DOWNSIZING

The next comments describe the way in which restructuring was implemented. To many managers at OilCo Chemical, the implementation was not seen in a positive light.

MANAGER, OILCO CHEMICAL: Several years ago, when we started the transformation, we spent a tremendous amount of time talking to people about the mission, vision, and values. I personally didn't understand the relativity of those values at that time. I thought of them as a purist would: belief in people, trust, and so on. We created expectations in people of a wonderful work place, where they would be valuable and important. I think we, and I, did an excellent job of creating that expectation.

Shortly after, we started talking about the employment contract. People heard that as: "As long as OilCo has use

This first comment makes a positive assessment. But it also shows how restructuring ran up against high expectations of "transformational values."
How should an organization in transformation handle a restructuring?

for me, I'm employed. If they don't, I'm not."

Then we started talking about a standard benchmarking scorecard, which compares manpower productivity between your site and other oil industry sites. It has messages like, "You've got 20 percent too many people for your output relative to top performing locations."

To achieve the required levels of productivity, we consolidated many jobs. We started talking about our need to do 80/20 work; instead of the 95/5 work on many items. Our point was, with a lot less energy you can turn in quality work that fits the need. You don't need to carry out the calculation of a distillation column to two places. But in a lot of people's minds, that meant we were asking them to lower their work standards—to turn in shoddy work.

Moving from a 95 percent style of perfectionism to an 80 percent style of perfectionism implies a recognition that perfectionism bears costs.

Then we initiated the pay freezes and PPP. People have made slightly more money, but they didn't trust the system or the target setting. And then we went through downsizing.

The workforce reduction was implemented almost entirely with transfers and voluntary retirements, yet it wasn't always perceived that way.

We, OilCo, as we always have in the past, downsized in the most socially responsible manner. But this downsizing shook people to their core; their foundation—their sense of job security, the implicit contract with the company.

MANAGER, OILCO CHEMICAL: We downsized almost 15% out of our several thousand people. It happened in the March or April time frame. People were asked to leave at the end of June. It was the right thing to do.

Is there a way to downsize in transformation without high emotional reactions?

But it was done with terrible implementation. We didn't take into consideration the human aspect of the project—the soft side issues. Timing, for example, is often everything in life. We had just come out with a record year for us financially, and here we were cutting back.

The structure of severance approaches at OilCo can send an unintentionally harsh message: "If you got offered a package, you are an unexceptional employee." See, for an example, an earlier comment (not from OilCo Chemical) on page 18.

CLERK, OILCO CHEMICAL: The biggest change morale-wise came in March, when they started talking about lay-offs. There were all sorts of rumbling going on. Then they announced that they were heavy on manufacturing and that would get hit hardest.

People started a rumor pool about the "15% club," how a huge number of people were being laid off. Then they announced the parameters: the packages. If you were an exceptional employee, you could get an exemption.

EXECUTIVE, OILCO Chemical: At the time the layoffs were happening, there were a lot of other issues—changes, transformational issues—that drained time away from spending it with employees. Managers were almost to the psyche where, "I can't go to time management school because I don't have time."

Did the work demands, as suggested here, contribute to lower quality of implementation of restructuring?

CLERK, OILCO CHEMICAL: I see that OilCo Chemical is trying. They're communicating things, but people don't want to hear it.

A letter came out about the second quarter results. The results are poor—not awful. We're not losing money, we have some opportunities. But people reading the letter heard, "OilCo's had a lousy second quarter, we're not doing well, but we're supposed to really buckle down and pitch in."

People feel that they have no way to make a difference, and that their PPP is going to suffer—even though the letter didn't say that.

When pay is based in part on organizational performance, it influences the perception of every communication about results.

MANAGER "A", OILCO CHEMICAL: Whatever actions that are being taken to empower people or build trust are not coming across in the intended vein.

At a workshop of about twenty-five first-level leaders, someone asked how the severance program was weighed against the mission, vision, and values of the company.

The reply, coming from a manager, was: "It wasn't done."

Here is a specific story about one workshop.

PRESIDENT, OILCO CHEMICAL, COMMENTING ON THIS STORY: At the top of OilCo Chemical, there have certainly been discussions about whether the downsizing was in line with our mission, vision, and values—especially at this

This comment was made during the validation (quote-checking) process. Decisions are made by the boards of the company, which consider multiple issues. However, these deliberations are not always widely known or understood.

The President, commenting here, did not know the identity of the managers in the story.

moment in time, after making good profits during the year before. We shared that kind of information with our internal board, the board that every business within OilCo now has under the new governance system. Before we went ahead, we informed OilCo's corporate board of directors, as well.

Many managers would not have known about those conversations. They might feel some frustration about being left out of the process. Weighing the severance program against the mission, vision, and values of the company may not have been well communicated, but to say, "It wasn't done," was not factually accurate.

How does one make decisions around core values?

How do you generate innovations around the tension between two core values that seem to be in conflict with each other (as, here, in the tension between "urgency," on one hand, and "belief in people," on the other)?

What is the ideal balance between high-level decision-making and self-direction in a tough situation like this one?

MANAGER "A", OILCO CHEMICAL, CONTINUING THE SAME STORY: Then at the same workshop the question arose: "Are you, then, expecting us to mirror that same mission, vision, and values to our employees?"

Someone else asked, "Why should I help OilCo Chemical become better? I can go work for OilCo Refining & Retail or another company."

People talked about how the purpose of building OilCo into the premier company no longer seemed so radical. Doesn't every company strive to be number one? Why not just join a company like Hewlett-Packard, that is already the best?

In change awareness work, you usually try to help people answer two questions: "How will this impact me?" and "What's in it for me?" After this workshop, I concluded that the leadership of our company has not helped us answer those questions.

◆ DESIGNING A DENOUEMENT

As the comments here suggest, the end of this story is yet to be played out. Despite the perceived problems in restructuring, business results have improved. A number of people speak of the future with a tone of concern. Many others look ahead with aspiration—for their own careers, and for OilCo Chemical as a whole.

PRESIDENT, OILCO CHEMICAL: If you look at the metrics of the downsizing, we have made a lot of good progress. That is a good aspect of our people: They don't like the change, but they do it.

How do external and internal forces interrelate in a single system?

The resistance to change is probably higher than I expected. Most people think that nearly all the downsizing has been layoffs. But there have been hardly any layoffs. Most people took packages voluntarily. But, whatever I say, they continue to talk about layoffs.

I think the deeper reason is that people are basically fed up with downsizing. They see it all around them in the United States. They still have their memories of the early 90s in OilCo. And there is a social trend, asking why corporations are doing this. You can read it every day in the papers.

One group of comments did not make it into the "major column," because they were too sensitive to quote directly. Several people wondered, in effect: "In the end, how sustainable will the new results be? Or will there be unexpected unintended consequences that will emerge later?"

How long does it take for the results of a difficult change to be assessed? What would be the most effective early indicators of success or failure?

Observers have noted two patterns of behavior at OilCo Chemical, and perhaps elsewhere at OilCo, that may relate to these dilemmas. First, does the high level of rationality in decision-making sometimes encourage people to overlook human implications? Second, do people tend to blame the leaders instead of finding a way to challenge them constructively?

EXECUTIVE, OILCO CHEMICAL: Over time, I'm convinced if we get this organization the way we think it should be, that the kind of people who will get into those management positions or leadership positions, I think they will be able to do it very well and we will become a great company as a result of it.

PRESIDENT, OILCO CHEMICAL: I think it will be harder to build back the winning spirit.

Everybody feels that winning spirit—or good morale or any other term you may like to use—is very important for activity and positive energy. It's important for our ability to accept more change.

The question one has to ask then: Can we successfully create a winning spirit in the next phase of the transformation while at the same time we have all those feelings about job security and suspicions?

That's a difficult question. It is, of course, very much on the plate here. You can't delegate that question.

CHAPTER 11

THE DIVERSITY CORPORATE INITIATIVE TEAM

A variety of cross-functional teams have been organized since the beginning of transformation. They include operational improvement teams, community service projects, and eight Future Imperatives teams, which report directly to the Executive Council. These last teams—six in 1994-1995, and two in 1995-1996—have been charged with developing approaches to critical strategic concerns for the company as a system.

The initiative teams came together as relative strangers. They figured out their own mandate. They gained confidence as they discovered that they had a significant task ahead of them. They muddled through the evolution of that insight, and then crystallized into understanding when they had a chance to look outside OilCo's traditional boundaries—in part by going to other companies. Finally, when they came back together, they faced inordinately tough deadlines and an uncertain fate: How should they present their material? What was their authority? And what would the aftermath be?

At OilCo, most of the teams had their formal task end at that point. Nonetheless, most of them found themselves feeling committed, in one way or another, to help follow up with the implementation of their recommendations. This comment comes from a staff member who was not on an initiative team, but who observed them first from a location outside Los Angeles, and later worked closely with one of the teams.

MEMBER, CORPORATE STAFF: The initiative teams were different from ordinary company practice. It looked like senior managers would have to come across with specific recommendations about how to run the businesses. It was

Could this be a model for other types of teams throughout OilCo?

not just cross-functional, but cross-business segment. The teams were being asked to learn about each other and work together for the first time.

We selected one of the eight teams to tell about in detail: The Diversity Corporate Initiative Team of 1995-1996. We chose this story because it was one of the two most recent stories, its work was relatively self-contained, it was ultimately seen as one of the most successful teams, and it focused on OilCo's efforts to deal with a critical transformational issue: The political and business "cases" for making OilCo's work force more diverse, and the pressures and opportunities that come with this diversity. In addition, the team's experience provides insight into the issues faced by all cross-functional teams as they propose change and take action.

◆ DIVERSITY: THE CASE FOR CONCERN

Why would diversity be a significant initiative for OilCo? Answers came from a variety of interviewees, who—in one way or another—expressed the idea that the homogeneity of OilCo's leadership was a critical limitation on the company's ability to succeed.

Support from the most senior corporate levels helped initiate these teams.

APPLIED LEARNING CONSULTANT: Diversity was a hot button for the CEO from the very beginning. He said, "We need to figure out what to do about it, because we're not where we need to be." But he didn't think it was the right project to do right out of the starting blocks, and we agreed with that assessment.

Many personal experiences were described by people we interviewed—in stories that explained their commitment to diversity.

MANAGER, OILCO REFINING & RETAIL: One of our senior managers was at a local gathering about a school issue, and there was a black man who was obviously in some leadership position in a parent's group. He gave a rousing talk: Moving, articulate, clear. People were on the edge of their chairs, and stood up and cheered him at the end.

Then the manager found out that the local school group leader was an OilCo employee. They had even been in meetings together. The way he conducted himself at OilCo, you would never have guessed that he and the civic speaker were the same person. He would come into meetings and be quiet and reserved and maintain a low profile.

It makes you wonder how much potential is out there.

MANAGER, OILCO CONSULTING: The first time I went to an OilCo leadership meeting, there were a couple of hundred people in attendance. I saw very little diversity of gender or race. In fact, the presenters even had common characteristics. Also, the format of the workshop did not provide a conducive environment for dialoguing. It was more of a listen and learn.

EXTERNAL CONSULTANT: I had the strongest reaction I ever felt at OilCo when I walked into that first meeting of the precursor to the Corporate Executive Team. It was like a 1970s locker room. I'm used to senior people in organizations being primarily male. But there were, I think, two women and no minorities out of one hundred or so people. The kind of conversation that was going on was very jocular—it was a shock. I hadn't seen that in the other companies I've worked in: GE, Merck, Ameritech, US West, and the financial district.

MANAGER, OILCO CHEMICAL: I hired two young people; both were minorities. One has already resigned. Will we be able to keep the other? I fear that we won't.

The problem is, minority people see us as a white company. "Why do I want to work there," they ask, "when everyone is white?"

They look at the managers in our group and see no minorities and one woman as a supervisor. Why don't we have more? Is this a company they want to work for?

MANAGER, OILCO CHEMICAL: We need to go out and find some people who are different from us—who smoke cigars spit on the floor, wear polyester suits, and want to raise

How many examples exist of similarly "untapped human resources"?

What would it take to engage them?

Two comments—one from an internal, and one from an external person—document the familiar "cookie-cutter" syndrome of the old OilCo.

Here is the gravest consequence of lack of diversity: loss of talent.

What happens when people learn the politically correct language but otherwise are no different?

Does highlighting diversity issues open "Pandora's box?'" What skills does an organization need to address diversity issues?

"Diversity of thought" seems "safer" to talk about than categories like race or gender, until you read comments like this.

This is perhaps the only skeptical comment that we heard about the need for diversity work.

In such a controversial arena, this lack of open skepticism is noteworthy.

It suggests that questioning the diversity initiative may be "undiscussable" at OilCo.

hell. Actually, that's sort of who I am. And you, leaders of the company, need to know: I will lead you into different places.

I will lead you into different jobs, different products, different ventures.

CUSTOMER SERVICE, OILCO CHEMICAL: You know, before I participated in a diversity workshop, I didn't think there was an issue. I've never been treated differently as a woman, and if I have, I didn't know about it. So, I thought, what's the big deal? I thought it was kind of sad that we had to spend so much time talking about it. That we couldn't just live and let live.

At the workshop, I was sitting in a group with all women, and suddenly I felt like "part of the oppressed." They could cite examples where they had been overlooked for a promotion, and Joe got it because he was male—but how do we know that? The stories just went on and on.

When I told them I didn't have a story, they didn't believe me at first. Maybe I'm one of the lucky ones.

◆ RECRUITING THE DIVERSITY TEAM

Like all members of the Future Imperatives teams, the candidates for the diversity team had been selected by senior executives, including members of the Executive Council. It was a difficult assignment to turn down. . . . and, because of the controversy of its subject, a difficult one to accept.

MEMBER, DIVERSITY CORPORATE INITIATIVE TEAM: My boss came in and said, "You're going to be a member of a strategic study team. Congratulations. It's going to be a great opportunity." Then he said, "Oh, by the way, it's going to be looking at diversity."

I had mixed feelings. To be honest, I wasn't sure whether OilCo was ready to take on the subject of diversity.

MEMBER, DIVERSITY CORPORATE INITIATIVE TEAM: When I was nominated, I had a crucial project that was taking me out of town three weeks out of every month. I didn't see how I could take something else on. My boss indicated that they would help out with the work load, but I was still uncertain. I went and talked to the adviser to the Executive Council, and she told me that it would be a great opportunity and experience. That pushed me over the edge, into accepting it.

Everyone we talked to from the diversity team had felt reservations upon being recruited.

MEMBER, DIVERSITY CORPORATE INITIATIVE TEAM: I knew that people on the first six teams thought it was a great experience. They learned a lot and met a lot of people at OilCo and did great things.

I was excited, but I also said to my boss, "Give me 'Cost'! Give me 'Growth'! Give me 'I.T.'! But don't give me 'Diversity'!"

Can the "great experience" of the initiative teams be replicated in teams throughout OilCo?

MEMBER, DIVERSITY CORPORATE INITIATIVE TEAM: Back in an OilCo training session, at least fifteen years before, the leaders asked us what legacy we would want to leave behind us. I said, after a lot of reflection, that I would like to be remembered as someone who made a difference.

I hadn't really known what that meant at the time, but I had thought I'd know it when I saw it. Now the offer to be on this team struck me, in terms of significance—both to the quality of life of the employees at OilCo and the effectiveness of the organization. This might be the best opportunity I would have to fulfill that dream.

MEMBER, DIVERSITY CORPORATE INITIATIVE TEAM: There was litigation pending against OilCo alleging race discrimination. Would we be prepared to bring those issues to the surface?

MEMBER, DIVERSITY CORPORATE INITIATIVE TEAM: We knew we needed to understand what the rules were and how far we were permitted to go. But none of us had a clue as to

This is an issue that couldn't be ignored. Yet, given the emotional backdrop, could it be carefully and cautiously approached?

what our final recommendations would look like when we were through. The Executive Council, while encouraging us to "do it well" and take it seriously, also had no clue about what they would end up supporting.

◆ DEFINING DIVERSITY AS A SUBJECT OF CONCERN

The first meeting of the Diversity Corporate Initiative Team took place in August 1995, with the Executive Council present. As with all the teams, the members had to define their own scale and scope of activity. They also challenged their sponsors. Was the council willing to expose tough issues around (for example) hiring practices or sexual orientation?

MEMBER, DIVERSITY CORPORATE INITIATIVE TEAM: If the Executive Council really wanted to avoid addressing diversity, they had the perfect out. The easy answer could have been, "Let's deal with it later, after this litigation is over." Instead, they said they had to deal with it now.

MEMBER, DIVERSITY CORPORATE INITIATIVE TEAM: This was also where the subject of sexual orientation first came up. In one of the breakout sessions, our team met to develop a plan. We listed categories of diversity—race, gender, ethnic background, et cetera—and someone suggested sexual orientation.

We include this story, which some people may find difficult to take, because it is typical of the way that highly charged issues get raised sometimes—almost by accident.

Talk about sexual orientation may clash with the privacy or consideration that some people feel they deserve from a workplace. Other people may feel that the ability to discuss this issue is a great asset.

How should a company handle the matter?

I presented the report back out to the full group, including the Executive Council. "We have a really diverse team," I said, and then described our own team according to our list of categories. "Half of us are left-handed and half of us are right-handed." And so on.

Then I got to sexual orientation, and I said, "Well, I guess I don't know about all of our differences. . . ." The whole room started laughing. I was laughing too.

But then I said, "We all laughed, but for all we know, there's someone here in the room who has a brother, sister, cousin or relative who is homosexual. Statistics say that 5 to 10 percent of our population is homosexual. Perhaps they include some people in this room. They're sitting here, laughing along with the rest of us because that's the politically correct thing to do in our culture."

There was silence, and just a bit of head-nodding. Sexual orientation had obviously not been on the radar screen when they chartered this team. Now, it had just come out.

I went on with the rest of the presentation. When we got our written feedback later, from the attendees, a couple of people said, "Be careful with this sexual orientation thing."

MEMBER, DIVERSITY CORPORATE INITIATIVE TEAM: We all understood now that this study would require courage. Both we, and the Executive Council, would have to respond to diversity issues as mature, seasoned, rational adults. It was very refreshing to me to see how the process would not come unglued.

MEMBER, DIVERSITY CORPORATE INITIATIVE TEAM: Even though we had support from the Executive Council, there was still some apprehension on the team as we developed our recommendations. Several times, we would say to ourselves: "We know they're on board, but they're only ten people. How is the Corporate Executive Team going to buy this initiative?" Would they have the time that the Executive Council had had to come around to see the value of diversity from a business standpoint, as well as from the more human aspects?

As the tough issues became clear, the team wondered about its support beyond the Executive Council.

Were they worried about what their peers would say?

MEMBER, DIVERSITY CORPORATE INITIATIVE TEAM: Our sense of our purpose evolved as we learned more about what the issues were at OilCo. Between focus group information, surveys, and challenge group sessions, we had lots of input from people in the organization. That input helped us define what the issues were, and from that our charter evolved.

MEMBER, DIVERSITY CORPORATE INITIATIVE TEAM: Originally, "valuing diversity" meant learning to accept things that

Note that this understanding emerged, in part, from conversations with people throughout OilCo.

were measurable. Race, gender, and some categories related to whether people came from a technical or a business background. At heart, we assumed that "doing diversity well" was about assimilation. How could you make everybody feel a part of the company, be comfortable, and not make wrong choices on the basis of factors like race and gender?

But we evolved into an understanding that people are genuinely different. They bring different things to the table. In driving toward assimilating everybody and having them be a "happy family," we drive out the richness of the differences. We need to see that there is value in being different, if it's done well. For me, that was a kind of wake-up call.

◆ THE EXPERIENTIAL WORKSHOP—A FIRST "DOING" EXPERIENCE

MEMBER, DIVERSITY CORPORATE INITIATIVE TEAM: In September, after only two meetings together as a team, we went through a diversity awareness workshop. The attendees were just ourselves, along with our Executive Council sponsor and two others.

MEMBER, DIVERSITY CORPORATE INITIATIVE TEAM: The workshop was emotionally draining. I wouldn't call it a "roller coaster," because there weren't many highs. I had a headache and couldn't sleep, because it had to deal with a lot of things I had tied up and suppressed away in a nice, neat bundle. When you start to see a little bogeyman coming back out again, that's not easy to deal with.

MEMBER, DIVERSITY CORPORATE INITIATIVE TEAM: The workshop was the first place where we had to own up to our part in the problem, and admit that we were part of it. We had not been placed on this team necessarily because we were known for being great at dealing with diversity at OilCo. Just the fact that we're all at relatively high positions in the company means that we've colluded, at a minimum, with diversity-related problems at OilCo or outside.

MEMBER, DIVERSITY CORPORATE INITIATIVE TEAM: It wasn't until I saw where I had assimilated—the things I've done to fit into the "OilCo way of doing things"— that I could recognize how other people were trying to fit in as well. There's a lot of stock, for instance, put into the ability to present somebody else's material: They throw you a pile of viewgraphs and you make a great presentation out of it, telling a good story even though you don't know the background of everything. But in having to present this way, a lot of people can't share all that they could otherwise bring to the table.

MEMBER, DIVERSITY CORPORATE INITIATIVE TEAM: I remember Team Member saying that he had never fully appreciated why OilCo's people of color did not trust the police. Then he heard stories of being pulled over and stopped. That made him understand, more clearly, his own manager-subordinate relationships.

MEMBER, DIVERSITY CORPORATE INITIATIVE TEAM: I found how naive I was. I never thought these events happened to people I knew. They took place somewhere else in the world. It had an impact on me to see racism alive and well, right here in my neighborhood.

MEMBER, DIVERSITY CORPORATE INITIATIVE TEAM: We talked about the isolation involved in being a high-level woman at OilCo. If you're female, you get used to hearing about your nickname. There's the Ice Queen, the Dragon Lady, the Wicked Witch. And you get used to always being "the only one" on a team or work group.

You don't develop the relationships with your male peers like they do amongst themselves, because of things they have in common that you don't share. And there aren't many women around, especially as you go up in the organization, to have those kinds of relationships

The use of the word "collude" suggests that everyone at a high level at OilCo has succeeded, in part, by playing and supporting a game; promoting only those who "fit in" with the culture (and themselves).

Is the term "collusion" reasonable? If so, what are its ramifications?

Others have mentioned this common "viewgraph" experience as something that never felt good.

If success in the old OilCo depended upon taking on the characteristics of the "traditional white male," what does success in the new OilCo depend upon?

with. Typically, you're the only one on your team who is a female. You don't necessarily want to be associated with the women, because you're trying to seem like one of the guys. Yet you can't be one of the guys, so you don't have that either. And, your spouse isn't tied into the OilCo network, like a lot of the men's wives.

All of this makes it difficult for women to feel a part of OilCo.

MEMBER, DIVERSITY CORPORATE INITIATIVE TEAM: We heard from several women who could recall a time when they were either unaware of this loneliness, or who denied that it was going on. They had been the first to say there were no problems, and had discovered only later, in retrospect, some of the sacrifices they had made in suppressing part of themselves. Then they felt a great sense of loss. In my view, that was a human tragedy that we ought not to perpetuate, and I became hopeful we could change it.

◆ MOVING TOWARD A SYSTEMIC UNDERSTANDING

Before making a presentation, all of the Future Imperatives teams were encouraged to conduct their own research and analysis, which generally included in-depth group work and bench-marking trips to other companies.

Complex systems exist in the eyes of the beholders. Studying systems requires a willingness to approach them from several points of view, until the nature of interrelationships comes into focus.

MEMBER, DIVERSITY CORPORATE INITIATIVE TEAM: Right after that experiential workshop, we said to each other, "This topic is too fluid. It's going to be a mess, and we need to take time to be messy."

The old OilCo engineering culture would have suggested: Let's map it out from Point A to B to C to D. But should we simply check off things along the line, and make sure we stuck to schedule? Or should we really try to understand our subject? Should we be flexible enough to change direction?

MEMBER, DIVERSITY CORPORATE INITIATIVE TEAM: That led us to do a systems analysis of the diversity issue. We put up dozens of issues on the wall that we wanted to try to tackle. Then, over several days, we refined them into a sense of the whole system.

MEMBER, DIVERSITY CORPORATE INITIATIVE TEAM: That system became the centerpiece for our work

MEMBER, DIVERSITY CORPORATE INITIATIVE TEAM: A lot of the differences among us came from our organizational culture upbringing. The advocates of a structured process brought some methodologies like project and process management—which didn't seem to apply so well in this type of problem.

At one point I remarked that if there were an event in the Olympics for anal-retentiveness, we should join, because we'd be gold-medal winners.

MEMBER, DIVERSITY CORPORATE INITIATIVE TEAM: We gathered data in a number of different ways. We were so time constrained, we had to have help, so we went over earlier surveys and studies. We read books—everything from Workforce 2000 to Dave Barry's *Guide for Guys.* We employed a consultant company to do some focus groups.

Another source of information surprised me. An e-mail message had announced the creation of this team and its members, and some of us got contacted by individuals—for the most part, around the sexual orientation issue. We did not know how to solicit any information about that, because it is so sensitive at OilCo. But people were willing to come forward to us, and try to influence something that was important to them.

MEMBER, DIVERSITY CORPORATE INITIATIVE TEAM: We understood the attitudes of technical and business professionals. But we did not have any refinery operators on our team. We had no members of the secretarial or clerical staff.

We began to discover that we had little understanding of the reality of what it's like to be a support staff or an

Something similar may have happened here.

Dealing with diversity issues extends beyond being able to confront the topic, and includes having a process, which tolerates diversity, for addressing the issues.

Another significant diversity issue concerns the different work backgrounds and roles of people at OilCo. Why is this set of differences so easy to ignore? What is the most effective way to address these differences?

hourly employee. We tended to forget that people like us—college graduates in management and professional jobs—made up a little bit more than a quarter of the population of OilCo. We were not getting the full benefit of the rest of our constituency.

MEMBER, DIVERSITY CORPORATE INITIATIVE TEAM: We visited seven other companies, plus the Army, to learn what they had done on the issue of diversity—in the case of Xerox, for decades. We wanted to learn about their trials and tribulations; what worked, what had happened. On every visit, we had at least one member of the Executive Council go with us; this was different from the other Future Imperatives teams.

MEMBER, DIVERSITY CORPORATE INITIATIVE TEAM: Most people don't think they have a whole lot to learn. We all think that our own view is already moral, upright, and legitimate. It was pretty clear that if a group of us came up with recommendations in areas that the Executive Council members thought they understood already, it would be very difficult for them to accept.

An example is the use of grass-root networks or affinity groups, where employees of shared background—people of color, African Americans, Hispanic women, white men—come together informally to talk about issues at work. For many years, these types of groups had seemed threatening. "They might get out of control." I am convinced that it was very powerful for the Executive Council to hear from other respected companies where these groups had been successful.

A typical situation in many organizations: letting the apprehension about sponsors' response dictate the activity.

How many groups have I been in where we got paralyzed, speculating about how a sponsor would react? Would our proposals get derailed? Would this be big trouble? In the end, all you have to do is check it out. Lo and behold, when you get facts instead of speculation, you discover that it's not such a big deal as you thought it was—or, if it is, you can deal with it.

MEMBER, DIVERSITY CORPORATE INITIATIVE TEAM: We also updated the Executive Council members continually. We had a program we called "Adopt-a-Leader." Each of us had the responsibility of updating one person on where we were or where we were headed, and getting feedback. "If you see something that might cause issues for you, tell us about it and then we'll explore."

Later, it would be easier to present our recommendations—and harder for the Executive Council to go against them—because we had involved the Council from the beginning.

MEMBER, DIVERSITY CORPORATE INITIATIVE TEAM: One of the Executive Council members told us afterward that he felt he had been set up on a particular visit. We had walked into the conference room at the corporation we were visiting, and met with a vice president and several other senior managers. There were only two white men in the room. "I had never been in a room that diverse in my life," he said.

One of us replied, "What do you think it's like for women and people of color at OilCo every day?" And the light went on.

A key part of the diversity team's strategy was to keep in close touch with the Executive Council, and tell them what they learned.

MEMBER, EXECUTIVE COUNCIL: The profundity of our diversity learning got to the core for all of us, emotionally, about where we were going wrong at OilCo. Our strong culture, which we had so jealously prided ourselves upon historically, was visibly manifest in the demographics of our organization. We were excluding people and excluding ideas, and denying that we had done this to ourselves.

◆ RECOMMENDATIONS AND AFTERMATH

Like most of the Future Imperatives eams, the diversity team presented about a dozen recommendations to the Executive Council—in this case, at a meeting in January 1996. One recommendation, accepted by the council, asked each business and firm to establish ten-year goals for "balanced work forces"—representation of all groups, minorities and women, at all levels of the company in a way that mirrored the external availability of these groups at the appropriate skill levels in society.

Creating accountability for diversity efforts is still a major problem in the field.

MEMBER, DIVERSITY CORPORATE INITIATIVE TEAM: We used some recommendations straight from the companies we had seen. Motorola, for instance, uses metrics to judge accountability for diversity, and we set up our recommendation the same way.

MEMBER, DIVERSITY CORPORATE INITIATIVE TEAM: We decided that, before presenting to the Executive Council, we wanted a first pass at the general OilCo population—first, on the content, and second on how accurately they perceived what we were saying. So in late November, we assembled a "challenge workshop": a diagonal slice of people, with different races and genders. General managers, managers, technical professionals, associate staff, a refinery operator, and a maintenance crafts person were present.

One interview (which could not be quote-checked for logistic reasons) described the response of a table of "white males" at this workshop. First they complained that the diversity goals were too much like affirmative action quotas. Then they began to talk out the issues, and acknow-ledged how the country's culture was changing, and they would have to be part of that change.

We made our presentation to the whole group and then broke into small groups for discussion, on the basis of various categories: Homogeneous groups of white men, all women, all minorities, mixed groups, and a group of relatively senior managers.

You would have thought we had given eight different presentations! Some said, "We really like it." Others said, "We really hate it."

The case for action, in other words, would have to be inclusive for white males. What would their role be?

It would also have to be strongly related to the business case.

MEMBER, DIVERSITY CORPORATE INITIATIVE TEAM: That challenge workshop would not have been feasible three years earlier. First, we would never have mixed general managers, operators, and secretaries in the same room, to ask all of them the same thing: "What's your thought? What's your reaction?"

And it would have been heresy to present a sensitive, controversial recommendation to a group before the senior management had seen it first, under a cloak of total confidentiality, so they could either endorse it or they could say no without having to deal with employee reaction.

MEMBER, DIVERSITY CORPORATE INITIATIVE TEAM: Everybody at the challenge workshop agreed on only one thing: "Hey, this is just another OilCo presentation." We had used viewgraphs and stood up there to explain them. That started us thinking that, with the Executive Council, we might do something different.

MEMBER, DIVERSITY CORPORATE INITIATIVE TEAM: They didn't want us to change the recommendation, but to repackage it: To put in more feeling and passion, and more of ourselves. That was a challenge, because we only had five weeks until report-out.

MEMBER, DIVERSITY CORPORATE INITIATIVE TEAM: We got professional help for a video. We were totally invested in the product, and we wordsmithed every word and frame in it. We also got help with our written report, which was uncharacteristic of an OilCo report. It read like a story. It talked about people and feelings, as well as the conclusion and recommendations.

MEMBER, DIVERSITY CORPORATE INITIATIVE TEAM: The presentation took place in January, to the Executive Council. We were second, after the Reward and Recognition Team. And we were nervous. We intermingled video snippets of our own stories with the statistics and other parts of our presentation. I don't enjoy having myself up there on video, and for days, knowing it would play, I wondered if it would be a big flop.

MEMBER, DIVERSITY CORPORATE INITIATIVE TEAM: Afterward, I knew it had gotten to them, in a way that an ordinary OilCo presentation would not, because they were talking: "How did you all do this?" And, "We ought to do this."

The new governance structure affected the abilities of the Executive Council to act directly.

How does the distribution of authority affect the ability of a company to initiate broader, often difficult, changes?

MEMBER, DIVERSITY CORPORATE INITIATIVE TEAM: The Executive Council went off to their room and had their private time to discuss the recommendations of the team. They came back the next day and said that they accepted the recommendations.

About a third of them were corporate-level initiatives that we knew they would carry through. But many of the decisions were up to the business units to implement.

I think the Executive Council was struggling with their role in this in light of the new governance.

MEMBER, DIVERSITY CORPORATE INITIATIVE TEAM: The resistance grows as you go deeper down. People say that the Executive Council or the Corporate Executive Team has nothing to lose. But they do.

Some people come up to me and challenge our purpose and findings. I don't feel I ever persuade them, but at least we have an exchange in dialogue. But I also think there's an underground, working within the system. I fear those who reject it but will not verbalize the rejection, and will operate against it as we try to implement it. That's just a subjective view of mine; I have no data to support it.

Dealing with the anticipated risks of truth-telling is still a pretty big hurdle for many people at OilCo.

MEMBER, DIVERSITY CORPORATE INITIATIVE TEAM: As part of this team, I gained a new appreciation for authenticity and the importance of telling your truth. The risks weren't as big as I thought they were. A lot of them were in my mind. When the CEO and the Executive Council say, "We want people to tell us how it is," that's what they mean.

What does this story suggest about the most effective way to get things done in the organization?

If you feel at risk, because you're saying things that are not expedient, you have to put your toe in the water gingerly. I came away with a real appreciation for the capacity of people to hear the truth and not punish you for it. If we can get that appreciation spread in the organization generally, it will be tremendous.

In the end, the CEO invited our team to make a shortened presentation to the OilCo Board of Directors. To my knowledge, it's not common for this kind of issue to be worked with the Board—not just diversity, but people-management issues in general. They tend to deal with capital budgets and barrels produced.

They gave us a half hour, and nobody told us what to say. Nobody made us schedule a dry-run rehearsal. That was an intriguing level of trust, contrasted with former times. We even told them that we thought bringing diversity to the Board would improve the quality of their deliberations. Nobody had apoplexy. When we finished, they invited us to stay for lunch.

CHAPTER 12

"WHO AM I?"

The corporate transformation that began in 1993 brings many OilCo employees to a painful choice. They realize that they must change fundamental ways of thinking, feeling, and acting, or risk their careers at OilCo.

Employees who have become involved with the company's transformation report benefits that carry over to every area of their lives: work, family, health, spiritual practices, and leisure. They report feeling more in tune with their essential selves. They gain confidence and visibility. In almost all cases, however, the personal transformation has included periods of confusion, fear, anger, mistrust, defeat, and even profound grief.

Many wonder whether a corporation should mandate this type of personal growth; or whether it is possible for a critical mass of people to undergo transformation. Other people see, in transformation, a threat to their attitudes about people, or to their core identity. Some feel a threat to their religious beliefs. They say, in effect, "I wish OilCo would quit trying to 'fix' me."

This theme exists for the consideration of personal issues raised by transformation. It is a very short theme, because transformation is still so new. It takes time for personal issues to come to the surface. We hope that, by raising them in conversations, people can feel as if their voice will be heard—and that they can still listen with respect to the voices of others.

◆ **WORK LIFE AND PERSONAL IDENTITY**

These quotes, from various interviews, illuminate the kinds of issues that will come to the surface, increasingly, as people think about aligning their personal aspirations with the corporate transformation.

How do we know that this fundamental type of personal change is going to make us a winning company?

No company has ever successfully completed a roll-out of organizational learning principles without dealing with this question of the perceived clash with existing religious beliefs.

Do we deal with it by confronting the issue head on? By restricting the transformation to issues unrelated to personal growth? Or in some other way?

MEMBER, EXECUTIVE COUNCIL: I think if you behave in a way to assimilate that's inconsistent with some of the things you deeply believe, it creates a sense of tension. Some people have called it "putting on a mask." I think if we could relieve that stress, it would create a lot of positive energy in the organization. That's why diversity, in the strictest sense, is so important: It lets people be who they are.

As my mask has come down, I've gone through the experience of being really surprised at what's inside there. The mask not only hid me from others, but from myself as well.

MANAGER, OILCO CONSULTING: Some people—and although I personally don't believe this, I understand where they are coming from—think the transformation has elements of "new age" religions built in. If you read Peter Senge's book, there are elements around the concept of personal mastery that seem somewhat opposed to Judeo-Christian beliefs, such as the idea of self-reliance. I know this has made some people extremely uncomfortable to the point where they say "this is really not for me." This reaction has manifested itself in private conversations and public forums.

There's a bit of cliquishness around this transformation stuff. You hear it in the jargon: "Share your left-hand column," the "ladder of inference," and "take off the masks." They make a lot of sense, but they're still viewed by many as "flavor-of-the-month." We had a great session with forty leaders at Georgia Pines. Three months later, we had another session for 180 people at the OilCo Hotel, where we kept talking about Georgia Pines. People started resenting this: "We weren't there. Quit beating us over the head about this 'mystical experience' you had."

Finally someone raised his hand and said, "We're at the OilCo Hotel now, not at Georgia Pines." The room erupted into spontaneous applause.

MANAGER, OILCO CONSULTING: For me, personal transformation has meant attitude changes: speaking your mind, learning to respect everybody's contribution, delegating work to people, and coming to realize that it takes all kinds of people to get results—not just the people who are "in my own image."

I think I have come to appreciate diversity of thought much more in the past year. The members of my management team bring different elements to the job—humor, aggressiveness, introspectiveness, analytical and technical abilities, but it blends together nicely to form something greater than the sum of the individual parts. In the past, I had often only trusted the people who looked and sounded like I did, so I missed a lot of the richness this mixture now brings me.

I would also have assumed that I could do it all better myself, if I only had the time. The OilCo model of a manager was: You got a bunch of little robots and programmed them. The robots couldn't think for themselves, so they would always come back and ask you what had to happen. As a result, the bottleneck in the group was the leader. That model, for me, has changed.

MEMBER, CORPORATE EXECUTIVE TEAM: At one workshop for the Corporate Executive Team, the external consultant running the workshop defined transformation as a "death and rebirth" process. We should get rid of the old thoughts and purpose, and be born again with something new. I stood up and said, "Bull---," in a rather assertive way.

"I haven't had a single invalid experience during my OilCo career," I said. "Everything that I've done has been valuable to me. By your definition, I'm not transforming. I think I'm growing." I haven't heard anybody ask us to stand up and take a blood oath to become reborn or get out.

I hadn't heard [CEO] stand up and give a pat definition for what it means to be a transformed member of the company. I think he expects us all to define that for ourselves in some meaningful way.

MANAGER, OILCO CHEMICAL: Recently I was at a committee meeting at my church. After making my own case, I

Can a person be an effective leader/employee without having to go through a transformation?

The skills of transformation, in this view, have value in the world outside OilCo. Does learning inside the work place reinforce learning outside the work place, and vice versa.

moved into inquiry mode to try and get people to explain their points more deeply for my own understanding and for the rest of the group.

I do that consciously now. I used to focus only on content, but now I am able to switch between content and context. My level of skill here is probably only an inch deep, but it's opened up a new world to me.

The next dimension is to build my awareness of where I am, what I am feeling, and what has impacted me at any moment.

Corporate transformation, in short, has raised a series of personal questions for many people at OilCo—questions that, in a stable "old-style" company, are easier to ignore:

- Who am I?

- What are the implications, for my identity, of engaging in the change process at OilCo?

- What are the implications for people who are close to me?

- What shifts of behavior have I noticed?

- What do these shifts imply?

- What shifts of behavior would convince me that the company is changing—or that I am changing—in a way that will help us move forward, toward where we want to go?

COMMENTARIES

CHAPTER 13

WHEN WILL WE LEARN?

Edgar Schein

◆ WHY READ THIS HISTORY?

When I first encountered this and other learning histories I was struck by their novelty. In all of our academic literature there is remarkably little novelty, either in content or form of presentation. The OilCo learning history is novel on several levels; it is interesting precisely because its novelty forces new reactions from the reader. One encounters real insights about organizational and personal realities; one encounters dramatic personal statements of the sort one rarely sees in printed nonfiction; one gets bored and wonders where all of this is going; and one discovers that while one section was boring another produced high excitement. At some level the learning history is a projective screen that stimulates the reader at so many levels that one encounters, in the end, one's own assumptions, predisposition, and biases. It is both a pleasant and an unpleasant experience. The point, however, is that it is an experience, not just a passive read of one more bit of academic research.

Let me now expand on the general statement by providing some of my own reactions and insights about this document. My comments are divided into two sections: first the learning history as a new form of research and intervention, and second this particular learning history as a source of insight into organizational change and learning.

◆ **THE OILCO LEARNING HISTORY AS RESEARCH AND INTERVENTION**

A NOTE ON DIAGNOSIS AND INTERVENTION

As readers who are familiar with my work on Process Consultation and Clinical Research will recognize, I find it increasingly difficult to separate the concept of research or diagnosis from the concept of application or intervention.[1] Anytime we are dealing with a living system, whether it be an individual, a group, or a larger human system such as an organization, the process of learning about it and the process of intervening in it are basically one and the same. Lewin's dictum, that one can understand a system only when one tries to change, it, was correct. He did not, however, make enough of the other side of the coin—if one intends to study a system, with no other goal, it can't be done without changing it, as physicists have known all along.

It is ironic that while the field of organization studies has so often attempted to emulate the hard sciences, it persistently fails in accepting what these hard scientists discovered long ago. *The very act of measurement changes that which is measured.* Our theories of change all talk piously of periods of diagnosis, scouting, surveying, and measuring prior to some process of "intervention." What is refreshing about a learning history is that it starts from the notion that diagnosis and intervention are a part of the same human process. A research document about an organization is not only an intervention at the stage of "gathering data." Beyond that, it can be made into a further intervention through the active involvement of the organization's participants in reacting to the data gathered. As they react they not only learn about themselves but also produce more data that deepens their own and others insights into the dynamics of what is going on at individual, group, and organizational levels.

The learning history as an approach to research and intervention should itself be studied to see the extent to which it represents genuinely new ways for researchers and their subjects to interact.

A NOTE ON WRITTEN PRESENTATION

In an important book on qualitative research and ethnography, John Van Maanen[2] reminds us that as researchers, interventionists, and/or writers we make some crucial choices when we decide to share our insights with "readers." We make a choice as to whether, on one extreme, to be the aloof interpreter, writing in the passive and distant voice, or, on the other extreme, to write a "confessional" in the first person, dramatizing our adventures and trying to buy credibility by confessing our various missteps. Our goal in both cases, of course, is to gain attention and credibility. We want our readers to believe us and we want to be interesting enough to keep the reader reading. In this domain of written presentation, the learning history seems to be a genuine innovation.

The essence of this innovation is to combine as many forms of presentation as possible into a single document. We have within the same few pages of any section of the learning history (1) the passive voice of the analyst looking at the whole case from an analytical and relatively dispassionate point of view, (2) the often passionate voices of many different participants reflecting different levels and functions in the organization, and (3) the voices of the change agents, consultants, and interventionists—both outsiders and insiders. This process takes the Rashomon approach to a new level. We are presented with critical insights from every angle and with many different points of view.

This approach is not without cost. You cannot read through the learning history the way you can read through a case because you do not have the single analytical thread that a case writer provides. Instead, you are battered by many voices, many of which disagree with each other or at least present orthogonal points of view. I find the format both interesting and irritating. I want a story. I want the written document to have a beginning, middle, and end. I want conclusions. Instead, I find myself reading intensely in some sections, skipping others, looking for quotes from certain kinds of participants, ignoring quotes from others, trying to short-circuit the process by reading the minor column analytical comments, and rereading other sections because of the sudden realization that I had not grasped a given point at all. In this way the learning history is seductive—which is, I believe, precisely what its authors want it to be. They want the reader to become involved and reflective, and they succeed remarkably well. In the end, then, the learning history is not only a tool for involving insiders in their own learning and change process, but has potential for vicariously involving readers in those same processes. In any case, the learning history is a great vehicle for satisfying organizational voyeurs.

A NOTE ON RELIABILITY, VALIDITY, AND APPLICABILITY

We write, presumably, in order to display our knowledge and insight to others, to influence their thinking, and to stimulate them. We do this in the nonfiction arena on the presumption that what we are presenting is reliable, accurate, valid, and useful. Usefulness a reader can judge for him or herself, but how is a reader ever to know about reliability and accuracy? In our more traditional forms of research presentation we fall back on careful descriptions of our methods, appropriate statistical analyses, and thoughtful reasoning. In studying living systems these methods often turn out be problematic precisely because the systems are alive. The systems change not only as a result of the research itself, but as a result of their continual interactions with their environments and their evolving internal dynamics.

My own sense about reliability and validity revolves more around our ability to replicate, to predict, and to understand intuitively. If I present a conclusion I have reached about some process in an organization that I have observed, I implicitly make the commitment that if the readers had been there, or in comparable situations, they would have observed the same thing. Most of us in the field of group dynamics learned from sitting in many training groups that certain phenomena were clearly visible to whoever would hang around to observe them. We found that the best way to deal with skeptics was to bring them into a group and let them see for themselves.

Since we were constantly intervening, we also learned that certain interventions repeatedly produced the same results. Replicating a phenomenon is a powerful form of validation. A level of predictability, provides the kind of assuredness that is presumably what we are all after as "scientists." What is frustrating in the social sciences is that we cannot achieve that level of replication, predictability and control in those areas that trouble us most. Take, for example, the prevention of conflict. The dynamics of how conflicts and other organizational phenomena play themselves out are describable and predictable, but still we go on having conflicts. Describability leads to a third criterion of validity—that readers understand and can relate to a description because it fits into their own experience in an immediate and intuitive way. Good organizational descriptions have the "ring of truth to them." It is this validity criterion that explains why good "fiction" often has more cred-ibility with managers (as well as, unfortunately, more impact) than acad-emic research.

The learning history is an important experiment in trying to reach all three of these criteria at once by form of presentation and choice of what to present. The analytical comments at the beginning of sections and in the minor column try to articulate the predictable and repeatable phe-nomena in an abstract way, but if the reader should not recognize or be able to relate to the general point, he or she can try to infer it from the quotes in the major column. At the same time, the analytical comments are formed as questions or observations rather than conclusions, which invites the reader to begin to construct his or her own model of what is going on. In the end, then, the reader does not have a set of "findings" or "conclusions" but comes away from a learning history with a rich, deep-er set of questions about what may have been going on. This situation is both frustrating and enlightening. As a reader I acquire less formal knowl-edge but maybe more skill in how to think about things. And, paradoxi-cally, if I become more skillful in thinking about things, I will become a more skillful observer/intervener which, in the end, is probably more valuable.

◆ INSIGHTS AND LESSONS ABOUT ORGANIZATIONAL CHANGE

The OilCo learning history is a story about organizational transformation. This is not your garden-variety tale of a few organizational changes that did or did not work. The transformation at OilCo is presented as a major change in all aspects of how the corporation works, and the lessons, therefore, are presumed to be lessons about what it takes to create this level of transformation. Without repeating all of the steps of the change process, I would like to comment on those that struck me as particularly relevant in terms of my own experiences as a change agent and change theorist. In other words, what in the learning history has the "ring of truth" to it? The points are listed in terms of a chronological sequence, but their operation as forces is cumulative and interactive. And, what is most strik-ing to me, is how many such forces have to be operating before trans-formational changes take place.

INITIAL DISCONFIRMATION

Much as we might wish that transformation could take place without a "burning platform" to motivate us, the evidence from this case reinforces the notion that people have to feel in trouble, economic or otherwise, before they really become motivated to tolerate the inevitable pain of change. But the interesting thing is that even when people experience a lot of disconfirmation, they can rationalize it away or ignore it altogether until some new direction can be perceived. That new direction is often provided by a new and visionary leader who not only takes advantage of the disconfirmation already present but adds his own "burning platform" data while providing, at the same time, a vision for how to move forward.

THE VISIONARY LEADER AS SAVIOR

Once the leader articulates a new direction, the organization mobilizes its anxiety and guilt into a positive drive to learn something new. We can only judge the success of transformational leadership after the fact. There are organizations that are in trouble, that have new visionary leaders, yet that do not succeed in getting on a transformational track. This distinction between effective and noneffective transformational leaders leads to two intriguing questions: (1) What are the distinguishing characteristics of transformational leaders who actually succeed in starting a transformation; and (2) who selected the transformational leader and was his ability to move the organization foreseen? The learning history does not have an answer to this question but it is one that should be asked because it makes explicit the influences of the OilCo board of directors. Did they pick a leader because they thought he could accomplish certain goals? Or were they surprised at the extent of change that their appointee pursued?

One of the big gaps in the study of organizational change results from the inability to get data about high level decisions around the anointing of CEOs. We do not know enough about how boards and corporate governance processes work in the selection of candidates, in the negotiation with candidates, and in the degrees of freedom they finally give to the new leaders that they select.[3]

THE LEADER'S THEORY OF CHANGE: ECONOMICS FIRST

I believe the most significant "finding" in the OilCo learning history is that the leader decided to start the transformation process by focusing on economic goals and economic education. Even though the difficulties lay in the human organization (the failure of lower levels to communicate what they knew, their complacency, and their dependence on higher levels to bail them out), the CEO chose not to attack those issues directly. Instead he brought in a business model of how to add value in every job and at every level, and supported the model with an educational program (the financial literacy initiative) that taught managers at all levels the meaning of adding economic value. The lack of openness and teamwork became evident later as the constraint on adding value. Openness and teamwork then became necessities, they were not merely general values that would be "good" for the company.

This sequence confirms my own general observation about culture change programs.[4] If they are not closely linked to business and economic goals, and embodied in new ways of working that clearly add value, they become merely the program of the month and are abandoned as soon as senior executives stop monitoring them. *So called "values driven management" only works if the leadership (1) defines the values in behavioral terms (the new way of working), (2) displays that new way of working in its own behavior, (3) redesigns the reward and discipline system to reinforce that behavior, and (4) continues to pay attention to and measure the consequences of the new behavior.*

If one wanted to dig deeper into the OilCo learning history one would explore how the CEO came to have such a clear insight and what gave him the strength to decide on an expensive economic education program in an organization that was already suffering financial difficulties. It should also be noted that this first step was imposed by the leader, not consensually arrived at. Later on, employees and managers at all levels became involved in the transformation, but the initial goals of 10 percent return in all jobs were nonnegotiable.

A FUNDAMENTAL CHANGE IN GOVERNANCE STRUCTURE

Organizations are notorious for changing structure to shake up the current system and thereby to send signals to the employees that something needs to change. However, most of these reorganizations have only business logic behind them, not "psycho" or "socio" logic. If the business logic is sound—decentralization, divisionalization, replacing geographic centers with business unit centers, and so on—then the changes are appropriate and accomplish business goals. But the nature of authority, the relationships among levels in the hierarchy usually remain the same. The "Federalist" ideas that emerged in Oil Co and the decision by the CEO to make many areas of operations autonomous or semi-autonomous reflected a more profound psychological and sociological reorganization than one typically sees in corporations.

These changes clearly challenged many of the sacred cows of corporate culture. Even if economic performance improves, the new governance process disconfirms what others have taken for granted and therefore causes unknown amounts of anxiety throughout the organization. I have seen many cases where innovations that clearly increased productivity were abandoned or actually squashed because the rest of the system could not adapt to the new form of governance that was implied. The most vivid of these was a case cited by Alex Bavelas in 1950 where an assembly line decided to work as a team and was able, as a result, to speed up the line by 100 percent. The project was abandoned because neither the unit supplying the line nor the sales unit receiving the line's output could handle the 100-percent increase.

The psychosocial issue usually revolves around deeply held assumptions about accountability and control. As McGregor[5] pointed out long ago, there is plenty of evidence that formal controls are less effective than self-control, that formal accountability is less effective than personal commitment, and that teams that feel accountable as teams can accomplish more than those same individuals separately, yet most of the corporate world operates by assumptions of hierarchical, individualistic, and formal controls and accountabilities. The top management of OilCo apparently succeeded in delegating accountability and allowing a measure of self-control, which would make it very deviant in the corporate culture world.

THE MOTIVATIONAL POWER OF PERSONAL LEARNING

The new governance structure clearly invited lower levels to learn to take on more responsibility and to become committed in ways that had not previously been possible. The door was opened to a level of personal learning that would make a substantial contribution to organizational performance. As the learning history makes clear, for many people the opportunity to commit to a learning process, a process of personal development, was extremely stimulating and energizing. This kind of energy is often released in workshops, in various kinds of organizational development programs, and in the kind of team-building activities that were invented in the OilCo transformation. People realize that there is a better, more personally rewarding way of working and being in an organization. And, not surprisingly, productivity improves as well, so everyone is a winner.

The problem is that the people and groups who discover these better ways of working find themselves out of phase with the larger systems in which they have to operate. The corporate culture of the rest of the oil industry, and the attitudes of the board of directors, are not necessarily in tune with the new ways of working at Oil Co. And, worse, the more committed and motivated the employees and managers within OilCo get, the more they create anxiety in the parts of OilCo that are slower to change or less enthusiastic about change. If the new way of working is not rewarded, then the newly committed employee will find him or herself faced with having either to regress or seek employment elsewhere. If the innovations are actually punished, the newly committed innovator becomes disillusioned, cynical, and leaves.

What is missing in many transformational learning processes is upward and outward influence. A group or entire organization invents a new way of working that is successful and assumes that the success will be its own reward, which the rest of the world will want to adopt. The members of the group cannot appreciate that it is their success that makes other parts of the organization anxious and hostile, because they do not understand the subtleties of what has gone on and how the success was achieved. If there is one critical skill that successful change agents must acquire it is the ability to move at a pace that educates higher levels especially and allows them to learn in the same way that they themselves learned.

We do not know to what extent the OilCo CEO was able to educate his own board of directors, nor do we know what will happen when he retires: will the transformation be complete in the eyes of many of the employees? One hypothesis to be considered (if only because it is so common in organizations) is that in the end, in any organization, what the CEO wants to do will run at cross purposes with some of the goals (implicit or explicit) held by the board or other key protagonists, in a way that is not sufficiently prepared for.

◆ CONCLUSION: LESSONS FROM THE HISTORY OF ORGANIZATION DEVELOPMENT

The lessons of the OilCo transformation are not really that new to anyone familiar with the evolution of the field of organization development (1950 to the present). One of the biggest discoveries was that people could learn from their own experiences in T-groups (training groups). That technology evolved rapidly and became the basis for many kinds of organizational change programs, most notably Blake's work on the "managerial grid."[6] It was recognized that the concept of groups studying their own behavior was countercultural and looked terribly unproductive. If this was to be done within organizations, top management had to be familiar with the ideas and accepting of them. One of the frequently cited "disasters" was when the CEO of Swissair wandered into a T-group and, after listening for a few minutes, decided that this was a waste of time and cancelled a carefully designed training program in midstream.

It is part of OD theory that the top has to be involved, and learning how to influence upward is one of the main elements in the training of OD professionals. In the OilCo case, one level of the top was involved, the local CEO, and that is why the transformation worked as well as it did. But did he involve the full organization sufficiently? Did people throughout OilCo understand what his concepts of federalism really were and what that meant for the future of the organization?

As any new set of ideas comes along to improve, transform, revolutionize how we work and how we manage organizations, we have to stay focused on the reality that to the extent to which the new ideas really work, they are inevitably countercultural. Counter-cultural ideas generally create anxiety and resistance in the systems above and around the innovation, triggering forces that subvert the innovators until the members of those surrounding systems have themselves learned what the innovators learned. In the OilCo story, we see an organization midway through this process, coming to terms with its own counter-culture, and learning what it means to absorb change.

CHAPTER 14

SENSE MAKING AS A DRIVING FORCE IN CHANGE AT OILCO

Karl Weick

Readers are eighty-five pages into this learning history before they read explicitly what they have sensed all along, namely, "planned change is never monolithic." This realization hit OilCo's CEO much earlier (page 131) when he acknowledged "that he didn't have the skills by himself to turn this ship around. He would need a lot of help." Both observations about change can be combined with an even more powerful image to suggest just what the top people at OilCo are up against when they try to transform the firm. This image, which retains the CEO's nautical analogy, comes from nothing less than Tolstoy's *War and Peace*.

> In quiet and untroubled times it seems to every administrator that it is only by his efforts that the whole population under his rule is kept going, and in this consciousness of being indispensable every administrator finds the chief reward of his labor and efforts. While the sea of history remains calm, the ruler-administrator in his frail bark, holding on with a boat hook to the ship of the people and himself moving, naturally imagines that his efforts move the ship he is holding on to. But as soon as a storm arises and the sea begins to heave and the ship to move, such a delusion is no longer possible. The ship moves independently with its own enormous motion, the boat hook no longer reaches the moving vessel, and suddenly the administrator, instead of appearing a ruler and a source of power, becomes an insignificant, useless, feeble man.[1]

The story of OilCo is clearly not a story of the enfeeblement of the top in stormy times. That's why it deserves to be taken seriously—and plumbed deeply for the lessons it carries for organizational change. Planned change is not monolithic. And it is this very shortfall that creates the surprises, the inconsistencies, and the ambiguities that seem to defy explanation and put a premium on a system's capability for sense making. The role of sense making at OilCo is tacit rather than explicit in the preceding narrative. Thus, the purpose of this essay is to call attention to processes of sense making[2] that occurred concurrent with the transformation. I offer a different interpretation from that of the consultants as to what is going on in the flow of events at OilCo. This alternative interpretation suggests a different set of driving events that influence the degree to which an organization learns and changes during times of upheaval, pressure, and ambiguity.

The commentary is organized into four parts. First, I describe briefly the official story of change at OilCo, briefly because that story is the core of this book. Second, I describe a longer alternative story that highlights events in the learning history that involve ongoing efforts to make sense of what is happening. In doing so I summarize basic themes in change and learning that are associated with a sense-making perspective. Third, I review the issues of transformation and episodic change in light of themes of sense making. And I conclude by suggesting problems that may be latent in the OilCo system if the sensemaking analysis is plausible.

◆ Change and learning at OilCo: The official story

Radically compressed, the story of OilCo's corporate transformation is one in which a new CEO inherits an apparently declining organization and wants to halt the decline. With the aid of waves of consultants, each wave specializing in a different aspect of upheaval, the CEO, working from the top down, strives to make OilCo into the premier firm in the oil industry by killing the old OilCo and rebirthing it as a less bloated, more aligned, more accountable firm of candid, interdependent actors. To realize this vision, business knowledge is driven deeper into the organization starting with the financial literacy initiative. In addition, accountability is shifted to intact units that are now treated as stand-alone businesses; efforts are made to articulate what the premier oil company now stands for; and people are dismissed, selected, and rewarded in proportion to their alignment of personal standards with those newly articulated by the firm. These changes are attempted against a prior history of guarded conversations, deference, hierarchical command and control, considerable slack in the system, basically good economic times until shortly before the learning history begins, assumptions of lifelong employment, an industry in which none of the players are obvious candidates for benchmarking, and insensitive measurement systems. At the point where the learning history concludes, the organization has become leaner, units have become both more autonomous and more accountable, employees are tapping a wider range of their skills in order to perform more complex jobs, issues of trust and trustworthiness have become more discussable, and there is general acceptance that there is no going back, that the old OilCo is now history, in form, if not in substance.

◆ CHANGE AND LEARNING AT OILCO: A SENSE-MAKING STORY

A different story, using essentially the same data as the official story, pays closer attention to a theme telegraphed in the introduction (page xxi), namely, "organizational learning is a process of collective sense making." This alternative story, since it is focused on finer-grained microdetails, is not necessarily incompatible with the official story. Instead, it suggests something of the infrastructure of so-called transformational change. It is the back room that makes the front of the house seem competent and on top of issues. But the contention is that this microinfrastructure is at the heart of whatever changes are observed. Furthermore, it is contended that change is continuous at OilCo. When we see transformation, what we are seeing is a change in the pace of continuous change, rather than the onset and then termination of episodic change. Thus, this case is an account of accelerations and decelerations in the rates and kinds of change that had been going on all along at OilCo. The trick is to spot the infrastructure that governs the accelerations and decelerations of continuous change.

The alternative interpretation begins the same place as does the official story. A growing financial crisis begins to capture everyone's attention. The overriding question in the face of decline becomes, "What's the story?" That question is translated into more specific probes such as, "Why the decline?" "Are there internal variations in the extent of the decline?" "Who is to blame?" "Is it us or the industry?" "Is it a transient decline or a permanent decline?" The answers to questions like this flow throughout the organization, and this is true whether consultants are present or not. Those answers can be characterized on at least three dimensions.[2] They have some degree of generality (answers have degrees of abstractness and may or may not apply to many different kinds of units). They have some degree of accuracy (answers fit the specific circumstances of a specific unit more or less fully). And they have some degree of simplicity (answers are more or less easy to grasp). If these three criteria are arrayed around a clock face with generality positioned at 12:00, accuracy at 4:00, and simplicity at 8:00, the dilemma in addressing the question, "What's the story," becomes apparent. A story that satisfies any two criteria is least able to satisfy the third criterion.

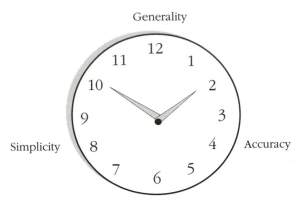

FIGURE 14-1

For example, OilCo's romance with financial literacy represents their infatuation with a 10:00 explanation of their troubles. "Improving Our Economic Value" is a general, simple explanation. It is general because the complex world of oil industry finance is reduced to a simple set of formulae, including admonitions to raise profitability and growth simultaneously. This admonition is relevant to many different kinds of units because of its high level of abstraction. The admonition and the matrix are also simple, accessible, and easy to understand. But what causes trouble for managers is that the overall OilCo financial analysis is an inaccurate description of the troubles in any one unit. Those troubles involve different variables from these two (e.g. unfixed compensation and skill problems, page 67). This inaccuracy creates ambiguity for those charged with implementing financial literacy (e.g., "it was beyond chaos here at Buxton Falls," page 123). To resolve that ambiguity, people must resort to richer communication media[3] such as conversation, face-to-face interaction, meetings, or negotiation, to create (not discover) some understanding of what this change actually consists of. The ambiguities that people face includes questions of what the change means, why it is necessary, what it will solve, and what it has to do with the routines they already have in place. What won't resolve these ambiguities are formal communication media such as videotapes, memos, placards, and spreadsheets.

Given the ambiguity created by financial literacy, the effectiveness or ineffectiveness of any change intervention is actually determined not so much by the content of the "Improving Our Economic Value" project, as by the quality of the interaction available to deal with the ambiguity created by that project. The success of the change depends on whether people are able to hammer out some joint understanding of what they face, why it is worth facing it, and what to do. The higher the quality of that interaction, the better able people are to shift away from general-simple albeit inaccurate diagnoses, toward those that are more accurate and simple (albeit less general and fitting for other units in OilCo) or more general and accurate (albeit more difficult to grasp and communicate within the unit or to top management). In the case of subunits in OilCo, as interactions are characterized by greater trust, trustworthiness, and self-respect,[4] participants are more willing to accept that they are not well informed about vision, values, and mission and more willing to reject formulations of these three that ring hollow. As conversations become more candid, people learn that it is possible to improvise their way to a better life at OilCo. They also learn that they have the capabilities to do so (e.g., page 109), that interdependencies will determine their fate, and that it is possible to align a non-work identity with a work identity, if people walk the talk embodied in a compassionate set of value statements.

The basic structure of this alternative story is that in the face of a stubborn crisis (e.g., Buxton Falls has the highest costs in the industry, page 119) or interruption (e.g., Buxton Falls has the worst safety record in OilCo, page 119), any old program will do as a pretext for change as long as that program

1. animates people and gets them moving and generating experiments that uncover opportunities (recall the CEO's comment on page 26 "If you give them that room, people can perform much better than we usually give them credit for");

2. provides a direction (recall OilCo's focus on a quest and a journey rather than a destination as the framework for pursuing financial literacy, page 41);

3. encourages updating through improved situational awareness and closer attention to what is actually happening (recall page 52 where a member of the Enterprise Leadership Group states that the more they drill down into the more specific details of the financial numbers. the less sense it makes and the more the financial literacy approach falls apart); and,

4. facilitates respectful interaction in which trust, trustworthiness, and self-respect *all* develop equally and allow people to build a stable rendition of what they face. (Recall the exemplary handling on page 95 by the President of OilCo Consulting of the query, "Is our purpose noble enough?" The questioner speaks up as a trustworthy reporter. The President trusts that people see things he misses, and has sufficient self-respect to admit to having glossed over what it really means to espouse a noble purpose).

What is important about these four aspects of sense making is that they are a plausible minimalist view of the infrastructure of change. What that means is that whether the program is financial literacy, or total quality, or learning organization, or transformation, or teachable points of view, or whatever, effectiveness will improve or decline depending on whether the program of choice engages or blocks these four. These four, by themselves, are sufficient to produce change. But since they require a focus or pretext for activation, some kind of surprise and some kind of content are necessary. In the case of OilCo, those prerequisites are met by financial literacy hauled out at a time of unexpected losses. But it is the thrust of this argument that there is nothing special about financial literacy that explains the improvement. Financial literacy was the vehicle for the activation of a more basic set of activities that produced changes that heightened effectiveness. The "Improving Our Economic Value" project "fostered inquiry" (page 48), was adapted to local needs (page 46), was the object of different interpretations (page 45), was the pretext for people to talk to one another about the business (page 43), and suggested linkages that people then examined more closely (page 42). Translated into the language of this essay, the project triggered varying intensities of animation, direction, attention, and respectful interaction. It is the pattern of these four activities that figured strongly in whatever impact the "Improving Our Economic Value" project had on operations.

REWORKING THE OFFICIAL STORY

I have suggested that themes of animation, direction, attention, and respect underlie learning and change. If we keep those four themes in mind as we retrace OilCo's transformation, we add even more richness to the OilCo learning history.

Consider transformation. From the standpoint of sensemaking, transformation is important partly because it has the potential, in its hyperbole, to get people moving. And when people get moving, if they have some guidance, they often stumble onto modifications and information that lead to improvements. The problem with transformation is that it is easy to talk the talk but hard to walk the walk. It is energizing to talk the talk of fresh starts, rebirth, zeal, deep change, conversion, challenge, sacrifice, risk, boldness, revolution, out of the box, etc. It is much harder to walk the talk of transformation because to do so means such things as

1. deep personal change (recall page 102 where this is identified as a need on the part of the members of the Executive Council),

2. chronic temptations toward hypocrisy in action (recall the discussion on page 159 of the distrust that was occasioned when the severance program at OilCo Chemicals was not weighed against mission, values, and vision),

3. wariness that one is trading off greater transformational zeal for lesser business skills (recall discussion of this point on page 151),

4. encouragement for impression management wherein the inexperienced rant and rave with their "rebel spirit" yet play it safe when out of earshot of transformational champions (recall page 153 where this issue arises),

5. selective retention of crucial institutional memory and fears that key memories are being lost (page 151),

6. riding roughshod over changes that were already under way (recall page 185 where an OilCo manager who had been engaged in con-

tinuous change becomes furious when he is told that it is time to be reborn),

7. likely association of the change with the sponsoring CEO only to be abandoned as soon as CEO succession takes place (recall page 116 where OilCo's CEO expresses this reservation),

8. adoption of a change strategy that actually is suited for a rather narrow set of contingencies,[5] and

9. inflated goals that in their unreachableness demoralize rather than energize.

My point is not to trash transformation. Instead, my point is that in the face of hurdles such as these, if a so-called transformation effort appears to improve organization functioning, one should look elsewhere than in the mechanics of revolution for the mechanism by which this improvement occurred. The effective triggering and functioning of collective sensemaking constitutes one such alternative mechanism.

It is easy, since the OilCo case is labeled a case of transformation, to miss the possibility that change was already under way before the official commitment to change was declared. More important, these precursor changes may have made transformation possible and may even have been the core that was consolidated in the transformation itself.[6] The rhetoric of transformation is seductive to researchers as well as practitioners. It tempts people to look for large, dramatic antecedents when they see large dramatic changes. They tend to underestimate the joint impact on systems of multiple small wins executed simultaneously.[7] These same small wins also represent small experiments that suggest what is more and less susceptible to change. OilCo is described as an organization "poised to change" (page xxi), but much of this "poise" seems due to units *already* engaged in transformation that were keeping a low profile (page 21), people trying "quick hitting things" without much success (forgetting that the results of change often lag the moment of intervention), clandestine changes (page 24), evolving commitments (page 64), early experiments at Buxton Falls intended to change their way of doing business (page 119), and latent willingness to make it up as they go along (page 59). Events such as these suggest that continuous change was as much a feature of OilCo as was its receptiveness to transformational change. Furthermore, without that continuous change, transformational change may have been impossible. It is the power of small wins to pave the way for transformation. And it is the power of small wins to lock in transformations after they have occurred. Both effects determine whether an episodic, transformational change will take hold or collapse. The crucial alignment furthermore may not be so much personal values with organizational values, as it is episodic change with the continuous change already under way. For example, the clandestine changes already under way at OilCo before the transformation is launched, suggest that there is some degree of autonomy and subsidiarity present *before* subsidiarity is officially declared as a component of transformation. Thus, when transformation is implemented it essentially ratifies existing practices tending toward subsidiarity rather than creates new structures. Obviously, this ratification does not apply across the board since not every unit at OilCo is a site for clandestine experiments. Nevertheless, those whose practices are ratified can become internal benchmarks for those whose practices have been less experimental and less consistent with subsidiarity.

LINGERING PROBLEMS

In an intervention as complex as this one, there are bound to be red flags that suggest continuing problems that may be incubating in the system and that could combine with other issues to undermine transformational gains. I will mention three that affect sense making.

For example, if people take seriously the "sense of urgency" as one of their key values, then they are likely to forego thinking about the week's events (page 89), the most economical way to do business (page 159), and the right way to deal with the issue of diversity (page 178). Sense making takes time. And if speed is allowed to dominate, then people tend to process incoming information by looking for confirmation of their a priori hunches rather than for disconfirmation.[7] In times of rapid change, trading confirmation for accuracy is a path to ruin because subtle differences that give momentary advantage go unnoticed. I see this veneration of urgency as yet another unfortunate by-product of the rhetoric of transformation. Reflective transformation is an oxymoron. Urgent transformation is a call to arms. Therein lies the trouble.

Systems in thrall to transformation often underestimate the value of controls and innovations they already have in place. We see that at OilCo. Consider the "self-defeating pattern of behavior" on page 77 that involves risk-taking. The number of risks taken is positively related to (the connected variables move in the same direction) the number of failures experienced, which is positively related to the number of people singled out for criticism, which is negatively related (connected variables move in opposite directions) to willingness to take risks, which is positively related to the number of risks taken.

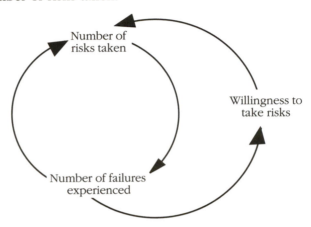

FIGURE 14-2

When set in motion this is a deviation-counteracting feedback loop that controls these events.[8] For example, the more risks that are taken the more failures that occur, the more people who are criticized, the *less* willing people are to take risks, the less risks taken the fewer the failure, the less the criticism the *more* willing people are to take risks, etc. Risk-taking varies but within limits, which is typically what organizations prefer even if they espouse a more daring ideology. The point is, risk-taking, as currently constituted in this system of causal connections at OilCo, is working. But, that reality is likely to be swept aside when the heavy hand of transformation starts with a blank sheet of paper. That's not necessarily a big deal. But what is of more concern is the possibility that this oversight may be indicative of a larger problem of insensitivity to causal sequences, processes, and interdependencies among events. On page 164 an executive at Chemical says "if we get this organization the way we think it should be . . . . we will become a great company." That description is unduly static and underestimates the degree to which organizations are sets of relationships in need of continual reaccomplishment.[9] An organization is not something one fixes once and for all and then gets on with business. It is that very mind set that allows things to deteriorate to the point where transformation, complete with annihilation of the old, is mandatory. I worry that the very upheavals involved in transformation tempt people to sigh, "I'm glad that is over!" and then to neglect from that point on the perpetual unraveling, on a daily basis, of what they have accomplished, and the necessity to rebuild and reaffirm it.

There seems to be a crucial problem in the move toward subsidiarity that is being missed. Subsidiarity is about simultaneous loose and tight coupling,[10] not just about loose autonomy as several managers seem to think. Simultaneous loose-tight coupling typically takes the form of tight coupling among units on a handful of core values (a cultural change), and loose coupling on everything else (a structural change). The red flag here is both that subsidiarity seems to be equated solely with looseness, and that structural change is seen as sufficient without there being any need to create culture change as well (page 73). The problem is that culture is the source of the tight coupling. If cultural coupling on tight values is slighted, then OilCo has created an anarchy rather than a federation.

CONCLUSION

We started with the image of OilCo's CEO stranded in a boat with an ineffective boat hook that didn't seem to have any effect whatsoever on the larger heaving ship of OilCo. But, as we looked closer, we spotted some driving forces that were having an effect on OilCo, an effect that was the indirect influence of the CEO's initiatives. It was suggested that the CEO set in motion the driving forces of animation, direction, attention, and interaction by means of programs of transformation, economic modeling, and value clarification. These driving forces engaged changes that were already under way, amplified them, diffused them, and institutionalized them.

The successful engagement of these driving forces is not inevitable. And that is the takeaway from this discussion. In the case of OilCo, transformation may have produced animation and some direction, but it is less clear that it improved attention or interaction. It was the addition of the EVA intervention that intensified attention and situational awareness and the dialogue intervention that supplied respectful interaction. *It took all of these programs to keep the full set of driving forces in play.* This outcome is important to note because most change programs ignore one or more of these driving forces. Consider a run-of-the-mill change intervention.

When a new program is imposed on people, they must continue to run the business the old way while they get accustomed to running it the new way. As they attempt this juggling act, people typically implement more than experiment, pay attention to compliance rather than to effects and outcomes, and listen more than they speak up. As we have suggested, when interventions curb animation, direction, attention, and dialogue, ambiguity increases. As a result, the rate of change is slowed rather than accelerated because problems of sense making interfere with adoption. People who are forced to deal with ambiguity without action that tests hunches, without a general direction that allows local adaptation, without close attention to details and consequences, and without candid dialogue to build consensual validation of what is happening, find themselves unable to reduce ambiguity. If the ambiguity persists, this becomes more and more stressful, which has the unfortunate effect of forcing people back onto first learned, overlearned earlier habits which are the very tendencies the change initiative was supposed to abolish.

In the OilCo case, we see intermittent threats to sense making. Respectful interaction is threatened when key people do all the talking (e.g., page. 103) and express ambivalence toward the value of humility (page 108). Clashes between old ways and new ways of doing business freeze experimentation, confuse the sense of direction, and scatter attention among a host of issues (e.g. pages 124-130). What keeps the change effort at OilCo going is that under the guise of self-organizing, people tackle new tasks and discover new capabilities. They continue to move in the direction of greater alignment of values and whatever they define as roughly northeast. They continue to notice, now in greater detail, just how much top management neglected and has left as their legacy for the units to clean up. And they become increasingly willing to speak up about what really needs to be remedied. All four of these activities—animation, direction, attention, respectful interaction—are crucial for adaptation, learning, and change in a turbulent world. But they are also the four activities most likely to be curbed severely in a hierarchical command and control system. Furthermore, there is no guarantee that highly touted change programs will necessarily restore them, renew them, legitimize them. The message of this essay is that if a change program leaves animation, direction, attention, and interaction untouched, it will fail.

CHAPTER 15

GOVERNANCE AND FEDERALISM

Charles Handy

The OilCo story is a classic case of an organization moving from a totalitarian state to a modified federation, and from a centrally planned economy to a more open-market situation where the component parts of the old organization become quasi-independent businesses. It is the kind of transition that many organizations of all sorts are being forced to make, not least the granddaddy of them all, the old Soviet Union.

As an aside it is perhaps ironic that the businesses that were, in the seventies and eighties, vociferously pro-market and anti-Communist, failed to perceive that they were themselves designed as centrally planned and controlled economies, not unlike the regimes that they deplored. Such systems were doomed in a fast-changing interconnected world where insulated cultures could not compete or even survive. The dislocations those regimes subsequently endured and are still enduring, the mixture of heady excitement for some and the loss of past certainties for others, the need for new relationships and new ways of working, these are all mirrored in this story.

The OilCo story reminds us that corporations are not pieces of architecture or engineering; they are communities of living people, in many instances bigger in terms of revenue than many a country. They are corporate states and as such, are subject to the rules and principles of political theory as much as their individuals, who are human beings rather than human resources, conform to the theories of psychology and sociology. It was when OilCo's senior executives realized that technological efficiency and financial logic were not enough, on their own, to harness the energies and talents of their people that they began to look for others models from other fields of theory and to talk a new language with words like "transformation," "vision," and "noble purpose."

With hindsight it is easy to recognize, at the start of the story, all the symptoms of a centrally planned system—the pervasiveness, for instance, of the "they" syndrome where "they," whoever they were, made all the decisions and gave the orders and everyone else tried to make sure that nothing went wrong. Success meant no mistakes. There was little room for personal choice or individual initiative but in return there was certainty and a quiet life. It was only when things turned bad and the certainty contract was repudiated that "they" were seen to be fallible and began to be distrusted—all elements readily observable in totalitarian regimes no matter how benevolent their intentions might once have been.

The series of experiments that make up OilCo's learning experience over the years of this history could have been made easier if the protagonists had seen themselves as working within a consistent framework. That framework could most appropriately have come from political theory. They intuitively realized this when they started to explore the idea of corporate federalism but there was more there to be mined had they looked deeper. It is always difficult, however, to graft ideas from one paradigm onto another and OilCo was still locked into the idea of the corporation as a sort of complicated machine for making money. People, in that model, are counted as costs, things to be minimized and controlled. Goals and rewards, in that model, are only financial. No one jumps out of bed in the morning excited to be making money for the shareholders but he, or she, might do so if more money came to them as well as to the shareholders. It is a model which takes a rather demeaning view of human nature, one in which any attempt to introduce "softer" motives tends to invite a cynical response.

Federalism, however, does allow tough and tender to work together. It separates the necessary from the sufficient. Profit, and cash in particular, are essential to the well-being of a federation and the center usually keeps a tight control over both, but that leaves the individual states the freedom to define their own particular versions of excellence or "noble purpose." There must, however, also be some overarching identity to which all the separate states or businesses subscribe, for federalism depends on the concept of "twin citizenship"—the idea that one can have two loyalties. No one would sacrifice local advantage of local heroes for the greater common good. The definition of that larger identity is, therefore, of crucial importance and OilCo was clearly reaching for it, although "premier" is perhaps both too diffuse and too simplistic to generate the kind of pride and passion that organizations thrive on.

Federalism is critically a matter of balance. It is both centralized and decentralized at the same time, but there is no general rule for what should be decentralized. It depends, and the balance is always changing. There are hints in the learning history that these arguments were pursued piecemeal and in corners rather than openly in the Executive Council. Which raises another issue—federalism distinguishes between legislative and executive decisions. The legislative, or policy, decisions are made by a representative body even if they are initiated by the executive group. This procedure—too cumbersome for the machine model of the corporation—does a lot to ensure that major changes, to the compensation system for example, are fully debated and accepted by representatives of all the business units before being "rolled out" by the executives. OilCo's reform of the governance system overlooked this aspect.

By making OilCo Consulting (services functions including information technology) a separate organization, the CEO apparently saw no need for a uniform information system, but information is the currency of a corporation and a common currency is a basic requirement of a federation—it is one of the things that binds it together, as the European Union realizes. It is because Britain has doubts about the federation that she is reluctant to commit to its common currency. Similarly, there needs to be a basic common law or, in corporate terms, a basic code of values, although individual businesses would, or course, be free to set their own dress codes, flex hours, and modes of address. It is another aspect of the larger citizenship which, if it is not maintained, leads to the break up of the federation and the synergy that should flow from that.

Synergy is, after all, the only reason for a federation rather than some sort of holding company. The individual parts of the federation should complement each other, just as the coastal states of the United States need the bread and food baskets of the center while they, in their turn, need the industrial power of the edges, and both rely on the center to maintain the arterial highways, physical or informational, and the means of defense. Coordinating devices are therefore required to link the different businesses together when the needs of the market so require, and individual businesses would be well advised to offer discounted prices to internal clients, as OilCo Consulting eventually found itself doing. In some organizations these discounts are repaid, up to a limit, from central funds in order to ensure that the federation makes the best use of its own resources.

Most crucially, however, federalism is more than a system of governance. It's a way of thinking that reaches down to each individual. Subsidiarity, or the idea that stealing people's proper decisions is wrong, was originally promulgated by Pope Leo X in the Renaissance years as a moral principle. Subsidiarity is different from empowerment because it assumes that the real power resides in the individual to begin with, rather than being given to him, or her, from above. The individual has to be helped to live up to the responsibilities that reside in the job and to delight in the ability to make a difference. The manager helps, or coaches, rather than controls. Implicit in this model is the necessity for the individual to know where the company is heading; otherwise the difference that he or she makes might be disruptive rather than helpful. Hence the importance of Visions and Missions, although these have to be translated down to the team level to be real and useful. Self-managed teams, of the sort developed at Buxton Falls, are a good example of subsidiarity in action, and the enthusiasm and sense of personal responsibility developed there are symptomatic of subsidiarity.

Buxton Falls realized that they were embarking on a major change in their culture. Not everyone will want it, particularly the "last-born," who grew up in another world and another model. They are only going to accept the new way of working if they can understand why it is necessary and that it is not another flavor of the month. Hence the need for an explanatory framework and massive amounts of education or, more truthfully, propaganda. Let us make no mistake: corporations are political creations and have to use the techniques of political power and influence if they want to bring their people with them.

Corporations are never going to be democracies in the normal sense of the word. Their employees are never going to vote for their leaders, except in their small groups. But corporations will be democracies in the original meaning of the word, namely that power ultimately belongs to the individuals who work there. To harness that power for the benefit of all—the shareholders, customers, and community as well as the employees themselves—is the task of the managers. OilCo instinctively realizes this at the higher levels and is inching its way toward ways of implementing this new understanding. This understanding does, however, need to be underpinned by a conceptual model of what a corporation needs to be in this new age when people really are the new assets of the business, more crucial than all the refineries, gas stations, and depots.

They might also find the changes easier to implement if they altered the number systems to reflect the new realities. ROI, for instance, is an out-of-date ratio in the information age. It encourages businesses to improve returns by the simple experiment of reducing investment, through outsourcing, and ignores the real investment in people who are still a negative number. Financial literacy is only a partial correction to this dilemma. OilCo's compensation complications might also be eased if the new profit-center businesses were true businesses in which the workers had notional shares entitling them to dividends on earnings and to capital gains on departure.

"Muddling through" has been a long-established Anglo-Saxon methodology, so OilCo's adoption of it is understandable, but it is painful, costly, and confusing even to those who do make it through. There has to be a better way. OilCo explored a limited number of conceptual schemes, looked at no organizations outside business, and, seemingly, read little. Education for changes of this magnitude has to start at the top and has to be of the mind-expanding rather than of the "how-to" variety. Consultants, no matter how good, are no substitute in the end for internalized ideas and visions, although the consultants can act as useful gatekeepers to other worlds. On the other hand, education was once defined as experience understood in tranquility. If that be so, then to reflect on the experience as captured in this history could lead them to the real understanding of their story and to even greater futures.

DISCUSSION GUIDE

CHAPTER 16

DISCUSSION GUIDE

Like most learning histories, the OilCo story was originally written for people at the organization being described. Learning history documents are generally commissioned to help the participants, observers, and other interested parties (inside and outside the organization) make sense of and learn from some significant organizational experience—an experience of organizational change, success, failure, or, more likely, all three. The form of the learning history document—narratives "spoken" directly by participants to the reader, with commentary and context alongside them—was invented in response to the shortcomings of the traditional ways in which organizational experiences are communicated. Only limited numbers of people can participate in company visits, oral presentations, and discussions with participants, while "business school" cases, best practices, benchmarking, and lessons learned often don't provide the depth or rich context that people need to make sense of events. The learning history provides depth and breadth in the form of direct data: the story in the words of its participants. This data not only gives readers an account of what happened, but also multiple perspectives from which to understand why things turned out the way that they did, and a basis for theorizing about how they might turn out in similar situations elsewhere.

The direct data of the "major column" transcript is augmented by several forms of perspective: in the "minor" column, in the introductions, and in commentaries written by noteworthy observers of management issues. The multiplicity of perspective is deliberate. If managers, and students of management, are to learn from OilCo's transformation through this learning history, then they must make up their own minds on what was important, and what they would do if they were faced with similar circumstances. In writing and editing the learning history, and designing methods for using the document in group discussions, we hope to provide materials and a process to help people engage in informed conversations about what happened (at, for example, OilCo) and how it might apply to them and their own situation. The conversation is the most critical part of the learning history process. Whether it takes place in workshops, meetings, classrooms, or informal settings, this is where individual and collective insights can be developed, tested, and considered.

The discussion guide you are reading may be useful in initiating and sustaining those conversations.. This guide is organized into four sections to provide the following material:

1. The context of OilCo (and how the learning history was used)

2. What has happened (since *Oil Change* was written)

3. The learning history process (and its design for discussion)

4. Guidelines for learning history conversations

◆ THE CONTEXT OF OILCO

The OilCo learning history, in its original form, was commissioned by a large American oil company for use as part of its ongoing transformation efforts. In other words, the document was intended to help carry forward the same initiative it was describing. The learning history effort began about three and a half years after the original Key West meeting that launched the transformation. Much had happened in the company since then, but the efforts had largely engaged OilCo's top leaders (primarily the 100-member Corporate Executive Team), the people who directly reported to them, and a few "early adopters" scattered through the OilCo work force. By some estimates, 3,000 (a significant fraction), of OilCo's employees had participated in some workshop, session, or meeting related to "transformation." Yet there was a perception that the initiatives hadn't made much impact. Some people were still responding to the shock of layoffs and cutbacks from a few years before; others were frankly skeptical of transformation as "one more management fad"; and a large number of people, particularly at OilCo's far-flung refineries and exploration and production outposts, had simply not paid much attention, at least in the view of the learning history's sponsors.

The company, in short, needed a way to communicate the realities of transformation candidly and openly, so people could make an informed commitment to it from all levels of the organization. This would require more than simply teaching people financial literacy techniques and "rolling out the message" by telling employees what changes were expected. The top leaders wanted to *engage* the broad employee population in thinking about the future of OilCo and its newly formed semi-autonomous enterprises. They hoped that the learning history would provide one credible, universally acceptable way to share the story of the top leaders and those engaged in transformation so that others could learn from and build upon that story. The leaders knew that as others became engaged, they would face the same kinds of challenges that OilCo's leaders and early adopters had already faced. The approach of sharing their own experience via the learning history, rather than executives preaching to employees, would be more inviting; it would lead to more open and honest conversations around the challenges of the changes required for OilCo's transformation. It was also made clear that credibility was paramount; we should not "whitewash" or minimize the challenges or problems of transformation, and we should focus our attention on some of the "difficult" cases—like the OilCo Consulting and OilCo Chemicals stories in chapters 9 and 10.

OilCo's Executive Council engaged the co-authors and seven internal employees to form what we called the Transformation Reflection Team to carry out this learning history project. The seven internal learning historians were carefully chosen by the senior corporate sponsors; they came from diverse parts of OilCo, all with a strong commitment to the evolution of the company and (by all indications) a well-developed sensitivity to OilCo's needs and an innate respect for the people they would be interviewing.

- Three were members of the Corporate Transformation Group (CTG), the group that had moved through the company training people in financial literacy. Two of these three CTG members were specifically chosen in part because they had spent a great deal of time out "in the field," working far from headquarters; they had an ear for the ways that transformation was perceived by plant managers, union members, and line employees who didn't always have clear channels of communication back to headquarters. The third had experience working directly with some of the most difficult episodes in transformation, such as the downsizing story described in Chapter 10.

• Another two internal learning historians came from the Human Resources organization, where they had been involved in more quantitative attitude survey work. This was their first opportunity to probe in depth in face-to-face interviews with a broad spectrum of people. One had recently joined OilCo from a large manufacturing company in another state that had undergone a large-scale change effort of its own. Taking part in the learning history effort was seen as a valuable orientation for this individual, a way to come quickly up to speed on OilCo's unique culture.

• The final two learning historians had come to the project from E&P's group of internal consultants, who had traditionally been distant from the work of either the CTG or HR. E&P is a distinct subculture within most oil companies, a subculture of geologists and drillers, of people who make informed gambles with millions of dollars, trying to find oil in remote regions of Alaska or under the Gulf of Mexico. These two internal people were, in effect, ambassadors between the two OilCo cultures.

• The external learning historians came from similarly diverse backgrounds. One (George Roth) was a social scientist trained in process consultation and action research, who had also been a line manager at a multinational corporation. Another (Art Kleiner) was a journalist and management book author, just then finishing a book about management subcultures (*The Age of Heretics*) which contained a great deal of material about the oil industry. Another (Ann Thomas) was an economist and educator who had worked recently in documenting organizational learning efforts in the auto industry. A fourth (Toni Gregory) was a scholar of social change, with a deep interest in social science methodologies, and a background as research director of the American Institute for Managing Diversity. The fifth (Edward Hamell) was a mental health professional with a background in hospital administration and in counseling.

These twelve people interviewed 150 people in eight weeks, nearly always in teams of two people—one insider at OilCo and one outside learning historian. The diverse mix of backgrounds among the group turned out to be one of its most important assets. Key themes emerged from the give-and-take not just between OilCo people and non-OilCo people, but among people from the various parts of OilCo. This often led to individuals taking strong stands that often filtered into the form of the document: a stand for giving union employees more voice, for emphasizing the "three siblings" more thoroughly, or for being more careful about our data-sifting methodology. Ultimately, as if we were a jury of OilCo's peers, the learning historians all had to approve of a theme if it were to become part of the final document.

The learning history document was refined after it was written in a lengthy quote-checking process, and in conversations with the sponsors and some of the key interviewees. It was introduced at the 1997 learning convention—an annual meeting of the top hundred leaders aimed at planning the next year's transformation. Following this meeting, the document was made available to OilCo's leaders to use with their direct reports and others further down in their organizations in talking about the transformation to date and what it would entail in the future.

In a version published under the auspices of the Society for Organizational Learning, the same material was introduced to the community of "learning organization" researchers, consultants, and practitioners. Now, in this Oxford University Press edition, it is available to a still larger academic business audience.

One of the greatest challenges in examining corporate change efforts is bounding the time frame that is studied. The boundaries imposed are mostly artificial and reflect the needs of those conducting the research rather than those who are studied. The same is true for OilCo. The learning history was commissioned to cover the four-year period of the CEO's focus on transformation, but it would be a mistake to assume that the story either began or ended with the boundaries of that four-year period (1993-1997).

The beginning of the story occurred sometime during the 1980s—perhaps in 1986, when the global oil price fell dramatically and forced most oil companies to reexamine their approach to profitability. In looking at that period while researching the document, we found that people couldn't talk about what happened without linking it to an earlier financial decline, and the layoffs, reengineering, and restructuring that brought the cash flow of the organization back under control. It was, in part, the set of business decisions that had be made in the past, decisions that many of the current managers participated in, that led to the focus for learning in the transformation. "How could we have let things get so bad around here?" and "Why was it so difficult to speak up when we saw things getting worse?," were the types of questions that OilCo managers asked. The pain that top managers, led by the CEO, recognized that the organization had brought upon itself was a powerful motivator for finding another way of working together and relating to one another.

Many people would say that the story continues today, as the CEO and a new generation of leaders continue to shape OilCo's future. Even in 1997, when this document was completed, it was clear that transformation at OilCo still had a long way to go. (Indeed, that was the primary reason why this document was commissioned—to be a tool in the ongoing "roll-out" of transformation.) The company was still in the early stages of its leaders' efforts to reenergize the work force and to develop a new vision and governance structure for the organization. While there had been much business improvement, no one could say with certainty that this would continue.

The document is thus like a snapshot of OilCo at a particular moment in time, a moment when the transformation was just evolving beyond the top 100 leaders and moving into the rest of the organization. And that leads to a kind of ambiguity in some parts of the document, because the reader does not know what happened next. Like a baseball player whose bat has cracked the ball into the field, the ball in the air and the speed of the runner are blurred as he runs toward first base. Whether the ballplayer makes it to first or beyond, or whether there are more hits to advance him, is uncertain at the time of the snapshot. We can, perhaps, see the confidence of the runner, and get excited by the photographer's ability to capture the blur of the player in motion. It leads those of us who are optimists to believe that he'll eventually score, and that his team will win too. Yet at the time of the snapshot we have little to go by and how we react to it tells us more about ourselves than the eventual outcome of the game. Which, in the learning history's case, is precisely why the snapshot is valuable.

Since this book is being published in 2000—three years after the learning history was originally distributed—we feel some responsibility to describe more recent events in an epilogue. Natural human curiosity holds sway; people will want to know what happened since the learning history ended. Knowing how things turned out may influence some to reconsider whether OilCo's transformation was a success or failure.

But we do not have a complete epilogue to offer. The story is still not finished, and we do not have much confidence in any interpretations— ours or anyone else's—of the events that have occurred to date. It is still too early to reconcile the various interpretations, that exist, and many of the pertinent details are still not available for public knowledge – in part, because it takes time for the results of a profound learning initiative to come to fruition. We have not been able to conduct in-depth interviews about the events since 1997; we have heard several informal versions of the story, but we have not verified or validated them, and we have not been able to accumulate multiple perspectives about them. Readers who take our version of "what happened next" as evidence to confirm or refute their conclusions are basing those conclusions on incomplete information. They may also be falling prey to the temptation to perceive only "what they want to believe" from the epilogue, with no compensating body of alternative ideas in the text.

Therefore, as you read the epilogue, do so with sensitivity to the possibility of error. Recognize that there are many factors not reported in the epilogue that might have influenced what happened. We have tried to limit it to "observable data"—facts that, like the noticeable results, anyone would agree have happened. But their significance is open to question and is already being interpreted in many different ways. In short, this ambiguity stems from the nature of corporate change itself. It is a rich and complex process, with, as the old saying goes, many fathers when it goes well and no one to claim parenthood when it doesn't.

◆   EPILOGUE: WHAT HAS HAPPENED SINCE 1997

Change has continued, if not accelerated, at OilCo. Both internal and external factors have influenced its development. Internally, the greatest shift has come through the governance structure—the shift to many new subcompanies, each governed semi-autonomously. In its structure and form, OilCo itself is very different from the company of 1994. It is composed of a number of smaller entities, many of which are more focused on their particular business.

Externally, the price of oil has dropped, putting increased pressure on oil-producing companies around the world to boost revenues and cut costs. Many companies, including OilCo, have responded through merger and acquisition, combining exploration, refining, and transportation resources—and in many cases, consolidating former rivals into one company.

OilCo has been an active participant in mergers and acquisitions, partly because of the head start that came from the new governance structure. Some of the new relationships take the form of alliances, in which OilCo is an equal partner, instead of mergers in which OilCo would have retained control.

Overall, OilCo's financial performance has improved amidst this turbulence. To be sure, the financial performance of some key OilCo businesses has declined—in some cases, far more than expected. Opinion is divided about the meaning of this. Many observers inside and outside of OilCo argue that the new governance structure made the company resilient and flexible in the face of a shifting market. Without the autonomous capabilities forged by the new governance structure, they say, profitability would have been lower. Others disagree.

Organizationally there are more questions than answers, and unfortunately the real world of global commerce doesn't let us run controlled experiments in which we can correlate change with results. There is only one certainty: OilCo's executive leadership is committed to continuing many of the components of the transformation in principle, including the work with financial literacy, team development, and personal change. The company's senior leadership continues to support the idea of organizational learning, and to create methods for instilling learning capabilities in people throughout the company. In the wake of financial turmoil, however, some things changed. By 1998, the idea of "transformation" had begun to seem faddish and misleading to many senior leaders and the term was dropped. Although the CEO did not intend the term this way, many had inferred it to mean a shift from one state of being to another, with an ending at the new destination. Over time, the pace of changes proved that kind of thinking naïve; the need for change is now seen as continual and unending.

The way people answered the question of whether they were better or worse off from the transformation, three years later, varied widely from individual to individual. Many continued to speak positively of organizational learning. They have been changed forever, in the way they see business, relate to their colleagues, and take meaning from their work. Those who were part of the transformation look back at the time as a period of development and increasing their capacities for effective action. They are proud of what they accomplished, and respectful of the OilCo leadership. In our opinion, they continue to exude a spirit of inquiry, a quest for continual personal and organizational development, and a reverence for the value (in both business and professional terms) of what the organization has been through.

◆ THE LEARNING HISTORY PROCESS AND ITS DESIGN FOR DISCUSSION

The learning history was designed to help others in OilCo participate in and learn from the ongoing transformation efforts. The general process by which a learning history is carried out has been described in detail elsewhere,[1] but for the convenience of the reader of this book is summarized in Figure 16-1. The participants from OilCo, who can unfortunately not be identified by name given the anonymity of the company, played a major role in all stages of the learning history process. Their guidance, probing, sensitivity, and continual feedback to the outsider learning historians are what make this an account of OilCo as an organization telling its story. Their involvement also ensured the accuracy and credibility of the document.

• First, a planning stage delineates the range and scope of the document as well as the audience seeking to learn from the organization's experience. The noticeable results of the improvement effort are initially specified in the planning stage. Including company people in the planning process develops their skills in planning and conducting assessments for learning.

• Second, there are a series of retrospective, reflective conversational interviews with participants in a learning effort (along with key outsiders), designed to gather perspective from every significant point of view. The interviewing process itself develops the skill for reflective conversation that provides benefits for the organization.

- Third, a small group of internal staff members and outsider learning historians "distills" the raw material (from reflective conversation interviews, documents, observations, and so on) into a coherent set of themes with relevance for those seeking to learn from the effort. This analytic effort, based on techniques of qualitative data analysis and the development of grounded theory, builds the capacity of the inside/outside learning history team for assessing and making sense of improvement efforts.

- Fourth, a document is written based on a thematic orientation, which includes extensive use of edited narrative from interviews. These quotes are fact-checked with participants before they are distributed in any written material (even though they are anonymous in all drafts).

- Fifth, a small key group of managers, participants in the original effort and others interested in learning from their efforts, attend a validation

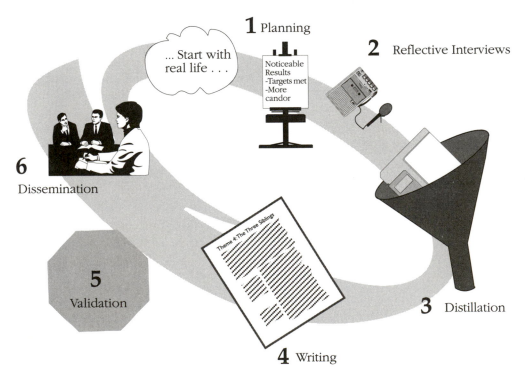

FIGURE 16-1 *Learning history process*

workshop after reading the learning history draft. This validation workshop allows those who participated in the improvement effort to reflect on and review for accuracy the material and their presentation in the learning history.

• Sixth, the learning history document becomes the basis for a series of dissemination workshops. In the dissemination workshops people throughout the company consider what has been learned, how to judge success, how to move forward in other initiatives.

The use of the learning history as part of the transformation required additional indexing so that leaders could connect it to the initiatives associated with transformation. An icon scheme and cross references were created to make the link with the Agenda for Corporate Transformation (see Figure 16-2) explicit.

In the way the learning history is organized, the second chapter, Genesis, provides an overall context for the story. The next three chapters (The Quest, Southern Company, and Governance) describe the business-related actions of transformation ("financial literacy"). The next three (Noble Purpose, The Glass House, and Buxton Falls) deal with issues of leadership and managerial development ("leadership"). The final four chapters (Roll-Out, Downsizing During Transformation, The Diversity Corporate Initiative Team, and Who Am I?) focus on cultural effects of transformation ("commitment").

FIGURE 16-2 *Agenda for Corporate Transformation*

◆ GUIDELINES FOR LEARNING HISTORY DISCUSSIONS

Learning is a process. For learning to take root, a cycle needs to be completed. Whether it is observe-assess-design-implement, plan-do-study-act, observation-reaction-judgment-intervention, or discovery-invention-production-generalization, all involve some form of action, followed by observation, a reflection on what was observed, the design of new action, and the taking of those actions. Without the ability to produce action that illustrates competency, it is hard to say, "I learned that." Therewith is a dilemma of learning histories for learning processes of students and managers. Without an active involvement in the learning history, and a connection to action, it is hard to illustrate or internalize learning from a learning history. A learning history is designed for, and intended to be used in, an active way.

The learning history itself is an organizational process for learning—involving investigation into organizational actions during a particular time period, reflection on those actions with participants and others who were affected, the presentation of those descriptions in a carefully written, edited, and fact-checked manuscript, and reading and reacting to the manuscript and the use of it as a basis for conversations. A learning history can inform conversations among a group of people interested in the phenomena itself, a team ready to take on a change initiative of similar style or scope, or a class of students applying and developing their managerial skills. Participants of the conversation are to be invited into a learning space, one where sharing reactions, surfacing ideas, suspending assumptions, and testing strategies can be supportively and safely done. Creating a low-stakes atmosphere for being "wrong," or having ideas that deviate from others' preconceptions facilitates the active experimentation and engagement that characterize adult and team learning processes. Good preparation, both in terms of having participants read the document in advance and in terms of providing them with helpful instructions for their reading, will help the subsequent group conversation be more effective.

We have found that in sending (or assigning) the learning history to be read, it is helpful to invite (or request) readers to:

1. read it with the mind set of a beginner, getting curious about why people are saying what they are saying,

2. notice their own reactions (when they find themselves bored or engaged, blaming or judging) and mark those reactions in their manuscript, and

3. come prepared to share their reactions, and link them to the place in the learning history where they were triggered, with others in the meeting or classroom.

Generally a cover letter or assignment instructions that go with the learning history are helpful in communicating these expectations. It is also important to note that depending upon the topic area of interest, only one or two chapters are assigned for close reading. We've found that it is not as helpful to excerpt chapters and hand them out separately. Excerpted materials inhibit the abilities of readers to learn more about questions on other sections that might interest them. Focusing on a reasonable amount of material, or breaking the whole into pieces for successive meetings, sets reasonable expectations and is a much more realistic request that can be achieved by all the individuals participating in the discussion.

The process for the discussion is much like that of good case discussions. We liken the dissemination of a learning history to book group discussions. What is read and understood by individuals can be magnified through the discussion of alternative interpretations and varied views on its implications. The better the engagement with the subject and materials during discussion, the greater the learning, development of shared understanding, and abilities of participants to re-enact their conversational experience in later real-world situations. Our approach to facilitating these conversations is to break them into two two pieces: first, people sharing their reactions to what they read and discussion of what happened, and second, why it happened and what the implications are for future change efforts. The implications for future change efforts is particularly important when the participants in the conversation are as a group contemplating similar change initiatives or working in similar settings (see Figure 16-3).

These questions are carefully designed to facilitate a learning cycle. They request that people "ground" their comments in the observable data presented as narrative in the learning history, reflect on the significance of what they choose to discuss, raise and discuss alternative interpretations of what explains the behaviors and outcome that were achieved, and consider how they would apply their insights into the design of their own activities and actions. We have found that it is too constraining to hold rigidly to this two-phase process, but rather to recognize that the discussion will be enhanced if there is a cycling between observations, reactions, explanations, and implications. Spending roughly half of the elapsed time in a meeting or class session in each phase seems to be a good rule of thumb for facilitating participants' learning.

Phase 1: "What happened?" and Reader Reactions

Focus on the learning history "data" and readers' reactions. Ask,
for instance:
- What happened here?
- What surprised you?
- Where did you find yourself judging, blaming, solving?

Phase 2: "Why?" and "What's next?"

Moving interpretations toward implications, with questions such as:
- Where did you interpret differently thanwhat is in the
  learning history?
- How do the experiences comparewith your own?
- What are the implications of these experiences relative to
  your initiatives?
- What learning do you see for you? Your organization?

FIGURE 16-3 *Guidelines for a learning history conversation*

The process that was developed and tested in learning history conversations very closely matches that of the U.S. Army's After Action Review, or AAR, process. The AAR was developed and tested over two decades to help the Army learn from its experience. Many in the Army attribute the AARs, along with the other investments the Army has made in its infrastructure for learning, as responsible for the organizations highly effective performance in Operation Desert Storm. The remarkable consideration for the U.S. Army's excellent operational performance is that it was accomplished during a time when new complex technology was being used "under fire" for the first time at a time when there was significant downsizing and reductions in capital spending.

When all is said and done, a learning history is much like life—what you get from it depends upon what you put into it. We hope that we've created a document worthy of the experiences of those who championed, participated in, and were affected by OilCo's transformation. We are indebted to them for their honesty in sharing their stories of personal and organizational development, and their courage in letting us publish their comments in a learning history that invites readers to engage in their own learning. We are equally hopeful that we have organized and presented the materials in this book in such a way that managers, students, consultants, and teachers who work with the material will find their time and efforts well rewarded.

ENDNOTES

◆ CHAPTER 3

1   Because some of the aspects of this financial literacy project have trade secret status, some details about the "Improving Our Economic Value" project have been omitted from this Oxford University Press edition. Every detail about the content of financial literacy in this book is specifically derived from either OilCo's leaders' own goals, or from the public-domain concepts of "financial literacy" and "open-book management." See the Box on page 44 for more information about sources. Readers may rest assured that the spirit and impact of the financial literacy initiative is rendered accurately, and that the most vivid and important aspects of the Quest—the response and innovation within OilCo—are related just as they were written for the original learning history

2   Details about the practice of financial literacy are adapted from *Open Book Management: The Coming Business Revolution*, by John Case, 1995: Harper Business, particularly pp. 63-68. Also see *The Great Game of Business* by Jack Stack (1992, Doubleday); *The Open Book Experience* by John Case (1997, Addison-Wesley); and *Open-Book Management: Creating an Ownership Culture*, by Thomas L. Barton, William G. Shenkir, and Thomas N. Tyson (1998, Morristown, NJ: Financial Executives Research Foundation).

◆ CHAPTER 5

1   See Charles Handy, Balancing Corporate Power: A New Federalist Paper, *McKinsey Quarterly*, Fall 1993 #3.

◆ CHAPTER 13

1   For the most recent reference to this point see *Process Consultation Revisited* (1999, Reading, Mass.: Addison-Wesley-Longman) and *The Clinical Perspective in Field Work* (1987, Newbury Park, CA: Sage), as well as the article "Legitimating

Clinical Research in the Study of Organizational Culture" (*Journal of Counseling and Development*, 1993, 71, 703-708).

2   Van Maanen, J., *Tales of the Field*, 1993, Chicago: University of Chicago Press.

3   See Lorsch, J. W., *Pawns or Potentates?*, 1989, Cambridge, Mass.: Harvard Business School Press and Demb, A. and Neubauer, F., *The Corporate Board*, 1992, New York: Oxford University Press.

4   Schein, E. H., *Organizational Culture and Leadership*, 1992, San Francisco: Jossey-Bass and Schein, E. H., *The Corporate Culture Survival Guide*, 1999, San Francisco: Jossey-Bass.

5   McGregor, D., *The Human Side of Enterprise*, 1960, McGraw-Hill.

6   Blake, R., Mouton, J., and McCanse, A. A., *Change by Design*, 1989, Reading, MA: Addison-Wesley

◆ CHAPTER 14

1   Tolstoy, L., *War and Peace*, Book 11, Chapter 12, page 988, cited in Sills, D. L., and Merton, R. K., *International Encyclopedia of the Social Sciences: Social Science Quotations*, 1991, Vol. 19, New York: Macmillan.

2   Weick, K. E., *Sensemaking in Organizations*, 1995, Thousand Oaks, CA: Sage.

4   Campbell, D. T., Asch's moral epistemology for socially shared knowledge. In I. Rock (Ed.), *The Legacy of Solomon Asch* (39-52), 1990, Hillsdale, N.J.: Erlbaum.

5   Stace, D., & Dunphy, D., *Beyond the Boundaries*,.1994, Sydney: McGraw-Hill.

6   Weick, K. E., and Quinn, R. E., Organizational change and development. 1999, *Annual Review of Psychology*, 50, 361-386.

7   Weick, K. E., Small wins: Redefining the scale of social problems, 1984, *American Psychologist*, 39, 40-49.

8   Fiske, S. T., and Taylor, S. E.) *Social Cognition,* 1991, New York: McGraw-Hill.

9   Maruyama, M. The Second Cybernetics: Deviation-amplifying mutual causal processes. *American Scientist*, 1963, 51, 164-179.

10   Weick, K. E., *The Social Psychology of Organizing*, 1969, Reading, Mass.: Addison-Wesley and Weick, K, E., *The Social Psychology of Organizing*, 1979, 2nd Ed. New York: Random

11   Peters and Waterman, *In Search of Excellence*, 1982, New York: Harper & Row

◆ CHAPTER 16

1   For a more complete explanation of the learning theory embodied in learning history work, the role of the learning history in learning from experience, and the need for reflection on the corporate agenda, see the readers guide in the first book in this series: *Car Launch*, by George Roth and Art Kleiner (2000, New York: Oxford University Press, p. 179ff). Also see the learning history web site at *http://www.fieldbook.com/rlearning.html*.

2   These varied representations of learning processes are from Fred Kofman (1992, MIT lecture slides), Deming (1992, from Shewhart Cycle in Quality, Productivity and Competitive Position, Ford Quality Education and Training Center), Schein (*Process Consultation*, Volume II: Lessons for Managers and Consultants, 1987, Reading, Mass.: Addison-Wesley) and Argyris and Schoen (*Organizational Learning: A Theory of Action Perspective*, 1978, Reading, Mass.: Addison-Wesley), respectively.

3   See *Teaching and the Case Method* by Louis B. Barnes, C. Roland Christensen and Abby J. Hansen (1994, Boston, Mass.: Harvard Business School Press) for description of what makes for good "thinking in education" and the creation of an environment for learning from cases.

4   For more information on the US Army's After Action Review process and its implications for learning in corporate environments, see pages 470 to 477 in *The Dance of Change: The Challenges of Sustaining Momentum in Learning Organizations* by Peter Senge, Art Kleiner, Charlotte Roberts, Richard Ross, George Roth and Bryan Smith (1999, New York: Doubleday/Currency).